Apartheid: South African Naziism

Mass grave of Jewish victims of Naziism along with symbol of German Fascism

Mass grave of black victims of apartheid *along with symbol of Afrikaner Fascism*

Apartheid: South African Naziism

by

Sipo E. Mzimela

VANTAGE PRESS
New York / Washington / Atlanta
Los Angeles / Chicago

To the victims of oppression, exploitation, and racism; and to those who struggle for liberation, human dignity, justice, and peace

FIRST EDITION

Published by Vantage Press, Inc.
516 West 34th Street, New York, New York 10001

Manufactured in the United States of America
ISBN: 533-05296-3

Library of Congress Catalog No.: 81-90724

Contents

FOREWORD

The year 1982, the year in which this book is being published, has special significance for the black South African people, who are struggling for their liberation from oppression and racial tyranny. It marks the seventieth birthday of the African National Congress—the movement founded to free the oppressed and to transform South Africa into a nonracial, unitary, democratic country.

For seventy years, the African National Congress has remained committed to that goal. We salute the founding fathers and mothers. We honor those who have suffered in the course of pursuing that goal—those placed under house arrest, banned, banished, detained, imprisoned, driven into exile, tortured, murdered. We hail those—both inside and outside South Africa—who have supported and continued to support this just struggle.

This anniversary coincides with the United Nations-sponsored International Year of Mobilization for Sanctions against South Africa. There are three reasons why there should be sanctions imposed against South Africa. First, under apartheid, 24 million blacks have been reduced to slavery by South African laws in flagrant violation of the Universal Declaration of Human Rights, which is embodied in the U.N. Charter. Second, the Pretoria regime illegally occupies the International Territory of Namibia in defiance of the lawful authority, the United Nations. Third, Pretoria militarily attacks independent African states. This policy of aggression is aimed at destabilizing and unleashing a reign of terror throughout the subcontinent. Occupied Namibia is used as a springboard for assaults on the People's Republic of Angola.

The call for sanctions is not new. For more than two decades, the victims of apartheid have consistently and persistently urged sanctions against the Pretoria regime with the conviction that this would be the only viable way to bring about peaceful change. The majority of the nations of the world have voted in favor of this measure. However, the governments of Britain, France and the United States have blocked implementation of this action by vetoes in the U.N. Security Council. They have argued that "sanctions will not work." In 1982, the advocates of this argument have themselves exposed its fallacy. The U.S.A. is frantically spearheading a drive for international sanctions against the Soviet Union for the latter's alleged involvement in the Polish crisis. The European Common Market countries are partly supportive of the U.S. position. Another victim of U.S. sanctions is Lybia. In the past the U.S. and its Western allies have imposed sanctions against Iran. The U.S.A. also maintains a trade boycott against Cuba.

At the same time, South Africa is being richly rewarded by the Western powers whose investments in and financial loans to the apartheid regime are at a record high and still growing. Why? Double standards? Profit motive? Convenient access to strategic minerals? Western arrogance? Racism? Ideology? Whatever the reasons, there can be no justification for the West's support of Pretoria.

Acknowledgments

In the course of preparing and writing this book, I have received assistance and support from many individuals, organizations, and institutions in many parts of the world. The list is far too long to be included here. That fact, however, does not in any way diminish my indebtedness and my sense of deep-felt gratitude to them.

Some of the material used in this book was originally used for my Ph.D. dissertation at New York University. I owe special thanks to the professors who guided me in my research, read my drafts, and also encouraged me to write this book. They are professors Lee Belford, Richard Hull, and Norma Thompson. I am also especially indebted to a multitude of scholars and authors who are not personally known to me. Their works were invaluable. Whether or not their names appear in my footnotes, I say, to them all, thank you.

Finally, I must mention the unfailing support and encouragement I received from members of my family. Nomusa and Lindiwe, because of their youth, are unaware of the tremendous inspiration they were to me during the course of writing. The English language cannot convey to Esther, my wife, *exactly* what I want to say to her. So, I must resort to my mother language, which is Zulu, and say to her: *Bayabonga abasemaNzimeleni.*

Sipo

Ventnor, New Jersey.
March 1982

Introduction

No two historical events can ever be identical in every detail. Times change; people change; conditions change. History moves. However, there are instances where history is repeated—to some degree at least. Such repetition may either be coincidental, or it may be deliberately engineered and influenced by humans.

In examining South Africa's *apartheid*—modern day's most inhuman and vicious system of oppression and exploitation—one searches the pages of history to see whether what we have in *apartheid* is a new and unique phenomenon or whether we are experiencing a repetition of history.

To be sure, man's inhumanity to man is not a modern phenomenon. It goes back to the day Cain killed Abel. The pages of history are so full of cases of injustice—murder, torture, wars, exterminations—that one is forced to conclude that, of all living creatures, human beings are the most cruel. To say that human beings sometimes "act like animals" is incorrect. The reverse is true.

In modern times, no period of history demonstrates man's inhumanity more dramatically than the period when the Nazis were the rulers of Germany. The Nazis of course did not invent tyranny, nor were they the last tyrants. What they did do was introduce a degree of racial tyranny hitherto unknown to mankind. Their tyranny was meticulously planned and executed with almost flawless precision. Their genius lay in their ability not only to indoctrinate almost an entire German nation but also to win support far beyond their borders. They proved to the world the effectiveness of propaganda and succeeded—for a while at least—in clothing evil in holy garb and selling it to the world as something good. The Nazis, therefore, must be credited with setting new standards as far as modern tyranny is concerned.

The only other form of race tyranny the world has known since the days of Naziism is *apartheid.* Progressive forces the world over have condemned *apartheid,* describing it variously as "inhuman," "repugnant," "abhorrent," "fundamentally immoral," "a catalyst of violence," and "a crime against humanity."

After the end of the Second World War, many, if not most, Germans claimed they did not know what the Nazis had been doing to the Jews. There is no way of verifying this claim. One thing is certain: South Africa's massive international propaganda campaign, which is heavily supported financially by the regime in Pretoria as well as by South Africa's international allies, has, like Naziism in the early stages, succeeded in clothing the evil *apartheid* system in respectable garb and selling it to the world, not as racial tyranny, which it is, but as "separate development," good neighborliness," "plural democracy," and "freedom and independence for blacks." This has caused a certain degree of confusion in the minds of many outsiders, even among those whose intentions are good.

It is not uncommon to find well-meaning people equating the struggle against *apartheid* in South Africa with the Civil Rights Movement, especially in the Southern states of the United States. For others, *apartheid* is just a policy of racial separation that will disappear with time. For others, there is now change taking place in South Africa, and, rather than keep pointing a finger at the regime in South Africa, it is better to give it support and thus encourage it in its praiseworthy efforts. Still, for others, *apartheid* is dead, though no one is willing to say when the funeral will take place. These are dangerous developments, especially when one remembers that, in the early stages, the Nazis denied that they were persecuting the Jews, claiming that they were merely putting into effect a policy of "separate development." Jews were to develop along their own lines, and Germans along their own. That policy led to the extermination of 6 million Jews, a world war, and the loss of 30 million lives. We must note, therefore, that the concept of "separate development"—unique now to South Africa—is of Nazi origin.

Because *apartheid* was introduced in South Africa for the first time just three years after the fall of the Nazis in Germany, one is compelled to search for the roots of *apartheid* beyond South Africa's borders. After all, when *apartheid* was introduced in 1948, whites in South Africa had already had contact with the indigenous black South Africans for 296 years. Since it came so soon after Naziism, one must determine whether there is any connection between *apartheid* and Naziism.

In order to do so, we must compare what is happening in South Africa under *apartheid* with what happened in Nazi Germany. We must examine whether there is any connection between the roles played by the Western governments, the transnational corporations, and the Western Church in *apartheid* South Africa and the roles they played in Nazi Germany. The Western Church must come under special scrutiny because of its long tradition of claiming to be the conscience of nations and the upholder of moral standards for the world. We need to ask once again what the Western Church did for the persecuted Jews in Nazi Germany and what it is doing for the persecuted blacks in South Africa today.

However, the crucial question is: What role did the authors of apartheid play during the Nazi era? It is the answer to this pivotal question that has led to the title of this book.

Apartheid: South African Naziism

1

Never Again?

The question of how Naziism could take root, grow, and capture the imagination of a large section of the population in a country with a long Christian tradition has baffled countless people throughout the world, ever since the true facts about Naziism have come to light. How human beings could have been led to participate in some of the worst atrocities in the history of mankind is something that bothers the consciences of most people who call themselves civilized. So painful is the question that many would like to think of Naziism as a one-time, unfortunate phenomenon in history, a thing of the past, something that was finally destroyed in 1945, something that can never happen again.

There are several reasons why many people think that Naziism is now dead and can never be resurrected. One of the reasons advanced is that Germany has been divided into two separate countries with two irreconcilable ideologies. Another is that each German state has formed an alliance with different countries. These different alliances would seem to make a resurgence of Naziism impossible. But perhaps the main reason why people think Naziism is a thing of the past is that, generally speaking, too little is known about the Nazis. For many people, "Naziism" is synonymous with the Holocaust. While the Holocaust represents the worst of the atrocities, it was the final—and logical—stage in a process that started long before the idea of gas chambers was conceived.

The history of anti-Semitism is something that is beyond the scope of this book. A very brief description of the factors that contributed to the hatred of Jews in general, and German Jews in particular, will have to suffice.

The Period Preceding Naziism

Anti-Semitism in Germany

Adolf Hitler and the Nazis were not the originators of anti-Semitism. In modern Germany, for more than one hundred years, philosophers, historians, journalists, theologians, anthropologists, and scientists had been conditioning the German mind to the point of accepting unquestioningly the idea that Germans were superior to other races.

The philosopher Friedrich Ludwig Jahn laid the foundation for this with his emphasis on the concepts of *Volk* and *Reich*. In his book *Deutches Volkstum* (German *Volk*dom), he pointed out that "A state without Volk is nothing—a soulless artifice; a Volk without a state is nothing—a bodiless airy phantom, like the Gypsies *and the Jews*. Only state and Volk together can form a Reich, and such a Reich cannot be preserved without Volkdom." [1]

Johann Gottlieb, regarded by many as the father of German nationalism, urged the Germans "to have character and to be German." He believed that it was the Germans who comprised the only perfect nation and who had the most to contribute toward human perfection. He regarded "Jewish ideas" as obnoxious. [2]

Some writers claimed scientific support for anti-Semitic attitudes. Christian Lassen claimed that historical evidence showed Jews to be selfish and exclusive and, unlike the

Aryan, lacking the harmony of psychical forces.[3] Arthur de Gobineau maintained that whites were superior to all other races; that, within the white race, the Aryan excelled; and that Germans were the predominant master race. Negroes and Semites were the "anti-types." [4] Houston Stewart Chamberlain wrote about the struggle between the virtuous Aryans and the "vicious Semites," which, he claimed, dated back to the days of Hellenism.[5]

Others defended anti-Semitism from the Christian point of view. Friedrich Ruehs maintained that Jews could not become German citizens. In his book, *On the Claims of the Jews to the Rights of German Citizenship,* published in 1815 he declared:

A foreign people cannot obtain the rights which Germans enjoy partly through being Christian. . . .[It is] forbidden by the very justice of Christian vis-a-vis each other. . . . Everything should be done to induce them [the Jews], in various mild ways, to accept Christianity and through it be led to a true acquisition of German ethnic characteristics and thus to effect the destruction of the Jewish people.[6]

A theologian who made a significant contribution toward the growth of anti-Semitism was Paul de Legarde (1827–1891). His name stands out because his ideas of Christian-Germanic faith were to have far-reaching consequences some forty years later. The theology of the *Deutsche Christen,* staunch supporters of the Nazis, was greatly influenced by de Legarde.[7]

In 1873, for the first time, the term "anti-Semitism" became identified with hatred for Jews. Wilhelm Marr, a German journalist is generally regarded as being responsible for this development.[8] Until 1873, Marr had been a struggling journalist, but this changed when his pamphlet *Der Sieg des Judentums ueber das Germanentums* (The Victory of Jewry over Germandom) became so successful that it went through

3

twelve editions in six years. In 1879 he formed *Bund des Antisemitismus* (Union of Anti-Semites). His influence in the literary world resulted in the formation of *Deutsche Antisemitische Vereinigung* (German Anti-Semitic Alliance).

On the political front, anti-Semitism became strongest in Berlin, where one of its chief advocates, Adolf Stoecker, founded the Christian Social Workers Party.[9] He characterized the Jews as "Godless," as "enemies of the Church and Christianity," and called for stern legislation against them. His views became so widespread that, in 1880, Heinrich von Treitschke, a distinguished history professor at Berlin University could say:

> Even in circles of the most highly educated, among men who would reject with disgust any ideas of ecclesiastical intolerance or national arrogance, there resounds as if from one mouth: The Jews are our misfortune.[10]

Anti-Semitism was not restricted to intellectuals. In 1880, the Christian Social Workers Party circulated an "Anti-Semite Petition" among the German people. The impact of this petition can be measured both by the large number of signatures affixed to it and also by the consequent attacks on Jews and their property as German people cried *"Juden raus!"* (Jews, get out [of Germany]!)[11]

Despite anti-Semitism, the Jews were able to make inroads and even advanced to leadership in some professions, particularly in industry, law, medicine, and finance. This advancement, however, was resented by many, and Jewish stereotyping and scapegoating were very much in evidence. Dawidowicz points out that:

> The stereotype of the Jew as international financier became more common. Catholics joined in using the Jews and the liberals as the sticks with which to beat Bismarck and the government.[12]

By World War I, there was enough acceptance of Jews in

the military that some had become officers. However, once more they were used as scapegoats. When Germany began to experience setbacks in battle, the Jews were blamed for the reverses suffered.

When Jews arrived in Germany as refugees from Eastern Europe, the situation was further aggravated. Hitler captured the mood of the times when he said:

> In the year 1916–1917 nearly the whole production was under the control of Jewish finance. . . The spider was slowly beginning to suck the blood out of the people's pores.[13]

With the end of the First World War, Germany became the Weimar Republic, and Jews were guaranteed equal status with Germans by constitution. This status was by no means acceptable to all German society. For example, the program of Hitler's National Socialist German Workers Party, officially published on February 24, 1920, rejected Jews as part of the German *Volk*.[14] A right-wing party made up of conservative Christians and Nationalists (German National People's Party) expressed opposition to the predominance of Jews in government and in public life.[15] Despite the constitutional guarantees in the Weimar Republic,

> Parliamentary democracy survived in Germany for barely one decade, which witnessed the seemingly irresistible rise of the Nazis, the proliferation of anti-Semitic associations and societies—as many as 430—and of anti-Semitic periodicals—as many as 700. Anti-Semitic bills were introduced with shameless regularity into State and National legislatures. The youth of the country, especially the students at the universities were overwhelmingly anti-Semitic. In Berlin's student elections in 1921 two-thirds of the votes were cast for anti-Semitic candidates.[16]

The Church remained neither silent nor neutral during

5

this period. Pfarrer Gerhard Jasper, Director of the Mission School in Berlin, and also editor of the student magazine, published an article by Pfarrer E. Schaeffer in the January, 1925, issue, containing the following statement:

Jews belong to the Semitic race. Compared to Aryans, the Semitic race is inferior. Because of their difference as well as their inferiority, contact with them is disastrous for Aryans, especially for the German Volk.[17]

In the same issue, another pastor, Pfarrer H. Kirchner, said, "It is indisputable; for us the Jews have become a Volks-plague which we must resist." [18]

In a study of Sunday church newsletters published by German Protestant churches between 1918 and 1933, Ino Arndt drew the following conclusion:

From 1918 to 1933 the Jewish question was of great prominence in the Newsletters of the Protestant Churches in Germany. Answers were given from an anti-Semitic point of view. The close connection between Protestant Christianity and Germandom and the strong after-effects of Stoecker's ideas produced a Nationalism, which saw in Jewry a natural enemy of the Christian National tradition and also held it [Jewry] responsible for the collapse of the monarchial order.[19]

The main readers of the Sunday newsletters were members of the middle class—farmers and craftsmen—who were opposed to both the Jews and industrialization. It is this class that formed the bulk of Hitler's followers, and the Sunday newsletters served as the primary means of communication for Hitler to spread propaganda for his anti-Jewish measures.

It was the combination of all these factors, sketched here very briefly, that created the conditions in which Naziism could so easily take root in Germany.

However, it was the formation of the National Socialist

Workers Party in 1920, with Hitler at its head, that marked the birth of an ideology in Germany, an ideology based on hatred for the Jews and one that would finally lead to large numbers of them being exterminated. The ideology was Naziism.

There had always existed strong ties between the Afrikaners of South Africa and the Germans. This was partly due to the fact that the Afrikaners were blood relatives of the Germans who settled in South Africa in the seventeenth and eighteenth centuries. The Afrikaners are, of course, a product of more than just Germans and the Dutch. They also have Malayan and African blood, something they would rather not mention. They are, however, extremely proud of their German blood.

When war broke out between the Afrikaners and the English at the turn of the century, the Germans sympathized with the Afrikaners. Likewise, during the first and second world wars, the Afrikaners sympathized with the Germans.

The Afrikaners had their own exclusive political party, which they called the National Party. The formation of the Nazi Party in Germany resulted in closer links between the Nazis and the National Party (Nats). Both parties decided they would cooperate and forge even closer links. At the time, neither the Nazis nor the Nats were in control of their respective countries. (The Nazis came to power in 1933 and the Nats in 1948.) Both were, however, engaged in strenuous efforts to recruit members in order to take over the government in Germany and in South Africa and change the course of history.

In 1918, the Afrikaners formed an exclusive organization called the "Broederbond" (league of brothers). It remained public until 1924, at which time it went underground. Its program called for not only the strict separation of blacks and whites but also for the absolute supremacy of whites over blacks. The organization was responsible for forging closer links with the Nazis. One of the methods used—one which proved most effective—was sending Afrikaner students to study in Germany during the formative years of the Nazi Party. Men who later held top government positions in South Africa after 1948, had studied in Germany. These included Hendrik Verwoerd and Jan Strijdom, both of whom later became prime ministers. It is important to note a comment about Verwoerd in Germany.

> Verwoerd studied in Hamburg, Leipzig and Berlin from 1924 to 1928. At that time he was said to have had very close relations with National Socialist circles in Germany. *Inter alia,* he was said to have inherited his Anti-Semitism directly from the racist Hitlerian theoreticians.[20]

In examining the statements made by Nazi theoreticians and leaders and then comparing them with racial statements of the Nats, certain clear parallels emerge. There was complete agreement on the following important issues:

Racial Purity

In their party program drawn up in 1920, the Nazis declared:

> Only a person who is of German blood can be a citizen of Germany. Jews, therefore, cannot be citizens of Germany.[21]

A few years later, Hitler, in his book, *Mein Kampf,* said:

> A people that fails to preserve the purity of its racial blood destroys the unity of the soul of the nation in all its manifestations. The most accursed of all crimes is cross-breeding. What we have to fight for is . . . our race and nation . . . and purity of its blood.[22]

In 1927, a leading German ethnologist stressed the importance, for Germans, of maintaining their pure blood. He said:

> Everywhere the running dry of Nordic blood, and its
> heedless dilution, meant the death of a whole culture.
> Where the Nordics, keeping their racial purity, settle
> over an unbroken area, some kind of popular government
> must come into being. . . . For areas with pure race some
> kind of republican system might well be fitting.[23]

After the Nazis came to power in 1933, they passed laws that
were designed to guarantee the so-called "blood purity" of the
German nation. The laws which are dealt with in detail in the
next chapter, were passed at the Nazi Party Congress in
Nuremberg in 1935. The preamble to the laws read:

> Imbued with the insight that the purity of German blood
> is prerequisite for the continued existence of the German
> people, and inspired by the inflexible will to ensure the
> existence of the German nation for all times, the Reich-
> stag has unanimously adopted the following law. . . .[24]

The reason for passing laws to ensure German blood purity
was given at the congress by one of Hitler's chief lieutenants,
Hermann Goering. He said:

> God created the races. He wanted no mixture. We
> therefore reject any attempt to adulterate this racial
> purity.[25]

In Germany, "blood purity" thus became a fetish.

As a result of the close cooperation that existed between
the Nazis and the Nats, the ideas of the German ethnologist
Hans Guenther were quickly echoed in South Africa in 1927,
the same year Guenther published them in Germany. Two
white professors in South Africa published an article in which,
among other things, they said:

> In regard to conditions in South Africa, it would seem

desirable that more attention should be given to the maintenance of racial purity.[26]

In 1942, when Nazi atrocities against the Jews were at their peak, Jan Strijdom who, in 1954, became Prime Minister of South Africa, said:

German National Socialism strives for race purity. That philosophy is certainly the nearest to our National-Christian philosophy in South Africa.[27]

When the Nats drew up the constitution of their party, which they called "The Programme of Principles," they included a clause on "blood purity." It read:

The party is strongly opposed to any attempt that might lead to the mixing of European and non-European blood.[28]

It is worth noting that the Afrikaners regarded themselves as Europeans until fairly recently. Their search for an identity that supposedly preserves their racial purity has led them in recent times to make the absurd claim that they are "the white African tribe." Like the Nazis, the Nats claimed, and continue to claim, that God was the author of their racial purity. Some of their leaders have said:

The maintenance of the Boers' (Afrikaners') tradition of racial purity must be protected at all costs and in every effective way as a sacred pledge entrusted to us by our predecessors as a part of God's plan for our people. Any movement, school or individual that offends against this tradition must be dealt with effectively by the authorities as a race-criminal.[29]

Yet another leader declared:

The racial policy which we Afrikaners should promote

must be directed to the preservation of racial and cultural purity. This is because it is according to the Will of God. . . .[30]

When the Nats came to power in 1948, they, like the Nazis in 1933, translated the so-called "theory of racial purity" into laws in South Africa. Those laws, which are dealt with in the next chapter, are still in force to this day. In Germany, the laws served to dehumanize the Jews. In South Africa, they had a similar effect on the blacks.

Master Race

The Nazis carefully worked out a doctrine of *Herrenrasse* (master race). According to this doctrine, the Jews were subhuman *(Untermenschen)* and the Germans (Aryans) were super human beings *(Uebermenschen)*. There was, of course a direct connection between this doctrine and the theory of racial purity. The Nazis described a marriage between an Aryan and a Jew as "a marriage between a human being and an ape."

To show that they believed that the Jews were the equivalent of apes, they not only forbade marriage between Germans and Jews but also passed laws against any kind of sexual intercourse between Germans and Jews.

The German doctrine of super and subhuman beings appealed to the Nats in South Africa. This fact is plain from the words of their leader, Jan Strijdom, who said:

> Our policy is that the Europeans must stand their ground and must remain *baas* in South Africa. If we reject the *Herrenvolk* idea . . . how can the Europeans be *baas?*[31]

For the Nats, marriage between black and white "is the same as a marriage between a baboon and a human being." This conviction led to the passage of the Immorality Act, which

11

makes sexual intercourse between blacks and whites a criminal offense. The law is dealt with in the next chapter.

A Chosen People

The claims the Nazis made about themselves needed some form of authoritative support if they were to be acceptable to the masses of the people whose support they needed. They, therefore, presented themselves as a people "chosen by God" to do his will. Being so chosen, they were immune to any form of criticism, because they were merely carrying out the "will of God." Hitler appealed to the Germans to carry out "the mission appointed for them by the Creator of the Universe." [32] He also said: "We believe in the task which Providence has laid upon us."[33] Afrikaner leaders have expressed similar convictions in such statements as:

> Indeed, the history of the Afrikaner reveals a will and determination which makes one feel that Afrikanerdom is not the work of men but the creation of God.[34]

From their church leaders, the Afrikaners hear that:

> We believe that as a people we have had a calling from God and we believe that we have a god-given task in relation to the non-whites in this African continent. God brought us here for a purpose.[35]

The Afrikaner leaders also see their so-called "calling" as evidence of their racial superiority. They have said:

> To achieve this calling the white man has been bidden to act as the guardian, master and spiritual leader of the black man. . . . We are in the process of setting the world an example since we know and believe that God wills it thus.[36]

12

This idea of being the chosen of God finds its strongest support within the exclusive Afrikaner Church, which is known as the Dutch Reformed Church.

Anti-Communism

On January 30, 1933, the Nazi party with Hitler at its head, became the new government of Germany. Less than a month later, on February 21, the Reichstag building (Parliament) in Berlin was set on fire. The government claimed that the Communists were responsible, and on February 28 took drastic measures against them, including arrests, closing of their offices, and confiscating of their property. For the most part, the public and the churches accepted the moves of the Nazis.

On February 28, the government persuaded the president, Paul von Hindenburg, to suspend certain sections of the Weimar Constitution so that the actions against the Communists could be legal. This led, in May, to the banning of the Communist Party. After that, anyone who criticized the Nazis they branded a Communist. Those who were not branded Communists were labeled tools or agents of communism. This was done by the Nazis in order to intimidate their critics into silence and to discredit them as traitors. The method proved very effective in silencing opposition to Naziism. The churches supported Hitler partly because they allowed themselves to be hoodwinked into believing that Naziism was a bulwark against communism.

The Nationalists came to power in South Africa in 1948. In 1950, they passed the "Suppression of Communism Act" and banned the South African Communist Party. What is interesting is that, by South African standards and practice, anyone who criticizes the Nationalist Party and its ideology of *apartheid* is branded a Communist or an agent of communism. "Communism" in South Africa is defined in law in such wide terms that the regime in South Africa is able to charge anyone or any organization with being a Communist agent or

have invaded both Tanzania and Mozambique, and thus Hertzog's dream of "a territory in central Africa stretching from the Atlantic Ocean (Angola and Namibia) to the Indian Ocean" (Tanzania and Mozambique), would have come true. Nothing would have prevented the Nats from terrorizing other African states. Worse still, *apartheid* would have spread from its home, the southern part of Africa, to most of Africa. The Cubans, therefore, were to the African people, in general, and to black southern Africans in particular, exactly what the Allies had been to countries in Europe that had been occupied by the Germans—namely, liberators. It must be remembered too that South Africa has an occupation army of some 100,000 men in Namibia in defiance of the United Nations and international opinion. That army not only terrorizes and murders the Namibian people at will, just as the Germans did in the countries they occupied, but also invades neighboring black states, such as Botswana, Angola, and Zambia. South Africa also constantly invades Mozambique, Swaziland, and Lesotho to kidnap and murder. These carefully planned acts of aggression and violence are no different from what Nazi Germany did to the rest of Europe.

Cooperation between the Nats and the Nazis

During the 1930s and early 1940s, there was much evidence of cooperation between the Nats and the Nazis in South Africa. This is mainly due to the fact that all the Nats students who studied in Germany during the twenties, and formative years of Nazism, returned to South Africa in the late 1920s and early 1930s. All of them held important and influential positions within Afrikanerdom. The thirties and early forties proved to be the formative years of *apartheid,* an ideology which, like Naziism, is rooted in the fallacy that there are super human beings and subhuman beings. For the Nazis, the Jews were the subhumans, and for the Nats the blacks are the subhumans. Contrary to popular belief, the

16

word "*apartheid,*" like Naziism, does not have a meaning. It represents an ideology. The word, which first surfaced in Afrikaner circles in the early 1940s, was used as a political slogan after 1945, and was put into practice after the Nats won the elections in 1948.

The architect of *apartheid,* as we have known it since 1948, was Hendrik Verwoerd. As has been mentioned above, he studied in Germany in the midtwenties, where he had close contacts with the architects of Naziism. On his return to South Africa, he became a professor of psychology at the exclusive Afrikaner university of Stellenbosch. In 1937, Jan Strijdom, a leading Afrikaner political figure, appointed Verwoerd as the first editor of the newly formed Afrikaner Nationalist mouthpiece *Die Transvaler.* In one of his first editorials, Verwoerd wrote:

Both in Italy and in Germany the systems have done much that is good for these countries, although of course they are not without fault. . . The Nationalists would be very remiss if they did not study the conditions existing in Europe, where new methods of state organization and new objectives are born out of the pressures of nation-building.[39]

The "new methods of state organization" Verwoerd was referring to were Fascism in Italy and Germany. The "new objectives" were domination. That is what Verwoerd aspired to. His aim was to destroy the parliamentary system of government that existed in South Africa at the time, and he pointed out that the way to achieve this goal would be for all the Afrikaners to become members of the Nationalist Party. He said:

The Parliamentary system as it exists in the Union today is of British structure. When the Republic comes, a change will be made; but as no change can be effected at this moment, Afrikaners must choose an instrument which can bring the best results under the existing British Parliamentary system—that best instrument is the Herenigde Nasionale Party.[40]

While a student in Germany, Verwoerd had heard Josef Goebbels, who later became Hitler's propaganda minister, denounce the parliamentary system of the Weimar Republic. In a speech Goebbels said:

We entered Parliament in order to supply ourselves in the arsenal of democracy with its own weapons . . . in order to paralyze the Weimar Republic.[41]

Verwoerd's editorials, which strongly and openly supported the Nazis, reached their peak when the atrocities committed by the Nazis against defenseless and innocent men, women, and children were also at their peak. This fact did not escape the attention of the English-speaking white South Africans, who, unlike the Afrikaner leadership, decidedly supported the war effort against the Nazis. The English-speaking press, therefore, attacked Verwoerd for his views. When in 1941 *Die Transvaler* misinformed its readers on the war situation, the *Star,* an English-speaking paper, said in its editorial:

Die Transvaler, which is published in Johannesburg though its spiritual home lies somewhere between Keerom Street and the Munich beer hall, has this week given a rather better example than usual of the process of falsification which it applies to current news in its support of Nazi propaganda. On Saturday the Bureau of Information supplied the Union newspapers with a sample of the broadcasts dealing with South African affairs which have been coming from Berlin. Like many previous ones it reiterated the assurance to South Africa that Germany does not wish to force its system of government upon other countries—"a statement," the Information Bureau's script remarked, "which is belied by what is happening in Europe."

18

Die Transvaler not only omitted this passage in reproducing the message, but made Zeesen's profession of benevolent intentions towards this country the occasion for a full dress article on the theme that Germany "would not deny the Afrikaners their republic," and the unwisdom of criticizing national socialism as practised within Germany. . . .

No one would so object had national socialism remained a domestic matter for that country. When its advent has resulted in sanguinary attack upon every country and other system of government which the Germans can reach in hitherto unheard-of excesses of cruelty and falsehood against them, and in a destruction of human resources such that it may take decades if not centuries to restore, the rest of the world not only has the right to criticize but the unescapable obligation to resist.[42]

Verwoerd sued the *Star* but lost the case because the court found that:

On the evidence he [Verwoerd] is not entitled to complain. He did support Nazi propaganda, he did make his paper a tool of Naziism in South Africa, and he knew it.[43]

Verwoerd's editorial support for the Nazis toned down when it became apparent that the Nazis would not win the war. In 1943, one of the German secret agents who was stationed in South Africa cabled Berlin to inform the Nazi officials that Verwoerd's newspaper, which was the mouthpiece of the Nationalist Party, had changed its attitude and was no longer openly supportive of Naziism. The telegram read:

The party press is extremely reserved with regard to Germany since the military reverse. O.L. recommend a frank explanation with the editor-in-chief Verwoerd.[44]

Although Verwoerd toned down his editorials and his anti-

Semitic pronouncements, as we shall see later, he remained a firm believer in Naziism.

Verwoerd was not a lone voice as far as support for Naziism was concerned. Nor did this support come from a few misguided Nats. The Afrikaner leadership was almost solidly behind Hitler and hoped and prayed for a German victory. For example, Ben Schoeman, who later became minister of transport in the first Afrikaner Nationalist government in 1948, said in 1940:

> The whole future of Afrikanerdom is dependent upon a German victory We may as well say that openly because it is a fact.[45]

A year later, the man who became the Nationalists' first prime minister in 1948 informed Afrikaner voters that:

> Perhaps 80 to 85 per cent of National Socialism has been taken up in the Nationalist Party programme, which the Party will carry out in letter and in spirit when it comes to power.[46]

The Afrikaner leadership was not simply involved in making public declarations in support of Naziism. There was also practical evidence to prove that the Nats were fully committed to the same ideology as the Nazis. The Nats went to great lengths in order to demonstrate to the Nazis in Germany that they were their allies. Such Nazi organizations as the Brown Shirts, the Gray Shirts, the Black Shirts, and the New Order, were all started in South Africa, and the membership was exclusively Afrikaner. The Afrikaner leaders even invited a prominent Hitler youth leader to South Africa to train their youth along the same lines as Hitler's Pioneers.

However, the most glaring and daring example of Naziism within Afrikanerdom came from the Ossewa-Brandwag, an ostensibly nonpolitical, cultural organization, which, by

1940, claimed to have a membership of more than 200,000. Despite its claims of being a cultural organization, the Ossewa-Brandwag was mainly involved in subversive, para-military, pro-Nazi activities in South Africa. It served as a Nazi secret army in South Africa and was involved in committing acts of sabotage against vital installations. John Vorster, who later became prime minister of South Africa was a general of the Ossewa-Brandwag. He was violently opposed to South Africa's joining the war on the side of the Allies, and his Nazi activities within South Africa led to his arrest in 1942. He was interned and only released after the end of the war.

The present South African leadership, therefore, not only opposed the Allies but actively supported the Nazis in the hope that the Nazis would win the war and subject the whole world to Fascism. In 1941, a leading South African newspaper, the *Sunday Express,* described the Ossewa-Brandwag as:

> . . . based on Hitler's National Socialism. The whole structure of the local organization, with special emphasis laid on discipline, is Germanic in its conception.[47]

For those who still doubted what the Nats stood for, John Vorster spelled out their stand in unequivocal terms. Addressing a rally of Afrikaner supporters shortly before his arrest in 1942, he said:

> We stand for Christian Nationalism which is an ally of National Socialism. You can call this antidemocratic principle dictatorship if you wish. In Italy it is called Fascism, in Germany National Socialism, and in South Africa, Christian Nationalism.[48]

The statement was made at a time when Germany was ravaging Europe and at a time when the Nazis were claiming that they had cleared Germany of Jews.

The Nazis lost the war in 1945, and in South Africa the

era of glorifying Naziism publicly came to an end. However, the spirit of Naziism lived on and found its living expression in what the Afrikaners called *apartheid*. All during the war, the Afrikaner supporters were systematically brainwashed in believing in such fallacies as "blood purity." They were also made to believe that Naziism was the only right path for them to follow since the principles of Naziism were ordained by God. After the Nazis lost the war, the Nats did not retract what they had been preaching. On the contrary, they continued with greater vigor. They only changed their tactics and used the newly coined word *"apartheid"* to express their old ideas. They continued to call attention to the "black peril" and promised their supporters that, if elected to power, they would solve the problem of blacks (black peril) "once and for all."

Because the Nats had laid the foundations of their ideology in the thirties and early forties, they were able to win the "general election" held in South Africa in 1948. The time had finally come for them to put into practice what they had been preaching.

When the Nazis took over the reins of government in Germany in 1933, they embarked on a program of legislation that finally controlled every aspect of Jewish life. Because of their admiration for the Nazis and their cooperation with them, the Nats were fully aware of these laws, just as most of the world was aware.

Once the Nats came to power in South Africa in 1948, they too embarked on a program of legislation designed to translate into reality their theory that blacks were subhuman.

Laws by themselves may reflect the thinking of legislators, but, unless they are put into practice, their importance is rather academic. In examining the anti-Jewish laws passed by the Nazis, therefore, it is important to bear in mind that the Nazis not only passed the laws against the Jews, but they also applied them ruthlessly. It must also be remembered that the Jews had no say in the making and/or execution of the laws. "Subhumans" could not have a say.

In the case of South Africa, the blacks had no say in the

making of the laws that have effectively reduced them to the status of subhumans, something the Nats claim for the blacks. The laws are ruthlessly applied in South Africa, just as they were in Nazi Germany. What remains is to determine whether Malan, the first *apartheid* prime minister meant what he said:

Perhaps 80 to 85 per cent of National Socialism has been taken up in the Nationalist Party programme, which the party will carry out in letter and in spirit when it comes to power.[49]

2

Similarities and Differences between Naziism and Apartheid

Weltanschauung (World View)

The Nazi Party Program of 1920 gave a clear and precise indication of what the Nazis were striving for and what they would do if elected to power. The document revealed the two most important ingredients of Naziism, namely nationalism and racism (anti-Semitism). In the document, the Nazis rejected everything that was non-German, maintaining that the Germans were a *Herrenrasse* (master race).

The Jews were singled out as a race unfit to be German citizens because they did not have "pure blood." What the Nazis envisioned, therefore, was a German nation free of Jewish blood and a German state free of Jews. This goal of an exclusive and master race had to be reached at all costs.

Upon assuming power, the Nazis embarked on a program that transformed their plans into reality. The program had three main stages. The first stage was the demoralizing and dehumanizing of the Jews through laws that discriminated against and oppressed them, simply because they were Jews, a reality they could not change even if they wished to. The second stage was the forced removal of the Jews from their homes, property, and businesses and their placement in ghettoes. The third and final stage was the Holocaust.

The Nazis based their claims to "exclusiveness" on the premise that God had created different nations and races because He did not want any mixture. Thus racism and nationalism assumed the status of religious dogma. All these elements are present in *apartheid!*

The main difference between Naziism and *apartheid* is that, at the time of this writing, the Afrikaner Nationalists have not embarked on a *formal* process of exterminating blacks as the Germans did to the Jews. As we shall see, under *apartheid* "genocide consists of dosing murder by various means and maintaining the percentage of the non-white population at a 'reasonable' rate."[1]

The Laws

As has been pointed out above, both the Nazis and the Afrikaner Nationalists passed laws that legalized racism and nationalism. In both cases, the core laws were those against mixed marriages and the laws providing for exclusive citizenship based on the concept of pure blood. These two sets of laws provided the foundations on which, in each country, hundreds of other laws were based, with the ultimate aim of producing pure races and pure states. In Germany, these laws finally controlled every aspect of Jewish life. The same can be said of South Africa as far as blacks are concerned. As was the case in Germany, the laws in South Africa are not only discriminatory but also oppressive.

It is not possible in a study such as this to compare and contrast all the laws passed by the Nazis and the Afrikaner Nationalists that affected the social, economic, political, and legal status of Jews in Germany and the blacks in South Africa. A selected few will have to suffice.

Certain parallels emerge when the Nazi laws and the Afrikaner laws are compared. In both cases, the underlying principle is the preservation of "racial purity"and superiority. In both cases, God is cited as the one who ordained racial separation from creation in order to protect racial purity and superiority. In both systems, while quoting the Scriptures to support the doctrine of racial purity, the marriage laws include provisions that nullify the Gospel teaching on marriage as found in Matthew 19:6.

In order to build a permanent wall between the Germans and the Jews, the Nazis enacted an elaborate set of laws, all of which worked to the disadvantage of the Jews. The Afrikaner Nationalists followed a similar pattern in their laws against the blacks.

In January 1933, the Nazis assumed control of the German Government. A little more than two years later, in September 1935, they held a party congress in Nuremberg at which legislation was enacted that had far-reaching consequences for the Jewish people.

The careful preparation leading to the passage of the famous Nuremberg Laws is worth noting. It was not by coincidence that Hans Guenther, the well-known anthropologist, was present at the congress to be honored for his work in ethnology.[2] His writings on the primacy of Nordic blood were of special interest to the Nazis and were most useful to them in the implementation of their anti-Semitic policies. Guenther was one of the leading advocates of "racial purity."[3]

No attempt was made to define "racial purity" or to document it scientifically, but several speakers at the Congress addressed themselves to the need "to protect healthy German blood," and to "prevent further bastardizing through mixed marriage with Jews."[4] One must agree with Phillip Tobias's observation that "under the Nazi regime, race purity became a fetish."[5]

The stage was set for the legislation that would regulate the lives of Jews living in Germany. The term "Jew" was used for the first time in this legislation. No longer could there be any questions about the meaning of "non-Aryan." It meant "Jew."

26

The first set of Nuremberg Laws was titled "Laws for the Protection of German Blood and German Honor." The Preamble read:

Imbued with the insight that the purity of German blood is prerequisite for the continued existence of the German people, and inspired by the inflexible will to ensure the existence of the German nation for all times, the Reichstag has unanimously adopted the following law, which is hereby promulgated:
Section I:
a) Marriages between Jews and citizens of German or kindred blood are forbidden. Marriages concluded in defiance of this law are void, even if, for the purpose of evading this law they are concluded abroad. [6]

The law specifically prohibited marriages between Germans and Jews. The stated purpose in the preamble was to preserve the purity of the German blood. However, there was no need to establish this purity since Germans were, by definition, "pure." By juxtaposing the terms "German racial purity" and "Jews," the term "Jews" came to mean those who threatened the very existence of the German nation. It is perhaps this single law that did most to condition the attitude of Germans toward Jews in the years following its passage.

It is not surprising that the reaction of the Germans was one of fear and hatred for the Jews. That which threatens survival can not be loved. By adding the provision that such marriages would be void even if concluded outside of Germany, the Nazis condemned not only Jews living in Germany, but the entire Jewish people. This should have raised questions for practicing Christians, in view of the Gospel teaching on marriage based on Matthew 19:6: "What therefore God hath joined together, let no man put asunder."

The Nazis were not satisfied with prohibiting marriage between Germans and Jews; they went a step further by encouraging divorce between those mixed couples who had married before the enactment of the law. The following decision by the courts illustrates this:

A person of German blood who refuses to have sexual intercourse with, or is totally alienated from his/ her Jewish spouse cannot be accused of failing in his/her matrimonial duties, let alone of breaking the marital vows as contained in Paragraph 49 of the Marriage Laws, because the healthy racial experience of the German Volk disapproves of the union of a German and a Jew.[7]

The second section of the laws passed at Nuremberg reads as follows:

Section II:
b. Extra marital sexual relations between Jews and citizens of German or kindred blood are forbidden.[8]

Moral considerations were not behind the passage of this law. The purpose was to further tighten Section I (a) in order to foster racial "purity." There is evidence to support this view.

In 1936 the Nazis began to establish human breeding institutions, which they named *Lebensborn*. The purpose was stated thus:

Lebensborn has to foster fecundity among the SS, to protect all mothers of good blood, as well as to care for them and to look after pregnant mothers and children of good blood. From this endeavor there will arise an elite youth of equal worth both spiritually and physically,— the nobility of the future.[9]

Heinrich Himmler, who was in charge of the elite *Schutzstafel* (SS) later said to his men:

All legitimate and illegitimate children of good blood

whose fathers were killed in the war will be brought under the sponsorship of specially chosen representatives of the Reichsfuehrer SS, responsible to me personally. . . . During the war the SS will be responsible for protecting the mothers and children, whether legitimate or illegitimate, from any immediate dangers or difficulty. After the war, if the fathers return, the SS will grant suitable financial assistance for the re-establishment of the family. [10]

Sexual promiscuity and adultery were apparently encouraged, but with an important qualification—the policy applied only to those of *pure blood.* Contravention of Section II of the law to protect German Blood and Honor was a serious crime, punishable by a prison term or death.

As late as 1942, when Jews were already being deported from Germany, Leo Katzenberger, a Jewish businessman, was hanged—despite insufficient evidence—after being accused and found guilty of having had sexual relations with Irene Seiler, a German businesswoman. Irene was sentenced to two years' imprisonment but was released after serving only six months.[11] The seriousness of the penalty for contravening this law reflects the importance attached by the Nazis to the preservation and promotion of German racial purity.

There was only one other law passed at the Congress in Nuremberg—the Citizenship Law. It read as follows:

A Reich citizen is a national of German or kindred blood only, one who through his conduct proves that he is willing and suitable to serve the German Volk and Reich faithfully.

Citizenship rights will be acquired by receiving the Reich Citizenship Document. According to law, only Reich citizens will have full political rights.[12]

The passage of the Citizenship Law was the culmination of the long-thought-out process designed to make Germany a country without Jews. The aim was clearly stated in the 1920 Nazi Party Program.

> Only those who are fellow Germans shall be citizens of our State. Only those who are of German blood can be considered as our fellow-Germans.
> Those who are not citizens of the state must live in Germany as foreigners, and must be subject to the law of aliens.[13]

Overnight, the Jews had become stateless. There was nothing they could do to change their Jewish blood into German blood. According to German law, they were condemned by their very nature.

In order to compensate for the lack of scientific definition of "racial purity," the Nazis called upon the ultimate authority—*God*. The fact that God had created different races was in itself proof that He wanted no mixture of the races. For a nation with a long tradition of Christianity, an appeal to the "Will of God" could not be taken lightly. Hermann Goering, one of Hitler's chief lieutenants, declared:

> God created the races. He wanted no mixture. We therefore, reject any attempt to adulterate this racial purity.[14]

The Nuremberg Laws were designed to make Germany a country free of Jews (Reichsbuergergesetz v. 15, Sept., 1935) and the German *Volk* free of Jewish blood (Gesetz zum Schutze des deutschen Blutes und der deutschen Ehre, v. 15, Sept., 1935). These two laws opened the doors to a flood of legislation that finally controlled every aspect of Jewish life.

Afrikaner Assumption of Power

The "Programme of Principles" which the Nationalists

used as a basic document for their 1948 election campaign contained the following statement:

As a basic principle of its attitude towards Natives and Coloureds, the Party recognises that both are permanent parts of the country's population, under the trusteeship of the European race. It is strongly opposed to any attempt that might lead to the mixing of European and non-European blood. It also declares itself in favor of territorial and political segregation between Europeans and non-Europeans in general and in residential, and as far as practicable, in the industrial spheres.[15]

As soon as they came to power, the Nationalists embarked on a program that would transform *apartheid* from an ideology into a living reality. One must note that they actually carried out what they had for many years said they would do if elected to office.[15]

The Prohibition of Mixed Marriages Act

One of the first measures the nationalist government introduced in Parliament was a bill that was enacted into law as "The Prohibition of Mixed Marriages Act." The act was amended in 1968 in order to close loopholes. The act reads:

Marriages between Whites and non-Whites are forbidden. Any such marriage entered into outside the Republic of South Africa is void and of no effect.[16]

When he introduced the bill in parliament, Theophilus Donges, Minister of the Interior, said the law was necessary in order "to check blood mixture and promote racial purity." He further stated that the measure had been "requested by the Dutch Reformed Church."[17]

The idea of racial purity looms large in the thinking of the Afrikaner Nationalists and is linked with Christianity. Daniel

31

Malan, in his capacity as Prime Minister of South Africa, made this clear:

> The Afrikaner's traditional fear of racial equality (egalitarianism) between White and Black derives from his aversion to miscegenation. The Afrikaner has always believed very firmly that if he is to be true to his primary calling of bringing Christianity to the heathen, he must preserve his racial identity intact. The church is, therefore, entirely opposed to intermarriage between Black and White and is committed to withstand everything that is calculated to facilitate it.[18]

He urged the whites to throw "an impenetrable armour around themselves—the armour of racial purity and self-preservation."[19]

This statement was made in 1954, and although blacks had been in contact with Christianity in South Africa for over three hundred years, they were still regarded as heathens. According to this reasoning, Christianity can only be preached by those who are racially pure, namely, the whites. Once again, racial purity is a prerequisite for self preservation, or, more precisely, racial purity is a prerequisite for continued existence.

The defenders of this law have gone far in trying to convince the world that intermarriage has disastrous social and cultural consequences. A Dutch Reformed Church minister supported the law by focusing on the offspring of such a marriage—known in South African terminology as "Coloured People." He said:

> Here we have a people who came into being through miscegenation with Whites. And as a mongrel race, they are, to us, the writing on the wall, a warning against what can happen with intermixture. They are Western in their code of living. They speak our language, sing our songs, live in our country, but they are a people notorious for their moral corruption. Lies are to them second

32

nature. They are absolutely unreliable in any matter, have little ambition and get their greatest pleasure from a bottle of wine and debauchery.[20]

The law specifically prohibits intermarriage between whites and non-whites. In South Africa, where there are different ethnic groups, the law and the concept of purity of blood are significant. The dark-skinned groups, for example, the Africans, "Coloreds," and "Indians," may intermarry. On the other side of the color line, Afrikaners, British, Germans, Italians, and white Americans may also intermarry with other *whites*. Because there had been intermarriage between black and white before the Nationalist government came to power, a solution had to be found for those Afrikaners who had some "impure blood" in their blood system. The answer was provided.

Nobody in South Africa need worry about a bit of non-white blood (mostly from Eastern people with a high civilization) which filtered in in the beginning as a result of mixed marriages. It has been diluted by pure blood from Europe with the result that the few families in question today have some of the blondest people among them. The blood composition of the Afrikaner people as a whole is today purer than that of many of Europe's and America's people.[21]

Despite the fact that medical science has not been able to provide any scientific distinction between the blood of black people and that of white people, in 1956, the Nationalists drafted legislation that required that the blood from white donors be kept separate from that of black donors. Although blacks may receive blood donated by whites, the blood from black donors may never be transfused into white patients. In order to avoid any accidents, the blood from black donors is kept in containers with black labels and that from white donors with white labels.[22]

Few people have been convicted for contravening this act,

primarily because it is so easy to enforce. A black person would find it difficult to pretend that he or she is white and vice versa. The convictions that have taken place have been in borderline cases where a "colored" person looks white. In such cases, as Marquard points out, "the police, probably on private and malicious information, suspect one of the partners, and a prosecution takes place."[23]

The importance of the Prohibition of Mixed Marriages Act lies in the fact that it is one of the major instruments used to guarantee the so-called "racial purity" and "self-preservation" of the Afrikaner people—their highest concern. Its power to void any marriage between black and white places the act in a position where it supersedes the law of Christ as stated in Matthew 19:6. This indeed may be a price the Dutch Reformed Church is prepared to pay in its commitment to prevent mixed marriages.

The act also gives practical expression to the implied notion that blacks are impure. When it was first passed in 1949, it served as a basis for other racial legislation as will become evident in the following pages. The conviction that whites are of pure blood, and the propagation of this idea, has made a major contribution to the shaping of the attitudes of whites toward blacks. The fact that such ideas are taught to white children in schools makes the task of changing such attitudes extremely difficult. Phillip Tobias says:

> The tragedy for our young children [white], the South Africans of tomorrow, is that some of our schoolbooks on History and Race Studies have many examples of this sort of thing [racial purity]. Small wonder that young people, nurtured on such pseudo-scientific fallacies grow up to approve policies based upon these very fallacies.[24]

The Immorality Act

In 1950, the year following the passage of the "Prohibition of Mixed Marriages Act," a bill to prohibit sexual intercourse between blacks and whites was introduced in Parliament. It was passed and became law that same year with the title "The Immorality Amendment Act No. 21, of 1950."

A law had been passed previously, in 1927, when James Hertzog was Prime Minister, prohibiting extramarital sexual intercourse between black men and white women. (Extra marital sexual intercourse between *white* men and *black* women was not prohibited by the 1927 law.) The 1950 amendment eliminated the distinction; black and white, male and female were included in its provisions. It also extended the prohibitions to all nonwhite races, not merely the Africans.

In 1957, the act was further amended, introducing severe penalties to be meted out to those who contravened it. The sentence recommended by the Immorality Act of 1957 was a maximum of seven years' imprisonment with hard labor.[25]

The aim of the law was not so much the control of immorality as it was—in the words of its sponsor, Theophilus Donges, Minister of the Interior—"to try to preserve some sort of *apartheid* in what one may call prostitution."[26] The purpose of this act was the same as that which prohibited mixed marriages, namely: to preserve racial purity. G. Eloff, in his book titled *Rasse en Rassevermenging* (Races and Miscegenation), wrote:

The maintenance of the Boers' tradition of racial purity must be protected at all costs and in every effective way, as a sacred pledge entrusted to us by our predecessor, as a part of God's plan for our people. Any movement, school or individual that offends against this tradition must be dealt with effectively by the authorities as a race criminal.[27]

The Prohibition of Mixed Marriages Act was not difficult to implement. The Immorality Act, on the other hand, has proven troublesome, since the methods of enforcement in-

35

fringe on the individual's right to privacy. Leo Marquard writes:

> Policemen shine torches into stationary cars at night and enter private houses and servants' quarters on suspicion.[28]

The application of justice to "race criminals" once they are arrested and brought to trial is even more questionable than the spying tactics used to apprehend them. According to the Immorality Act, morality is judged by the color of the skin: An action that is not immoral for people with one skin color *becomes* immoral when it is performed by persons with a different skin color. Gwendolen Carter points out that:

> . . .African females have been found guilty and sentenced while their European male partners have in a separate trial, been acquitted.[29]

The Immorality Act tightened the loopholes and extended the provisions of the Prohibition of Mixed Marriages Act. But there was another safeguard needed to assure success to the Nationalist Party's design to produce a race of "pure blood" and to protect its privileged condition.

Citizenship in South Africa

In 1936, the limited franchise that a few blacks enjoyed was abolished.[30] This disenfranchisement was formalized legally in 1959, when the passage of the "Promotion of Bantu Self-Government Act" took from blacks all rights of citizenship in South Africa. [31] There had been a steady progress toward this point for many years.

In 1942, the Nationalist Party Programme clearly stated its policy regarding the rights of "the Natives":

> It [the Nationalist Party] also declares itself in

favour of territorial and political segregation of the Native, and of separation between Europeans and non-Europeans in general, and in the residential and—as far as is practicable—in the industrial spheres.[32]

In 1947, Johannes Strijdom, later Prime Minister of South Africa, said:

The Nationalist Party policy is division and *apartheid*. The Native is to live his own life in his own area. The Native must only be allowed to leave his area to come to work in the European areas as a temporary worker. His wife and children must remain behind.[33]

This is the same man, it will be recalled, who considered Naziism as "most certainly nearest" in philosophy to the National Christian philosophy in South Africa.[34]

In 1948, when the Nationalists came to power, they immediately embarked on an elaborate law-enacting program designed to translate into a reality the promises they had made to the all-white voters who elected them, regarding political and territorial segregation of blacks. The accomplishment of the deed was evidently not happening quickly enough to satisfy the white constituency. In 1950, the Minister of Native Affairs had to assure the white electorate that blacks in South Africa would have "no political or social or other rights equal with Europeans."[35]

It can be seen that the "Promotion of Bantu Self-Government Act No. 46 of 1959" was the actual fulfillment of political promises that helped win the election for the Nationalist Party in 1948. It also marked the legal birth of South Africa as a totally white nation and the reduction of blacks to the status of aliens in their own land.

The Act abolished the Parliamentary representation of Africans. It recognized eight African national units—North Sotho, South Sotho, Tswana, Zulu, Swazi, Xhosa, Tsonga, and Venda—and provided for the appointment

37

of, initially, five Commissioners-General to represent the Government in African areas. The constitution and powers of Bantu territorial, regional, and tribal authorites were more clearly defined; and it was laid down that representatives of territorial authorities would be appointed in urban areas.[36]

In 1964, whites needed assurance from the government once more. The presence of large numbers of black workers in South African mines and factories was a cause of alarm to them. Hendrik Verwoerd, the Prime Minister, assured them that this was not a sign that the government had deviated from its policy of establishing a South Africa for whites only. He stated:

The mere presence of large numbers of Bantu in employment does not amount to integration. It is only when there is intermingling of those people in social life or in the political or religious spheres that one really gets integration. The mere fact that foreigners are employed in a community or in another country does not constitute integration.[37]

An inference is drawn by Verwoerd in the above statement that is worth noting, namely, that the laws already passed by Parliament—which functioned as a rigid wall between the races in the social, political, and religious spheres—had, in fact, reduced blacks to the status of foreigners. This is stated explicitly elsewhere when he points out that blacks are allowed to work in South Africa "like Italians who go to France to take up employment there."[38]

This is merely a selective account of the laws passed by the Afrikaner Nationalists against the blacks in South Africa. Leslie Rubin, author of a brief commentary on *apartheid* legislation, states:

Since the present Government came to power in

South Africa in 1948, a vast body of legislative enactments has come into existence designed to give effect to the new policy of *apartheid*. Hundreds of laws have been passed by Parliament; thousands of regulations, proclamations and government notices have been issued under those laws. In addition there are numerous by-laws made by the municipal councils of cities and towns throughout the country. All these combine to institute the legal apparatus which regulates the daily lives of more than four-fifths of the population of South Africa, that is, the 15 million non-whites.[39]

It is important to remember that the laws passed by the Nazis against the Jews were ideological laws, designed expressly to oppress them and to control every aspect of their lives. This is what made Nazi Germany a totalitarian state. The Nats copied both the laws and the method of enforcing them, namely, brutality.

The Nazi Education Laws

When the Nazis came to power in 1933, both Jewish and German children attended the same schools except in the case of Confessional schools. Even in such schools, it was religion rather than race that determined attendance. But the Nazi concept of racial purity could not be reconciled with mixed schools for Germans and Jews, so, in order to correct this state of affairs, the Nazis passed a law in April 1933, titled "Law against the Overcrowding of German Schools and Universities."[40]

This law provided for the reduction of the number of Jewish children in schools and of Jewish students in institutions of higher education. The number permitted in any school was based proportionately on the number of Jewish persons living in that particular area. Thus, for the Jews, admittance to a school became a privilege rather than a right.[41]

But this partial exclusion was not satisfactory to the Nazis; it was not quite consistent with the ideal of racial purity. Therefore, on November 15, 1938, the Minister of Education decreed that "all Jewish children be expelled and excluded from German schools."[42] From that date on, Jewish children could attend only Jewish schools, and consequently social mixing was prevented at a very early stage in life. The effects of such harsh legislation did not seem to concern the authorities. The historian Raul Hilberg writes:

> Although the school segregation measures created a very serious problem for the Jewish community, they provoked less discussion and less controversy in the upper levels of the German bureaucracy [43]

The Afrikaner Nationalist Government Education Laws

In 1953 the Afrikaner government enacted legislation that created, for the first time in the history of South Africa, a government office to deal exclusively with the education of blacks. The "Bantu Education Act No. 47 of 1953" gave the government jurisdiction over all aspects of "Native" education: It reads:

> As from the date of commencement of this Act. . . .the control of native education shall vest in the government of the Union subject to the provisions of this Act;
> It shall be the function of the Department under the direction and control of the Minister, to perform all the work necessary for and incidental to the general administration of native education.[44]

Six years later, university education was included with the passage of the Extension of University Act, No. 45 of 1959.[45] This provided for:

> . . . the establishment of separate university colleges for

40

Black students and for the progressive exclusion of these students from the previously open universities.[46]

When the minister of Native Affairs, Hendrik Verwoerd, introduced the Bantu Education Bill in Parliament, the Prime Minister, Daniel Malan, gave the following reason why blacks had to receive a separate and inferior education:

For a white minority to face a large majority of civilized and educated non-whites, wishing to share our way of life, and striving for equality in all respects [would make] the fight for a White South Africa immeasurably more difficult.[47]

To this, Hendrik Verwoerd added:

I just want to remind hon. members that if the Native in South Africa today in any kind of school in existence is being taught to expect that he will live his adult life under a policy of equal rights, he is making a big mistake.[48]

The major concern for the Nationalists in drafting these laws was that educated Africans would refuse to accept the inferior status required to achieve "racial purity" in South Africa. Designing an inferior grade education for blacks would ensure this inferior status and protect the superior status of whites.

The difference between the German laws and the Afrikaner Nationalist laws is that, in South Africa, primary school education was always segregated, whereas, in Germany, there was a time when German and Jewish schoolchildren attended the same schools. However, at university level, the laws in both countries had the same effect, that is, of separating the students on the basis of race, and the students had no choice in the matter. In Germany discrimination and oppression became entrenched through the manipulation of education, and the same can be said of South Africa.

41

Freedom of Worship in Nazi Germany

On April 7, 1933, the Nazis passed the "Law for the Reestablishment of a Professional Civil Service." Section 3 (I) of the law read: "Non-Aryan officers are to be pensioned." Section 15 of the law read: "The same can be applied to white-collar workers and labourers."[49] Non-Aryans were to be separated from Ayrans not only in the civil service but in all areas of employment. The law did not mention the Church explicitly but the idea of separation in practice, included all spheres of human activity. The application of this law in the German Protestant Churches is discussed in chapter 3.

On November 13, 1933, powerful supporters of the Nazis within the Protestant Church declared:

> We expect our Church to speedily implement the Aryan Clause without any modifications and further to group together all Protestant Christians with foreign blood and to found a separate Jewish Christian Church for them.[50]

Many Churches did in fact exclude Jewish Christians from their congregations, and the whole question of "racial purity" within the church became a major controversial issue between supporters and opponents of the measure.

The Nazis, while stating that there was religious freedom in Germany, did not allow the Church to participate in political matters.

> The religious practice of the Church in National Socialist Germany has never been hindered by any State or Party measures as long as the practice remained within the realm of the religious and was without political character. Every German has the possibility to practice religion freely.[51]

What the Nazis expected of the Churches was a pietistic form of Christianity, concerned solely with matters that are incomprehensible in earthly terms, such as "faith or belief in the Divine."[52] They were not supposed to raise questions about social, economic and political injustices, since these matters belonged to the realm of "issues under the sole jurisdiction of the National Socialists."[53]

Freedom of Worship in South Africa

In 1957, the minister of Native Affairs introduced a bill in Parliament which would give him power to prohibit mixed church services and church-related meetings. The bill was passed after long and heated debate and became known as the "Church Clause." Its official title is "Native Laws Amendment Act, No. 36 of 1957." Section 29 (b) reads:

The Minister may by notice in the *Gazette* direct that the attendance by natives at any Church or other religious service or Church function on premises situated within any urban area outside a native residential area shall cease from a date specified in that notice, if in his opinion:
(i) the presence of natives on such premises or in any such area traversed by natives for the purpose of attending at such premises is causing a nuisance to residents in the vicinity of those premises or in such area; or
(ii) it is undesirable, having regard to the locality in which the premises are situated, that natives should be present on such premises in the numbers in which they ordinarily attend a service or function conducted thereat; and any native who in contravention of a direction issued under this paragraph attends any Church or religious service or Church function shall be guilty of an offence and liable to the penalties prescribed . . .

In view of the fact that there were already laws that separated the residential areas of blacks and whites and also restricted the movements[54] of blacks, mixed worship services in South Africa were an exception rather than the rule. Moreover, the Dutch Reformed Church and the Lutheran Church already had separate churches for blacks. The other denominations had separate churches for the different racial groups, but their members were free to worship in the church of their choice. It was to these denominations that the Christian Council was referring when it issued a statement saying:

> We shall be forced to disregard the law and to stand wholeheartedly by the members of the Churches who are affected by it.[55]

However, since the Christian Council was not a church, this statement had only the weight of moral support for the affected churches.

The law itself was designed to serve a much more important function than to prevent a relatively small number of blacks from worshipping with whites. It was self-preservation that was the motivation, as was pointed out by *Die Transvaler*, the mouthpiece of the Nationalist Party.

> It is not so much the overwhelming numbers of the non-Europeans but the destruction of the feeling of difference and otherness which is the great danger for the preservation of the European and his civilization in this multiracial land. As long as liberalistic bishops and canons, professors, students and politicians can freely attend Church and hold socials together, *apartheid* will be infringed in its marrow.[56]

Freedom of worship in South Africa does not include the right to criticize and challenge unjust laws. In 1976, the Prime Minister of South Africa warned against criticizing government policy, "under the cloak of religion." To quote:

From the pulpit which stands in the house of the Lord

the Word of God must be proclaimed. Men must not abuse the pulpit to try to attain political ends in South Africa. From that pulpit we expect the Gospel of Christ to be preached.[57]

The Prime Minister overlooked the fact that the Gospel is opposed to separateness *(apartheid)* and calls for unity. Jesus prayed, "Father, I pray that they all may be one" (John 17:21 – 23). The Prime Minister was objecting to any form of criticism of *apartheid*. The Church had to support and not oppose *apartheid*. It will be recalled that the Nationalist Party claimed to be carrying out God's will regarding racial separation. As long ago as 1948, the government warned the churches not to attack its policy of *apartheid*.

Churches and societies which undermine the policy of *apartheid* and propagate doctrines foreign to the nation will be checked.[58]

One notes that the Prime Minister was not concerned with whether or not the doctrines were true or false. *Apartheid* had to be accepted as the true doctrine, and anything that challenged that position was false and had to be dealt with accordingly.

Despite the restrictions on what the clergy may or may not preach, the authorities maintain that there is religious freedom in South Africa, as the following statement made by the Prime Minister in 1971 indicates:

It has become the fashion in certain circles to talk about a clash between Church and State. The State has never at any time taken action against Churches.[59]

The wording of the statement is deliberately deceptive. It is true that churches have never been shut down because of their opposition to *apartheid*. But the government has taken action against churches by either deporting, banning, or arresting Church leaders opposed to apartheid. Similarly, the Nazis took no actions against the churches. What they did was arrest Church leaders who dared to challenge Nazi policies, placing some in concentration camps.

Nazi Amusement and Entertainment Laws

Any attempt to maintain "racial purity" required that Jews and Germans be prevented from mixing on the social level. A number of anti-mixing decrees were, therefore, introduced in order to make social mixing illegal. On September 9, 1933, a Reich Chamber of Culture was established, with responsibility for directing all German cultural life including music, art, literature, theater and cinema. Jews were excluded from membership.[60]

Five years later, in 1938, Jews were prohibited from visiting any German cultural events including theater, concerts, lectures, cabaret, and circus shows.[61]Jews were also barred from resorts and beaches[62] and from dining cars,[63] and friendly relations with Jews were prohibited.[64]

All these measures failed to isolate the Jews completely, so, by 1941, a stern warning had to be issued.

> Lately it has repeatedly become known that, now as before, Aryans are maintaining friendly relations with Jews and that they show themselves with them conspicuously in public. In view of the fact that these Aryans do not seem to understand the elementary basic principles of National Socialism, and because their behavior has to be regarded as disrespect toward measures of the state, I order that in such cases the Aryan party is to be taken into protective custody temporarily for educational purposes, and that in serious cases they be put into a concentration camp, graded for a period of up to three months. The Jewish party is in any case to be taken into protective custody until further notice and to be sent into a concentration camp. [65]

This order marks one of those rare periods in history when the maintenance of "friendly relations" was considered a crime of such magnitude that it warranted severe punishment. But there was to be discrimination even in punishing those involved in these relationships. The Germans could expect leniency, whereas no mercy was to be shown towards the Jews.

The South African Amusement and Entertainment Laws

The laws that govern social contact in South Africa, especially in the area of recreation, are embodied in one broad law known as the "Separate Amenities Act, No. 49, of 1953." The purpose of the Act is:

To provide for the reservation of public premises and vehicles or portions thereof for the exclusive use of persons of a particular race or class, for the interpretation of laws which provide for such reservation, and for matters incidental thereto.

1. In this Act, unless the context otherwise indicates:

"public premises" includes any land, enclosure, building, structure, room, office, hall or convenience to which the public has access, whether on the payment of an admission fee or not but does not include a public road or street;

"public vehicle" includes any train, tram, bus, vessel or aircraft used for the conveyance for reward or otherwise of members of the public.

2. Any person who willfully enters or uses any public vehicle or premises or portion thereof or any counter, bench, seat or other amenity or contrivance which has in

terms of subsection (I) been set apart or reserved for the exclusive use of persons belonging to a particular race or class, being a race or class to which he does not belong, shall be guilty of an offence and liable on conviction to a fine not exceeding fifty pounds or imprisonment for a period not exceeding three months or to both such fine or such imprisonment.[66]

"Under this Act beaches have been segregated in many parts." [67]

Although the Nazi and South African laws are phrased differently, the purpose is the same, namely, to keep the races apart through law. In both cases, the penalty for breaking the laws is imprisonment. The difference between the Nazi penalties and the South African penalties is the severity of the punishment. The Nazis meted out heavier penalties. [68]

Employment Laws in Nazi Germany

On April 7, 1933, a law was passed in Nazi Germany that eliminated Jews from the civil service. On July 6, and July 25, 1938, measures were promulgated affecting the employment of Jews in other fields. The decree enacted on July 6 curtailed Jewish employment in certain commercial areas. It read:

Jews and Jewish businesses are prohibited from engaging themselves in the following commercial areas:

Guard services; credit information offices; real estate agencies; brokerage agencies; visitors' guides: marriage agencies; catering to non-Jews and peddling. [69]

The decree went into effect on December 31, 1938.

The decree of July 25 withdrew the licenses of doctors. From September 30 on, Jewish doctors could only treat Jewish patients and members of their own families. The second part of the decree was intended for those Jews who had German spouses.[70] Commenting on these measures, Raul Hilberg says:

> Under the terms of these laws there was no transfer of enterprises from Jews to Germans. Only the customers, patients and clients were transferred to German patronage. [71]

These laws brought hardships to those who depended on the income from their profession and also removed Jewish participation from large sections of German commerce, industry, and the professions.

Employment Laws in South Africa

The "Industrial Conciliation Act, No. 28 of 1956" prohibits blacks from performing certain types of work in commerce and industry and also prohibits them from qualifying for certain professions.[72] As amended in 1959, the Act gives the Minister of Labour authority to determine which jobs should be reserved for whites only. For example, in mining, blacks may not be employed in the sampling, surveying, and ventilation departments. They may not, by law, hold senior positions in the engineering, motor vehicle, clothing, and construction industries. The Act also prohibits blacks from supervising whites.[73] These new and far-reaching provisions were added to the original act in order to make *apartheid* more effective.

The Nursing Act, No. 69 of 1957, makes it an offense for anyone:

> To cause or permit any White nurse, midwife or student to be employed in any hospital or similar institution or training school under the supervision of a Black nurse. [74]

In discussing discriminatory employment practices in

South Africa, Muriel Horrell pointed out that:

> Black doctors have not been allowed to treat their own patients in provincial hospitals if this involved their being placed in a position of authority over white nurses. Further, black doctors have been prevented from serving in senior specialist capacities in large hospitals serving black communities if this placed them in a position of authority over junior white doctors, interns, or medical students. Black doctors are not allowed to treat white patients.[75]

Although *apartheid* calls for the separation of the races, this has not been possible in commerce and industry. *Apartheid* is, therefore, applied by reserving certain jobs for whites only and by leaving the top positions in the hands of whites only.

In Nazi Germany, the principle of "free choice of employment" applied to Germans only and was legally denied to Jews, on the basis of race and not ability. In South Africa, the discriminatory laws leave certain avenues of employment completely inaccessible to blacks by virtue of their belonging to a race that is not white, for example, civil service, the diplomatic corps, and the judiciary.

Collective Bargaining and Wages in Nazi Germany

"Jews who are Employed have a Separate Labor Status."[76] These "special regulations" concerned the rights of Jews to sell their labor on the competitive market at competitive prices.

Prior to this law, the principle that unemployed Jews could be forced to work on construction and reclamation projects, and also that they had to be separated from other laborers, had already been established. [77]

In practice, the separate labor status meant that the labor offices decided where Jews were to be employed. No special arrangements were made for invalids, and no distinction was made between the type of work to be done by youth and that to be done by adults. Jews were to be employed in groups arbitrarily formed by the German labor offices.[78]

The earnings of the Jews were drastically reduced and fringe benefits were removed from their pay. They were paid for "actual work done." Hilberg comments:

> Industry had been given the right to almost unlimited exploitation: to pay minimum wages for maximum work.[79]

Collective Bargaining and Wages in South Africa

The "Native Labour (Settlement of Disputes) Act, No. 48 of 1953," as amended in 1973 and 1976, prohibits blacks from forming registered trade unions. The Minister of Labour, Ben Schoeman, justified this law on the grounds that blacks would use the trade unions "as a political weapon" for the purpose of creating industrial unrest and chaos. "We would probably be committing race suicide if we give them that incentive," he said.[80]

The Industrial Conciliation Act, No. 28 of 1956, as amended by Act 41 of 1959 and Act 18 of 1961, established "a system of self-government in industry by means of collective bargaining between employer and employee."[81] Blacks are excluded from this, since the Act defines a trade union as "any number of employees in a particular undertaking, industry, trade or occupation associated together, etc." The Act defines an "employee" as "any person [other than a Bantu] employed."[82] The Bantu Laws Amendment Act, No. 19 of 1970, empowers the courts of law to order the removal of blacks from urban areas in order to work on farms, institutions, or rehabilitation schemes, where they are detained for such a period and ordered to perform such labor as may be prescribed by law.[83] All these measures apply to blacks only.

Since 1924, it as been illegal for blacks to strike (Industrial Conciliation Act). However, the Native Labour (Settlement of Disputes) Act, No. 48 of 1953, as amended in 1955,[84] further tightened the Act by providing severe penalties for black strikers. The penalties include a fine of 1,000 Rands or three years' imprisonment, or both. This law does not affect any other population groups in South Africa.

Without the protection afforded by the trade union, the employers could pay black workers whatever they wished. The Minister of Labour said the principle of equal pay for equal work applied to whites only. As a result of the dilution of work following mechanization, numbers of operations had been allocated to black semiskilled workers at wages that were far below the living wage paid to whites.[85] The government showed no concern over the fact that blacks were forced to survive on substandard wages.

Property Rights in Nazi Germany

Decree for Acquiring Jewish Property, December 1938:
Article II
A Jew can be required to sell, within a given period of time, his farm, forest, other property connected with his farm and forest, his real estate or other property, either together or separately. This decree can be accompanied by an injunction.[86]

The provisions of this decree were stated in such general terms they could include virtually all Jewish property. Since the decree does not make any mention of exceptions, it can be assumed that the Nazis intended to leave the Jews with no property at all. Clause Seven of this Article II read: "No Jew may purchase real estate." On January 1, 1939, a law was passed providing for the removal of Jews from the houses they owned, and placing them all together in "Jewish houses."[87] A day earlier it had been decreed that Jews would not be eligible for rent subsidies. It is hardly necessary to note that these

52

measures seemed designed to cause the Jews considerable hardship and suffering.[88]

Property Rights in South Africa
The Group Areas Act, No. 41 of 1950

In introducing the bill that called for separate residential areas for the separate racial groups in South Africa, the Minister of the Interior said in Parliament: "The Bill is endorsed by public opinion which is nurtured by the instinct for survival."[89]

This Act separated blacks from whites in residential areas, and also what is far more important, took away the freehold rights of blacks. The then Minister of Native Affairs, Hendrik Verwoerd, said that blacks would be entitled to only thirty years' leasehold in the urban areas without the automatic option of extension.[90] In the urban areas, blacks would all live in "locations." Verwoerd assured Parliament that blacks would never own the locations. The property belonged to whites, "and the natives who reside there reside there just as native farm laborers live on a farm of a European owner."[91]

The Native (Urban Areas) Amendment Act, No. 16 of 1955, as amended by Act No. 19 of 1970, empowers the Minister of Native Affairs to order the demolition of a location and to move all blacks to another site without consulting them. The only requirement is that the government consider it necessary to move them. The law gives the Minister of Native Affairs wide powers. He can determine not only where blacks shall live, but also for how long they will live in a particular area.

Racial Classification in Nazi Germany

The "Law for the Reestablishment of the Professional Civil Service," which was enacted on April 7, 1933, effectively divided German citizens into two categories: Aryans and non-

53

Aryans, and, from that date, Jews who were civil servants lost their positions, and this profession was henceforth closed to Jews. These two terms continued to be officially used until the 1935 Nazi Congress at Nuremberg where, for the first time, the terms "German" and "Jew" were used instead of Aryan and non-Aryan respectively. Altogether, a total of sixty-five laws and decrees were passed against the non-Aryans between April 1933 and September 1935.[92]

Racial Classification in South Africa

"The Population Registration Act, No. 30 of 1950" was "the logical corollary to the Mixed Marriages Act and Amendment to the Immorality Act." In introducing the bill to Parliament, the Minister of the Interior, Donges, said:

We cannot expect any government to enforce the existing laws, which provide for a certain amount of discrimination if we withhold the machinery necessary for the application of that form of discrimination.[94]

The Act provides for a rigid system of racial classification, so that everyone in South Africa would be classified as "Coloured," "Native," or "White." The 1973 amendment was designed to further tighten the provisions of the Act, especially with regard to persons classified as "Bantu." The Act regularized the *de facto* exercise of power delegated by the Secretary of the Interior to the head of the Bantu Reference Bureau and his personnel. It authorized government officials to notify blacks who had been issued identification documents (passes) that they had been classified as members of an indicated ethnic group, and to seize any documents from them in which their race was not reflected as "Native" or "Bantu."[95]

In practice, classifying people according to race and ethnic group is more complicated than it sounds. In the case of the Nazis, Hofer points out this difficulty when he says:

> How difficult it was, apparently, sometimes to determine clearly this racial membership, is clear from the further regulations that a grandparent would unquestionably qualify as a full Jew if he was a member of the Jewish faith. Well, what an intellectual criterion to determine the so-called biologically definitive racial membership! If anywhere, then it is here that the whole absurdity and contradiction about the pseudo-scientific and manipulative character of anti-Semitism, is revealed. No wonder that a man like Goering could say: I decide who is a Jew![96]

In South Africa there also have been problems, as Tobias points out:

> No wonder we were told in 1957 that seven teams had to be created to classify the races in South Africa—and we have yet to learn that a single physical anthropologist or human geneticist was included in those teams. No wonder, too, that it was reported in the *Star* on 13 January 1958, that the special committee which the Minister of Interior had appointed four years previously to coordinate the different (and often conflicting) definitions of races in various South African statutes, had had to report that they had found the task impossible. This was a fair report, since they were indeed being asked to attempt the impossible. Unfortunately, the Minister's response was to reappoint the committee and ask them to have another try! A year later, the committee was still bogged down on the definition of "Native"—and had not even started trying to define a "European" or "Coloured."[97]

These two statements are quoted at length to show to

what extent the apostles of "racial purity" are prepared to go to justify it. In Nazi Germany, the classification—arbitrary as it was—had far-reaching consequences. The ghettoes, concentration camps, and gas chambers were all designed primarily for those classified as Jews.

In South Africa, those who are classified as black automatically lose their South African citizenship and are arbitrarily assigned to one of the nine Bantu homelands.

Identification Documents in Nazi Germany

In 1938, the Nazis enacted a law compelling Jews to carry identification documents. It read:

> Jews who are German subjects, in accordance with their characteristics as Jews, have until December 31, 1938, to apply at their respective police stations for identification cards. For Jews who are born after this decree comes into effect, an application must be made for the card within three months of the date of birth.
>
> As soon as they have the identification cards, Jews over the age of fifteen must, upon official demand, prove their identity by producing the identification card.
>
> Failure to comply with these regulations will be treated as an exceptionally serious offense.[98]

Identification Documents in South Africa

In 1957, the Afrikaner Nationalist Government enacted a law, "The Natives (Abolition of Passes and Coordination of Documents) Act, No. 67 of 1952, as Amended by the Native Laws Further Amendment Act, No. 79 of 1957." This law compelled blacks of sixteen years and over to carry an

56

identification document known as the "reference book." The law requires that:

    a) All Native males and females who have reached the age of sixteen be issued a Reference Book.

    b) All such Natives to have the Reference Book on their person at all times and to produce it on demand.

    Any Native who fails to produce the Reference book on demand shall be guilty of an offence and liable to the penalties proscribed.[99]

The books issued contained information relating to the permanent residential address, employer's name and address, payment of government taxes, and additional information.

The feeling of blacks toward the "Pass Laws" is summed up by Leo Marquard:

There are few aspects of European administration that Africans resent so bitterly as the pass laws and regulations. They consider passes as badges of inferiority; they resent the constant interference of the police; the fines imposed are out of all proportion to the offence or to the income of the offender; and the conviction stands as a "previous conviction."

And, to show how ruthlessly the law is enforced, Marquard says:

There can be few adult Africans living in European areas who have not, at some time or other, offended against the pass laws. [100]

Almost two thousand Africans are arrested daily because of "Pass" offences.[101]

Freedom of Movement in Nazi Germany

> Jews may not leave their places of dwelling after 9:00 p.m. in summer and after 8:00 p.m. in winter.[102]
> It is prohibited for Jews to leave their residential areas without having on their person written permission from their local police.[103]

Shortly after the outbreak of the war in 1939, the movements of Jews were curtailed. In addition to suffering restrictions of the curfew laws, Jews were also prohibited from entering certain areas which were reserved for "Germans" only.[104] The movements of Jews were further restricted when the ghettoes were established in late 1939. The local authorities established specific regulations for each ghetto, but all of them restricted Jews. In Lodz, for example, Jews were not allowed to move freely within the ghetto and were to be off the streets between 7:00 p.m. and 7:00 a.m.[105] In the Warsaw Ghetto, Jews were not allowed to change residence and were forbidden to be on the streets between 9:00 p.m. and 5:00 a.m.[106]

Freedom of Movement in South Africa

The "Pass Laws" referred to above, which cause the arrest of almost two thousand blacks a day, are one of the most widely used methods in South Africa to monitor and control the movements of blacks.

The Native Laws Amendment Act, No. 54 of 1952 describes all urban areas as "proclaimed areas." This means that blacks must have special permission to be in urban areas. The law states that a local authority has full powers over the movements of blacks in each urban area.

> A local authority shall issue to any native who has been permitted to remain in any such area a permit indicating

the purpose for which and the period during which such native may remain in that area.[107]

Local authorities are also empowered to enforce local curfew laws which apply to blacks only. In most cases, curfew laws are in force between 10:00 p.m. and 6:00 a.m.[108] John Dugard summarizes the plight of blacks when he says:

The right of an African to move freely within South Africa is non-existent, despite the fact that he is a South African National.[109]

Failure to comply with these government regulations leads to arrests, fines, or imprisonment.

Opinion and Expression in Nazi Germany

The Nazis enacted laws that denied the Jews their right to vote. Having done that, the Nazis forbade the Jews from publishing newspapers, magazines, or from forming political organizations. They were denied the fundamental right of expressing themselves freely. They thus became voiceless.[110]

Freedom of Opinion in South Africa

The Nats, after assuming power, wasted no time in legally denying every black person in South Africa the right to vote. This is in keeping with their claim that "South Africa is a white man's country." They followed this action by banning all black political organizations. In addition to that, black newspapers were banned. In effect, the blacks of South Africa had become voiceless in the land of their birth and of their ancestors.[111]

Sports in Nazi Germany

Soon after taking over the reins of government, the Nazis decided to control all sporting activity in Germany. Jews were then forbidden from serving on governing boards of athletic organizations and were later barred from joining German clubs. The next step was to exclude them as spectators from sporting events. At the Winter Olympic Games in 1935, Jews were not allowed to attend. At the gates were signs that read "Jews are not permitted." These were only removed after an international outcry. However, later in the same year, an American swimming team swam in Berlin before an exclusively Aryan audience.[112]

The Nazi policy on sports was summed up in the following statement:

> German sports are for Aryans. German youth leadership is only for Aryans and not for Jews. Athletes will not be judged by ability alone, but also by their general and moral fitness for representing Germany.[113]

Sports in Apartheid South Africa

The policy of the apartheid regime toward sports was announced by the Minister of the Interior, Theophelus Donges, in 1955. The law includes the following points:

1. White and non-White sport must be organized separately.

2. No mixed sport within South Africa's borders.

3. No mixed teams to represent South Africa abroad.

4. International teams must respect South African laws by not including non-Whites in teams that visit South Africa.

5. Non-White sportsmen from abroad can only compete against non-White South Africans.

6. Non-White organizations seeking international recognition must apply through the white South African organizations.

7. The government would not issue travel documents to non-whites who are critical of South Africa's policies and who seek South Africa's expulsion from World competition. Donges described such efforts as "subversive."[114]

The man who in 1942 declared that Naziism and *apartheid* were one and the same thing, summed up the policy of the Nats when, as Prime Minister, he said:

I, therefore, want to make it quite clear that from South Africa's point of view no mixed sport between non-whites and whites will be practiced locally, irrespective of the standard of proficiency of the participants. . . . We do not apply that as a criterion because our policy has nothing to do with proficiency or lack of proficiency.[115]

As in Nazi Germany, sports in South Africa are an equal part of a political ideology.

Police Power in Nazi Germany

Police were given full authority to arrest and detain Jews without a warrant. Jews were denied the right to appear and be charged before a court of law. Nor did they have any right to sue for redress. There was also extensive use of the secret police (Gestapo), who officially terrorized the Jewish population.[116]

Police Power in South Africa

The Nats have given full authority to the police to search the premises of blacks; to arrest only blacks without a warrant, to detain them, and to banish them to so-called "homelands." There is heavy reliance on the use of secret police and police informers. The regime's ministers, such as the Minister of Justice, have powers which far exceed those of the courts. These powers are used to detain, without trial, opponents of *apartheid* indefinitely.[117]

Nazi Methods of Jewish Control

The Nazis concentrated the Jews in ghettoes and labor camps. They then established "Jewish Councils" *(Judenraete)* to be in charge of the ghettoes and camps. The councils were made up of Jews. However, they had no power of their own but were there to carry out Nazi instructions to the full. Thus, the Nazis used Jews to oppress Jews.[118]

The Methods of the Nats for Controlling Blacks

Like the Nazis, the Nats have concentrated blacks in ghettoes and labor camps, which they call "hostels." In order to control these establishments without being physically present, they have established "Bantu Councils," whose membership is black. The members of the councils are appointed by the Nats, and their duty is to carry out the instructions of the Nats. They have no power either to legislate or to modify existing legislation. They are instruments of *apartheid*. Having copied from the Nazis, the Nats use blacks to oppress blacks.[119]

The Nazis and the Japanese

The Nazis were at pains to dupe the world into believing that all their intentions were good. They argued that they were not racist but were merely promoting a policy which would allow the Germans and Jews to develop separately. The Japanese, however, were unhappy with the distinction "Aryan and non-Aryan," feeling that this placed them in the same position as the Jews. The Nazis finally decided on giving only the Japanese special treatment. They called them "honorary Aryans."[120]

The Nats and the Japanese

With growing opposition to *apartheid,* the Nats have tried, and continue to try, to sell *apartheid* as a humane policy, which seeks only to ensure that each "race" in South Africa "develops separately." The Japanese showed displeasure with the distinction "White and non-White," especially because it placed them in the same category as blacks. Because the Japanese are an important trading partner of the Nats, the Nats decided to meet Japanese objections by giving them special treatment. They are officially known as "honorary whites" and are legally treated as whites. All other Asians in South Africa and the world over are known to the Nats as "non-whites."[121]

It would take several volumes to compare and contrast all the laws which the Nazis passed against the Jews with those passed by the Nats against the blacks. The Nazis began with their anti-Jewish legislation in April 1933. The reason was that the Nazis were determined to construct a legal framework for their inhuman actions. By the time they declared Germany "free of Jews," they had passed legislation which controlled every aspect of Jewish life. That legislation took away the voting rights of Jews, their homes, their property, their citizenship, their freedom of expression and opinion, their rights to fair trial, to appeal in a court of law, to choose their friends and marriage partners, schools for their children, professions, their places of worship, how to spend their leisure time, where to spend it, their freedom of movement. That legislation destroyed family life, broke up families, enslaved Jews, and reduced them to subhumans.

Although it was too late, the world finally acted to bring an end to Naziism. However, this did not happen out of compassion for the Jews or out of outrage at the Nazi atrocities. It happened out of self-interest.

While the Nazis were busy legislating against the Jews, the Nats in South Africa made no bones about their admiration for the Nazis and promised that, if elected to power, they would follow in the footsteps of the Nazis. Even at the late hour when the rest of the world went to war against the Nazis, the Nats remained their loyal supporters.

The moment the Nats had long been waiting for came in 1948, when they won an election in which 80 percent of the population was not allowed to participate, because the color of their skin was black. On assuming power, they embarked on a program of legislation that consisted primarily of incorporating Nazi legislation against the Jews into the South African Statute Book, with blacks, instead of Jews, as the target.

The Nazis had built their flood of legislation on two basic laws which laws gave practical expression to their claims of "racial purity and superiority." These were the marriage laws and the citizenship laws, which together guaranteed German exclusiveness. A close look at all the other anti-Jewish laws reveals a total commitment to reach the goal of absolute exclusiveness and domination. The Nats have been meticulous in following the example of the Nazis.

The Reaction of the Different Churches to the Rise of Naziism

Protestant

As early as 1932, an influential group of Protestant pastors and lay people within the Protestant churches formed the *Bewegung Deutsche Christen* (Movement of German Christians), with Pastor Joachim Hossenfelder as their leader. Their stated aim was to revitalize Protestant Christianity by transforming the Church into a German *Volkskirche* (Folk-church). Control of this church would rest with pastors, and the laity rather than bishops and superintendents.[1] They espoused what they called "Positive Christianity"—a term used by the National Socialist German Workers Party (Nazis) in their program.[2]

The Nazi Party Program, officially published in February 1920, included a section on Christianity. Point twenty-four of the twenty-five-point program stated:

We demand freedom for all religious denominations in the state so far as they are not a danger to it and do not militate against the customs and morality of the German Volk. The party as such stands for *Positive Christianity,* but does not bind itself in the matter of creed to any particular denomination. It fights the spirit of Jewish materialism within and outside of our ranks and is convinced that our nation can achieve permanent health from within only on the principle: "Common welfare comes before individual welfare." [3]

The statement was phrased in such a way that it would find broad acceptance within the different Christian denominations. Those within the churches who were zealous to convert Jews to Christianity were pleased with this stated intention of the Nazis. It could also find acceptance by German patriots, whether or not they were Christian.

Within the Nazi party were two powerful forces. One, represented by men like Alfred Rosenberg (who later became Reichsminister for the Occupied Eastern Regions), wanted to see Germany become an atheistic state. The other, represented by men like Hanns Kerrl (who later became Reichsminister for Church Affairs), supported the idea of "Positive Christianity." The *Deutsche Christen,* therefore, had powerful allies within the Nazi party.

Kerrl and his associates recognized the power of the churches. In fact, SS and SA men were required to attend church services in their uniforms. Hitler, himself, mentioned "the Almighty" and "Providence" at his rallies, and also attacked Marxism and Atheism. [4]

Many Germans left the Church during the economic crisis that was part of the Great Depression, especially between the years 1930 and 1933. With Hitler's rise to power, however, this trend was reversed. The Nazi statements had found ready and receptive ears in German Christian communities. [5] The presence of leading Nazi members at Church services and the attacks on Godless Marxism, Jewish Materialism, decaying morals, and destructive authors—together with the government's call for the exercise of authority and leadership and the renewal of morals—reinforced the impression that the Nazis were pro-Christian. So much, in fact, that the year 1933 became known as "The Year of the Church." [6]

The Nazi Assumption of Power

On January 30, 1933, the Nazi party, with Hitler at its head, bacame the new government of Germany. Less than a month later, on February 21, the Reichstag building (Parliament) in Berlin was set on fire. The government claimed that the Communists were responsible and on February 28 took drastic measures against them, including arrests, closing of their offices, and confiscation of their property. The press on the whole welcomed the measures taken against the Communists. For the most part, the public and the churches were silent.[7]

On Febrary 28, the government persuaded the President, Paul von Hindenburg, to suspend certain sections of the Weimar Constitution so that the actions against the Communists would be legal. This led, in May to the banning of the Communist Party.[8] On March 24, 1933, the government won yet another victory in the form of the "Enabling Law."[9] In effect, this law suspended the constitution and gave the government authority to enact laws without consulting Parliament. And this meant that the government could enact laws for the next four years even if the laws were clearly unconstitutional.[10]

With the new powers in hand, the first measure against the Jews was planned. In response to what the government and party described as "the abominable agitation by Jews in and outside Germany" the *Voelkischer Beobachter,* the official mouthpiece of the Nazis, on March 29, 1933, published an article calling on all Germans to boycott Jewish businesses on April 1, 1933.[11]

There is no evidence of any official protest from the Protestant Church against this organized boycott. On the contrary, there *is* evidence of support. Otto Dibelius, General Superintendent of Kurmark, Berlin, commented:

Finally, the government found it necessary to organize the boycott of Jewish businesses in the correct assumption that the foreign pressure [on Germany], which is a result of the international connections of the Jews, will only end when German Jewry is in danger.[12]

On April 7, 1933, the Nazis passed the first anti-Jewish law, known as the "Law for the Restoration of the Professional Service."[13] Jews who were already civil servants were forced to retire, and no Jews were allowed to join the civil service after that date. This law, sometimes known as the "Aryan Clause" became a source of controversy between the *Deutsche Christen* and the Confessing Church.[14]

While these developments were taking place on the political front, the Protestant Church was involved in an internal struggle. Although there was no opposition to the idea of uniting all twenty-eight provincial churches into one Church, controversy developed when it came to the question of control. There were those who favored a church that was organizationally independent of the state and others who favored a church under the direct control of the state.[15] The *Deutsche Christen* supported the latter position.

Hitler tried to prevent an open struggle between the two factions. His efforts won him praise from some of the Church leaders, including Provincial Bishop Rendtorff of Mecklenburg, who demonstrated his gratefulness by joining the Nazi party and identifying himself with . . . "Adolf Hitler, the leader sent to us by God." [16] Another move by Hitler in his efforts to win over the provincial leaders was the appointment of Ludwig Mueller, a conservative churchman, to be in charge of Church affairs, rather than the radical *Deutsche Christen* leader, Joachim Hossenfelder.[17]

Mueller was appointed as an interim Church leader until such time that Church elections would be held. The churches were assured that their rights would not be abused, and their relationship to the state would not be changed.[18] When the time to elect a Reichs bishop came (May 2, 1933), Ludwig Mueller, who was favored by both the government and the *Deutsche Christen,* was defeated by Friedrich V. Bodelschwing, a favorite of the anti-*Deutsche Christen* forces.[19] Because Bodelschwing was unacceptable to the government, he was forced to resign.[20] His position was taken by Ludwig Mueller. The government appointed other Church officers as well, and most of the appointments came from the ranks of the *Deutsche Christen*.[21] Hossenfelder, now one of the Church officials, ordered "thanksgiving services" to be held because the Church was now "freed" from "its lack of order." [22]

On July 14, 1933, all twenty-eight provincial churches accepted a new constitution for a unified German Protestant Church.[23] It soon became clear to the opponents of the *Deutsche Christen* that the unified *Deutsche Evangelische Kirche* (German Protestant Church) was under the control of the *Deutsche Christen* and therefore would be used to promote Naziism.[24] These fears were confirmed when some of the churches started applying the Aryan Clause.[25]

On September 21, 1933, under the leadership of Martin Niemoeller, Gerhard Jacobi, and Eitel-Friedrich v. Rabenau, the opponents of the *Deutsche Christen,* formed the *"Pfarrernotbund"* (Pastors Emergency Union). Within a week, more than two thousand pastors had joined the union, and by January 1934, the union had more than seven thousand members.[26] Martin Niemoeller was elected leader of the consistory. The membership of the union was limited to clergy who were opposed to the *Deutsche Christen's* views on Church organization as well as their understanding of what constituted a church. The controversy was both ecclesiological and theological and an internal Protestant Church matter. There is no evidence to support intent on the part of the *Pfarrernotbund* to challenge any of the policies of the new Nazi government.[27] When, for example, Hiter unilaterally withdrew from the League of Nations in November 1933, Martin Niemoeller sent him a telegram congratulating him for what he called a "national deed." [28]

Faced with this split within the Protestant Church, Reichs Bishop Mueller decided not to enforce the Aryan Clause in the churches. His efforts at reconciliation were torpedoed by the *Deutsche Christen,* who, on November 13, 1933, held a huge rally at the Berlin Sports Palace, at which they passed resolutions calling for the dismissal from the Church of all pastors who were "unwilling or incapable of completing the German Reformation in the spirit of National Socialism." In effect, they called for the disbanding of the *Pfarrernotbund.* They also called for the introduction of the Aryan Clause in the Church; the establishment of separate churches for Jews; the introduction of German church services that would be free of foreign influence; and a *volks* church that would be compatible with the totalitarian demands of the National Socialist State.[29] On their part, the *Pfarrernotbund* claimed they stood for the "right theology; truth as opposed to lies, love as opposed to force." They opposed the application of the Aryan Clause to the churches.[30]

The question of the Aryan Clause became the main source of conflict between the *Deutsche Christen* and the *Pfarrernotbund.* The members of the *Pfarrernotbund* supported the continued presence of baptized Jews in the Protestant Church on theological grounds. They argued that Jews who had become baptized Christians were part of the Christian Community, and to deny them membership in the church would be un-Christian because such an act "would negate the Communion of Saints."[31]

The other provision of the Aryan Clause, if applied to the churches, would mean that all pastors who were of Jewish blood would be forced into retirement. In rejecting this demand, Martin Niemoeller revealed the dilemma facing many Protestant Church leaders in 1933. He said that for him, Jews were *"Gastvolk"* (foreigners); that the Germans had suffered a great deal under the influence of the Jews; that it demanded a great measure of self-denial in spite of suffering to fight for the rights of non-Aryans to remain in the church, and finally:

Thus it so happens that a fundamental position is demanded of us, whether or not we feel comfortable about it.[32]

The *Pfarrernotbund* concerned themselves with the Aryan clause only in so far as it affected the Church and not in its wider implications. Article Four of their resolutions (drawn up by Niemoeller), states that the application of the Aryan Clause to the churches is incompatible with the confession of the Christian faith.[33]

Dietrich Bonhoeffer

Dietrich Bonhoeffer differed from his colleagues in the *Pfarrernotbund* in that he was concerned with the *whole* Jewish question and not just the question of the Aryan clause in its relation to baptized Jews. Writing to a friend, Erwin Sutz, a week after the enactment of the Aryan clause, he criticized the approach of the *Pfarrernotbund:*

> ... The Jewish question is causing the Church great difficulties and responsible people have totally lost their heads and their Bibles.[34]

As Bonhoeffer saw it, by enacting the Aryan Clause, the Nazis presented the Church with two related but distinct problems. The first problem arose out of the fact that the Nazi law made it impossible for Jews to become civil servants simply because they were not Aryans. The second problem was the extension of the Aryan Paragraph into the churches. For Bonhoeffer, the Aryan Paragraph raised theological, moral, and humanitarian questions.[35] He declared,

> The Church cannot treat its members according to the dictates of the state. The baptized Jew is a member of our Church. For the Church, the Jewish question is different from what it is for the state.[36]

Bonhoeffer maintained that the Church had three important responsibilities in its relationship with the state. First, the Church had to make sure that the state acted responsibly.

Second, the church had a duty toward those who suffered from the actions of the state, since it was the duty of the Church to be on the side of victims, even if these victims did not belong to any particular denomination or Christian congregation. Third, the Church had a duty beyond the rescue of victims of oppression; it must try to destroy the *causes* of oppression. He admitted that the Church would have to enter the political arena to do this but maintained that this would be necessary if the state failed in its duty to maintain law and order.[37]

Bonhoeffer felt so strongly about the whole Jewish question and in particular about *Pfarrernotbund's* preoccupation only with theological questions, that he considered leaving the Church. In a letter to Karl Barth, he asked for advice.[38] Karl Barth persuaded him to remain in the Church "at least for the time being."[39]

Although he followed Barth's advice, he became isolated within the *Pfarrernotbund*. In a letter to Barth, he wrote:

> I feel that in some way I don't understand I have somehow got up against all my friends. My views about what should be done have seemed to cut me off from them more and more. . . . It seems to me that at the moment it is more dangerous for me to make a gesture than to retreat into silence.[40]

This letter was written from London, where he had "retreated into silence" in September 1933.

Before leaving for London, Bonhoeffer and a few members of the *Pfarrernotbund* had been asked by the members to prepare a document that would clearly spell out the role of the Church in the new situation created by the Nazis' rise to power and the support given them by the *Deutsche Christen*. Because of the disagreement between Bonhoeffer and his colleagues, the document was never published.[41] Eberhard Bethge remarks that the document, known as the *Bethel Confession,* "was emasculated by those bodies whose voice carried authority."[42] It is during the preparation of this document that a discussion of *Bekenntnis Bewegung* (Confessing Movement) and *Bekenntnisfrage* (Confessing Question) took place within the *Pfarrernotbund* for the first time.[43]

The Birth of the Confessing Church

Despite the fact that the Protestant Church had at least two opposing factions within its ranks, the *Deutsche Christen* and the *Pfarrernotbund,* Hitler and the Nazi Party saw the unified Church as the only answer to the internal struggle and throughout 1933 made several efforts to unify the Church.[44]

On the surface, there seemed to be no reason for conflict within the Protestant Church. For example, when Ludwig Mueller was elected Reich Bishop on September 2, 1933, he said:

> The whole German movement for freedom with its leader, our Chancellor, is for us a present from God, given in a time of decision, when the enemies of Christ were doing their best to destroy our people both inwardly and outwardly. In the triumph of this German freedom movement we hear the call of our God, and it is our honourable and sincere duty to listen to this call and to act accordingly. . . . The old has passed away. The new has begun. The political struggle in the Church is over. Now begins the struggle for the soul of the people.[45]

On their part the *Deutsche Christen* had this to say:

> We, the *Deutsche Christen* believe in our savior Jesus Christ in the power of his cross and his resurrection. Jesus' life and death teaches us that the way of struggle is at the same time the way of love and the way of life.[46]

Although these two statements suggest a desire for

73

reconciliation and harmony within the Church, the *Pfarrernotbund* remained unimpressed by either. In May 1934, the *Pfarrernotbund* met at Barmen, where, after deliberating for two days, they adopted *"Die Barmen Erklaerung"* (Barmen Declaration). This was a six-point theological document based on six texts taken from the New Testament. They can be summarized as follows:

1. The Church is built on God's revelation (John 10:1–9).
2. The Church has the right to speak on issues affecting society, especially in the social and political spheres (1 Cor. 1:30).
3. Attention is called to the question of brotherhood, especially within the ranks of the Church (Eph. 4:15–16).
4. Collective leadership is called for within the Church (Matt. 20, 25, 26).
5. The Church is called on to oppose totalitarianism (1 Pet. 2:17).
6. The continuation of a *Volkschurch,* and its freedom (2 Tim. 2:9).

The document is basically the work of Karl Barth[47]; its adoption is generally regarded as the birth of the Confessing Church, [48] with the six points serving as its foundation. The Confessing Church maintained that a church could only *be* a church if it remained faithful to its calling, a calling embodied in the six principles. Friedrich Zipfel points out that the Confessing Church did not aim at being an opposition group in the sense of opposing the state, but members were free to voice opposition to the state in a private capacity.[49]

Since the state recognized Mueller as the Reich Bishop and the Confessing Church refused to recognize him, conflict was unavoidable. In August 1934, Mueller called a national synod. At this synod, laws covering the administration of the Church and the leadership of the Church were passed. These actually provided the Reich Bishop with a basis for exercising dictatorial powers.[50]

Mueller tried to bring the *Pfarrernotbund* into line by making it compulsory for every pastor and church official to take the following oath:

I, NN, take an oath to God the Omniscient and Holy, that I, as a chosen servant in the present office of proclamation as well as in all other spiritual offices, will, as is befitting a servant of the Gospel in the German Protestant Church, be faithful and obedient to the leader of the German *Volk* and state, Adolf Hitler, and I pledge to serve him in a way that befits a German Protestant man. . . .[51]

The Confessing Church called on all pastors to ignore the oath.[52]

In the autumn of 1934, when Mueller was officially accepted as Reich Bishop, many leading members of the Nazi government attended the celebrations, giving evidence that the state supported Mueller and, therefore, the *Deutsche Christen*.[53] Although Mueller's efforts to unify the Church had some success, two large provincial churches refused to be drawn into the union. They were Wuerttemberg, whose Bishop was Theophil Wurm, and the Church of Bavaria, whose bishop was Hans Meiser.[54] Both bishops were placed under house arrest by Mueller's assistant, August Jaeger, who had the title "Administrator of the Reich Evangelical Church." There were protests in support for the bishops[55] and Hitler finally ordered their release.[56]

The actions of Mueller and Jaeger, particularly the use of force in their efforts to achieve Church unity, led to the convening of the Second Synod of the Confessing Church,[57] called the Reich Confessional Synod, in October 1934, at Dahlem. At the synod, attention was drawn to the fact that Mueller had acted contrary to the Church constitution of July 11, 1933; he had ignored all pleas from the Confessing Church; and, by calling for "one state," "one *Volk*" and "one Church" Mueller had turned the Church into an instrument of the state. The Confessing Church, therefore, was making use of emergency power to form a "Council of the German Protestant Church." Martin Niemoeller was a member of this council.[58] Bishops Meiser, Wurm, and August Marahrens, Bishop of Hannover, were invited to confer with Hitler.[59] They suggested that Mueller resign as Reich Bishop, but Hitler did not accept their suggestion. Jaeger, however, did resign his position.[60]

On November 22, the Council of the German Protestant Church, together with the bishops of the provincial churches, formed what they called *"Vorlaufigen Kirchenleitung,"* (Temporary Church Leadership) with Bishop Marahrens of Hannover as leader.[61] Some leading members of the Council of the German Protestant Church, including Karl Barth and Martin Niemoeller, were unhappy with the choice of Marahrens.[62] Mueller, citing the Church constitution of 1933, declared the newly formed organization unconstitutional, and asked that pastors and Church officials refuse to become members.[63] His request went unnoticed, and the new organization functioned until 1936, when internal conflict caused it to disintegrate.[64]

Until the end of 1934, the Church struggle was purely an internal conflict,[65] the "Aryan Clause" being the basic contention between the *Deutsche Christen* and their opponents, as illustrated in the following citation:

(1) The *Deutsche Christen* decided to introduce the Aryan Paragraph in the churches (decision of the General Synod of the Old Prussian Provincial Church, dated September 6, 1933). (2) The law was suspended (Law of November 16, 1933). (3) The suspension was suspended (Decision of the Reich Bishop, January 4, 1934). (4) The suspension of the suspension was suspended (Paragraph 1 of the Church Law for the Settling of the Church situation, dated April 13, 1934). (5) The suspension of the suspension remains in force (Paragraph 4 of the same law).[66]

It soon became obvious to the Nazis that Bishop Mueller was incapable of bringing about peace between the *Deutsche Christen* and the Confessing Church. Although he continued to hold the title of Reich Bishop, "from 1935, no one took notice of his existence."[67] The government decided to play a more direct role in the affairs of the Protestant Church, and, to gain direct control, decided to reorganize the Church.

The first step in this process was taken on March 11, 1935, when "The Law for the Administration of Protestant Church Property" was enacted. Other measures followed. On June 26 of the same year, an act to control the legal aspects of the Protestant Church was passed.[68] On July 16, 1935, the *Reichskirchenministerium* (Reich Church Ministry) was established. Hanns Kerrl, formerly Minister of Justice, was appointed Minister of Church Affairs. Prior to this, church affairs had been handled by both the ministries of Culture and Interior.[69]

On September 24, 1935, the "Law for the Safety of the German Protestant Church" was passed. This law gave the Minister full powers in church affairs, stating:

The Reich Minister for Church Affairs is empowered to reestablish orderly conditions within the German Protestant Church and in the provincial churches, and to issue legally binding decrees. The decrees will be published in the *Reichsgesetzblatt.*[70]

Armed with these powers, Kerrl proceeded to reorganize the Church. He established Church commissions made up of members of the Confessing Church and *Deutsche Christen* and made them responsible for the administration of local and national Churches. A passage in the Declaration of the National Church Commission read:

We welcome the National Socialist popular evolution on the basis of Race, Blood and Soil.[71]

Niemoeller and his followers protested against this statement, just as they protested when the *Vorlaufige Kirchenleitung* agreed to hold Thanksgiving services when Saarland became part of the Reich.[72] The fact that Bishop Marahrens's faction of the *Vorlaufige Kirchenleitung* did not protest suggests that there was a difference of opinion between the two factions of the official representatives of the Confessing Church.

While the Church was preoccupied with its internal affairs, the Nazi regime was busy enacting laws and issuing decrees against the non-Aryans. Between April 1933, when the first such law was passed, and July 16, 1935, when the *Reichskirchenministerium* was established, over sixty laws and decrees had been passed against non-Aryans, all of them based on the Aryan Clause, and designed to deny non-Aryans the right to become professionals. They made it impossible for the non-Aryan students to attend the same schools and universities as Germans. They prohibited non-Aryans from serving on juries, from becoming honorary members of organizations, from publishing and selling newspapers.[73]

How the non-Aryans felt about the measures enacted against them is perhaps best reflected by Marga Meusel, who later played an important role in helping Jews leave Germany. In an article titled "On the Situation of the German non-Aryan," she wrote:

> This situation is desperate. In the face of this sea of hatred, defamation and meanness the situation becomes desperate not only for those who are affected but much more for a nation *[Volk]* that allows all this to happen. . . . [74]

The Confessing Church held its Third National Synod at Augsburg, from June 2 to June 4, 1935. (The first was held at Barmen and the second at Dahlem.) At the first two synods, the Jewish question had not been discussed. On May 24, 1935, a week before the National Synod met at Augsburg, the Chief Adviser of the *Vorlaufige Kirchenleitung* on non-Aryan affairs requested that the forthcoming confessional Synod draw the attention of the Confessing Church, in an appropriate manner, to its duty toward Protestant non-Aryans.[75] The synod took no stand on the Jewish question. In despair, on June 25, 1935, Karl Barth wrote a letter to his friend, Pastor Hermann Hesse, in which he said:

> [The Confessing Church] has yet shown no sympathy for the millions who are suffering injustice. She has not once spoken out on the most simple matters of public integrity. If and when she does speak, it is always on her own behalf.[76]

Dietrich Bonhoeffer also found fault with the Augsburg Synod because, among other things "it had remained silent on the Jewish question."[77] However, the real first major test for the Confessing Church came with the passage of the Nuremberg laws.

The Nuremberg Laws were designed to make Germany a country free of Jews (Reichsbuergergesetz v. 15, Sept., 1935) and the German *Volk* free of Jewish blood (Gesetz zum Schutze des deutschen Blutes und der deutschen Ehre, v. 15, Sept., 1935). These two laws opened the doors to a flood of legislation that finally controlled every aspect of Jewish life.[78]

Reaction of the Confessing Church to the Nuremberg Laws

A week after the passage of the Nuremberg Laws against the Jews, a meeting of the Prussian Synod was held at Steglitz. For the first time in the history of the Confessing Church, an official of the Church Ministry, Dr. Stahn, addressed the delegates and stressed the need for cooperation with his ministry.[79]

Dr. Stahn informed the synod that his ministry would set up finance departments, which would be in charge of all

Church finances. Once again, differences emerged within the ranks of the Confessing Church. Marahrens's faction accepted the arrangement, while Niemoeller's faction opposed any kind of secular interference in the affairs of the Church.[80] Wilhelm Niemoeller says:

> Among the Prussians, the tendency was very strong to speak, not only about the question of the non-Aryan Christians but generally about the Jewish question and, therefore, about the persecution of the Jews.[81]

At the Prussian Synod of the Confessing Church, the following resolution was passed:

> With shame and pain, we ascertain that there are Church councils that prohibit the baptizing of Jews. That is a sin. We may not make the administration of the Word and Sacrament dependent upon criteria outside of Holy Scripture. That is why we may not deny the Jews baptism which they desire because of their faith in Jesus Christ, the Son of God. Anyone of the Church who considers the baptism of Jews treason against the Church defames the Sacrament of Holy Baptism. So speaks our Lord and Savior Jesus Christ: "To me is given all power in heaven and on earth. Therefore, go and teach all people and baptize them in the name of the Father and of the Son and of the Holy Ghost, and teach them to keep all what I have commanded you. And lo, I am with you all the days until the end of the world."[82]

This resolution was prompted by the fact that some churches, especially those under the control of the *Deutsche Christen,* "either refused to baptize Jews or expelled from their churches those already baptized."[83]

That the Nuremberg Laws raised fundamental moral and, more important, theological questions for the Church did not escape some members present at Steglitz. However, "the unpleasant discussion" on the Jewish question was referred to the Council of Brethren for further action.[84]

Dietrich Bonhoeffer, who was not a member of the Prussian Synod because he was not a parish pastor, attended the synod as an observer. Bethge says Bonhoeffer returned from the synod "in a depressed state of mind" because

> To Bonhoeffer, the synod was a vital opportunity that had been thrown away. For he believed that Steglitz had allowed financial autonomy and state recognition to be foisted upon it as its principal theme instead of breaking new ground by insisting on a discussion on how they could become a voice for the voiceless. It had, he felt, shown itself culpably dilatory in restricting its statement to the subject of Jewish baptism while leaving the remainder of the question to be dealt with by the council.[85]

The Split within the Confessing Church

A week after Stahn had addressed the Confessing Church at Steglitz, his immediate superior at the Church Ministry, Hanns Kerrl, announced the formation of Church commissions to be responsible for the administration of the churches. The highly respected General Superintendent of the Confessing church, Wielhelm Zoelner, was appointed chairman of the National Church Commission. Many within the Confessing Church believed that the era of Bishop Mueller and his assistant Jaeger (an era characterized by authoritarianism and support for the *Deutsche Christen)* was over and that it was now possible to work with the new Church administration. Niemoeller was one of those who did not share this view. In a letter to members of the Confessing Church, he wrote:

> We are in danger of losing God's grace through our own disloyalty. Therefore we must ask our brethren to exam-

ine their hearts to see if they are ready for the future struggle. . . . In recent months we have been waiting for the decisive success of our Church administration and for the official recognition by the state of the Confessing Church. But we have only received one disappointment after another. Many of us are therefore tired and despondent. But we must recognize that it is our faithlessness which has caused us to put our trust in men rather than in God.[86]

Not all the members of the Confessing Church shared Niemoeller's fears. Many Protestant clergy felt that to oppose the new arrangements would weaken Germany internally and encourage her enemies abroad. It was time, therefore, to be loyal and to demonstrate national unity.[87] Martin Niemoeller remained unimpressed, and, in January 1936, he issued a pamphlet *The State Church Is Here,* in which he attacked Kerrl's attempts to control the Church and his use of the Gestapo to enforce his directives.[88]

From February 17 to Febrary 22, 1936, the Fourth Synod of the Confessing Church was held at Bad Oeynhausen. High on the agenda was the question of the relationship between the Confessing Church and the Church commissions. It is on this question that the Confessing Church split into two "Confessing Churches." One group, known as the "Dahlemites," because they adhered to the principles enunciated at Dahlem, was led by Niemoeller and refused to have anything to do with the Church commissions or with Kerrl's office. The other group, led by Bishop Marahrens and known as the Conservatives, accepted cooperation with the Church commissions in principle.[89] The break was finalized on March 12, 1936, when Niemoeller's followers formed "The Second Provisional Administration of the Confessing Church." The leading members in the group were Fritz Mueller, Fricke, Albertz, Boehm, and Froeck. In Marahrens's group were Bishops Wurm, Meiser, Breit, Hahn, Lilje, and Beste.[90]

To demonstrate that they did not recognize the authority

of Kerrl and his Church commissions, the Second Provincial Church Administration, together with the Reich Council of Brethren, decided to address themselves directly to Hitler. In a memorandum drafted in May 1936 and hand delivered to the Reichskanzelei on June 4, 1936, they drew attention to a number of grievances. Among the points raised were the deviations from the accepted Church Constitution; the meaning of "Positive Christianity"; anti-Semitism, which led to hatred of Jews; the deification of Hitler; concentration camps, spying, and eavesdropping.[91]

It must be pointed out here that the Confessing Church was not without its own anti-Semitism. In March 1936, three months before the memorandum was delivered to Hitler, the Rhineland branch of the Confessing Church issued a statement on the Jewish question in which the following was said:

> Forty to sixty percent of leading posts serving the Bolshevist cause are filled by Jews; in important fields such as foreign politics, trade with abroad, etc., the proportion of Jews in leading posts is as high as 95 percent.[92]

When Hitler failed to respond, the full text of the protest was published in overseas papers. This proved disastrous for the Confessing Church. They were accused from all sides of disloyalty and of plotting with Germany's enemies abroad. The Lutheran Council publicly dissociated itself from the memorandum. The Provincial Council issued a statement declaring that it was not responsible for the publication of the memorandum and went so far as to cooperate with the Gestapo in its search for the culprits.[93]

In an effort to show their loyalty to Germany, the drafters of the May memorandum produced a watered-down version of the original, in which no mention of concentration camps, anti-Semitism, or the glorification of Hitler and the German nation was made.[94] The idea was to have the memorandum read in all the churches. The Provisional Administration not only met with resistance from the Church Ministry—which was to be expected—but the Lutheran Council rejected the memorandum and in November declared:

> With the Reich Church Commission we wholeheartedly support the Fuehrer in the struggle for the life of the German people against Bolshevism.[95]

With the Confessing Church clearly split, the *Deutsche Christen* tried to take advantage of the prevailing climate by making the question of baptizing Jews a central issue. However, the Church ministry showed no particular interest in taking drastic steps. From time to time, the National Socialist Press would protest the baptism of Jews or the presence of baptized Jews in German congregations. But these were isolated cases. Officially, the baptism of Jews and their membership in German congregations were not prohibited until the outbreak of World War II.[96]

The Confessing Church and the Nazi Office for Church Affairs

When Hanns Kerrl was appointed by Hitler to be Minister for Church affairs, he set himself the task of transforming the German Protestant Church into an ally of the state, under state control. Throughout 1937 and 1938, he made speeches designed to win over both National Socialists and Church leaders to the view that National Socialism and Christianity were compatible.[97]
To his fellow-Nazis he said:

> The National Socialist not only fully recognizes his obligations to God and the Divine order but lives them. The true National Socialist was he who knew God's commandments in his conscience and his blood. Thus the state itself is the living form of the national community—faith in God expressed in experience.[98]

84

To the churches he said:

> Christ did not teach us to fight against the National
> Socialist doctrine of race. Rather he waged an unprece-
> dented warfare against Judaism which for that reason
> slew Him on the Cross.[99]

And to both the Church and the National Socialists, he
declared:

> National Socialism is the fulfillment of the will of God
> which is demonstrated to us in our blood. . . . Chris-
> tianity is not dependent upon the Apostles' Creed. . . .
> True Christianity is represented in the party, and the
> German people are now called by the party and es-
> pecially by the Fuehrer to a real Christianity. . . . It is
> not the Church which has demonstrated that faith which
> could move mountains. But the Fuehrer has. He is the
> herald of a new revelation.[100]

However, neither the National Socialists, nor the Confessing
Church, nor the *Deutsche Christen* was convinced, and Kerrl's
idea of unifying the Protestant Church faded away with time,
much to the irritation of Hitler.[101]

The conflict between the Confessing Church (Dahlemites)
and the Church ministry reached a high point in 1937. In
June of that year, forty-eight prominent Dahlemites were
arrested,[102] and, on July 1, on the direct orders of Hitler,
Martin Niemoeller was arrested.[103] Some seminaries were
closed down, and many pastors were forbidden to preach or to
lecture. By the end of 1937, over seven hundred pastors had
been arrested, because they defied orders issued by the Office
for Church Affairs.[104]

The dilemma of opposing Hitler's Church policies on the
one hand, while remaining loyal to him as leader of the
German nation, placed the Dahlemites in an extremely
embarrassing position. On March 13, 1938, Austria was
annexed by Germany, and, as a sign of gratefulness to the

Fuehrer, Friedrich Werner, a member of the Ecclesiastical Council of the German Evangelical Church, called on all pastors to take the following oath of allegiance to Hitler:

I swear that I will be faithful and obedient to Adolf Hitler, the Fuehrer of the German Reich and people, that I will conscientiously observe the laws and carry out the duties of my office, so help me God. . . . [105]

Werner added that:

Anyone who was called before this decree came into force . . . is to take the oath of allegiance retroactively. . . . Anyone who refuses to take the oath of allegiance is to be dismissed.[106]

For the *Deutsche Christen,* the oath was welcome, judging by the telegram sent to Hitler, which read:

My Fuehrer, I report: In a great historic hour all the pastors of the Thuringian Evangelical Church, obeying an inward command, have with joyful hearts taken an oath of loyalty to Fuehrer and Reich . . . One God—one obedience in the faith. Hail my Fuehrer.[107]

Within the Confessing Church, there was the usual theological discussion on whether or not the oath invalidated the ordination vows.[108] The vast majority of the pastors accepted the oath. Only a few Dahlemites refused to take it. Karl Barth, no longer in Germany but in Switzerland, wrote:

I am most deeply shocked by that decision and the arguments used to support it, after I have read and reread them. . . . Was it possible, permissible, or necessary that this defeat should come about? Was there and is there really no one at all among you to take you back to the simplicity of the straight and narrow way? . . . No one to beg you not to hazard the future credibility of the Confessing Church in this dreadful way?[109]

And Bonhoeffer added his voice:

Shall we learn from this? Will the Confessing Church be willing to confess publicly its guilt and disunion? Will it give to prayer for forgiveness and a fresh start the place that it now needs? Will it be able in that way to honor the truth to revive again the disunited brethren's consciences which are simply anxious to reach the truth, and to bind them again to God's Word? . . . Does it see how it had endangered its word through its latest session? Today these are open questions.[110]

It was on July 31 that the Confessing Church (Dahlemites) decided on the oath. On August 8, the *"Fuehrerblaetter"* published a circular, dated June 13, and written by Martin Bormann, Hitler's deputy, in which he pointed out that the decision regarding the oath had been taken without the "decision of the Fuehrer" and therefore could only be regarded as an internal Church affair. There would be no disciplinary measures taken against those who had refused to take the oath.[111]

Since September 1935, the Nazis had passed over one hundred laws that were specifically designed to have adverse effects on Jews, [112] and Bethge points out that the Confessing Church took the oath to the Fuehrer "when it already knew that a regulation was coming out by which non-Aryans were compelled to have a large 'J' stamped on their identity cards."[113] That regulation came into effect in October of the same year.

Politically, the Nazis continued to feel that they had the support of all sections of the population. They continued, therefore, to pass more and more legislation against the Jews. They even passed a law replacing the designation "non-Aryan" with "Jew" so that no one should doubt that the measures were meant for the Jews.[114]

The November Pogrom: Reichskristalnacht (The Reich Night of Broken Glass)

On November 7, 1938, a seventeen-year-old Polish Jewish student, Hershl Grynszpan, who was studying in Paris, shot and seriously wounded a German civil servant, Ernst v. Rath, who was at the time serving as Third Secretary at the German Embassy in Paris. The news quickly reached Germany. Von Rath died on November 9.

On November 8 and 9, Nazi-inspired meetings were held throughout Germany to discuss the Paris incident and to plan measures to be taken in retaliation. On the evening of November 8, Nazi supporters set fire to some Jewish homes, synagogues and businesses.[115] But it was not until November 9, after the death of v. Rath that the state approved organized revenge against the Jews.[116] Jewish homes, businesses, and synagogues were ransacked and destroyed by fire; at least thirty-six Jews lost their lives and an order was given to arrest all able bodied male Jews, especially the wealthy. The night of November 9 thus marked the beginning of the pogrom and earned the title of *"Kristalnacht"* because of the amount of glass shattered that night.[117]

Joseph Goebbels, who was Propaganda Minister in Hitler's Cabinet, and also directly responsible for the actions of November 9, denied that the government had had anything to do with the violence against the Jews. In an official statement he said:

> . . . It is said, the spontaneous reactions of the German *Volk* were a result of organized teams. How little knowledge these *Zielenschinder* [hack writers] have of Germany! How serious this reaction would have been had it been organized! . . . [118]

On November 11, Reinhard Heydrich, who was the Chief of Police, gave a report to Martin Goering, his senior, on the extent of the damage done to Jewish property. The government held the Jews fully responsible for all the damage and ordered them to pay a total of one billion Reich Marks in compensation. Between November 11 and November 29, no fewer than twelve anti-Jewish laws were passed by the state. Most of them were designed to eliminate Jews from German economic life.[119]

The Reaction of the Confessing Church to the November Pogrom

Almost two months before *Kristalnacht,* the Confessing Church had celebrated a liturgy at which they prayed that war would be averted. At about the same time, on the occasion of the invasion of Czechoslovakia, Karl Barth, acting independently in Switzerland, wrote a letter to a friend in Prague, saying:

Every Czech soldier who fights and suffers will be doing so for us too and—I say this unreservedly—he will also be doing it for the Church of Jesus, which in the atmosphere of Hitler and Mussolini must become the victim of either ridicule or extermination.[120]

The Nazis were quick to connect the liturgy and Barth's letter, referring to them as "treasonable actions in clerical garb." The Confessing Church, finding itself on the defensive, dissociated itself from Barth's letter, saying:

We have nothing to do with this democratically ideologized political theology directed from Switzerland against our fatherland; there is no connection between Barth and the special prayer or the spirit of this liturgy.[121]

But Hanns Kerrl, knowing of the split within the Confessing Church, saw an opportunity to deal a blow at the Dahlemites. He summoned Bishops Wurm, Meiser, Marahrens, and Kuehlewein (all opponents of the Dahlemites) to a meeting.

After the meeting, the bishops issued the following statement:

> We categorically state that the circular issued by the
> Provisional Church Administration on September 27,
> 1938, regarding the holding of prayer services in connec-
> tion with the danger of war, is unacceptable to us for
> religious and patriotic reasons, and has been rejected by
> our churches. We condemn in the strongest terms the
> attitude therein expressed, and dissociate ourselves from
> those responsible.[122]

This statement was announced by the German News Agency
in the beginning of November.

When the Jews were attacked on November 9 and 10, the
Confessing Church was in disarray and unable to speak with
one voice, and so it chose not to speak at all. It was silent just
as it had been after the passage of the Nuremberg laws and
the other anti-Jewish measures (which numbered 170 by this
time).[123] It was because of this silence that Bonhoeffer,
according to Eberhard Bethge, pronounced his statement:
"Only he who cries out for the Jews may sing Gregorian
chants."[124]

One week after the events of November 9 and 10, the
German Protestant Church celebrated its annual event
known as *Buss und Bettag* (Day of repentance and prayer).
The biblical text assigned for that day was Jeremiah 22:29 (O
Land, Land, Land, hear the Word of the Lord). Theodor Dipper
says:

> It would have been very helpful if at that time the
> Church leadership, in view of the unique and clear
> situation, had issued a statement to the congregations
> and at least given a short introduction to the text for the
> day.[125]

None of this happened, but at least one pastor, Julius von

Jahn, was brave enough to preach a sermon, on November 16, 1938, in which he said:

The passions have been released, God's commandment ignored, God's buildings which were holy to some have been burned down with impunity, the property of others stolen or destroyed. Men who have faithfully served our German *Volk* have been thrown into concentration camps simply because they belong to another race. This injustice may not be admitted in official circles—the healthy national consciousness feels it clearly, even where one dares not speak about it.[126]

For this sermon, Jahn was attacked by a pro-Nazi mob and, finally, sent to prison.[127] The majority of the pastors of the Confessing Church were horrified at the sermon. Bishop Wurm, in whose province von Jahn served, was critical rather than supportive. In a sermon preached on December 6, 1938,— at which time von Jahn was in prison—Wurm said:

It goes without saying that when a servant of the Church preaches he must avoid everything that is the equivalent of forbidden criticism of concrete political events.[128]

And in a letter to Franz Guertner, Minister of Justice, the bishop said:

I in no way challange the right of the state to fight Jewry as a dangerous element. From the days of my youth I accepted the views of Heinrich Treitschke and Adolf Stoecker about the destructive influence of Jewry in religious, moral, literary, economic and political spheres.[129]

At the beginning of Advent, the Confessing Church held a Church conference at Steglitz. There a statement was issued, and it was read at most of the churches that were under the control of the Confessing Church. The statement read:

> Dear brothers and sisters: Many of you are deeply troubled by the fate of fellow-Christians. As a result of the action against the Jews, some have preached about the Ten Commandments seriously and have been persecuted for that.[130]

On the whole, however, the Confessing Church was silent. Provost Heinrich Grueber (see below) said:

> In a few meetings of the Confessing Church there was a call for a protest. But what were the few who protested compared to the millions who went along or remained silent, who at best buried their heads in the sand or stuck their hands in their pockets.[131]

On the same subject, Grueber said, in 1958: "We Christians—out of fear and cowardice—kept our mouths shut."[132] Commenting on the same issue, Pastor Julius von Jahn had this to say: "We were all afraid to touch on the point that was very sensitive to the regime."[133] Without an official plan of the Confessing Church to help the Jews, it was left to individuals, like Pastor Jahn, to do so.

Humanitarian Work

The anti-Jewish measures which the Nazis passed—in particular, those that affected the economic situation of the Jews—made life increasingly difficult for them. It drove many of them to seek help. Provost Heinrich Grueber, a Protestant pastor in Berlin, saw the need for an office that would be of assistance to Protestant non-Aryans. The office was established in Berlin with the support of some leading members of the Dahlemites, among them Albertz-Spandau, the Confessing Church's legal adviser, Friedrich Perels, and Pastor

Hermann Maas. The main function of the office, particularly after November 9, was to facilitate the emigration of Jews, in particular those who were members of the Protestant Church. This is clear from the name of the office. It was called *"Kirchliche Hilfstelle fuer evangelische Nichtarier"* (Church Welfare Office for Protestant non-Aryans).[134]

Grueber's office worked closely with the Church ministry, the Ministry of Interior, the Ministry of Foreign Affairs, and the Gestapo.[135] Kurt Meier believes that the Nazis allowed Grueber's office to function because they believed that it would facilitate the emigration of large numbers of Jews. However, when it became obvious that the rest of the world was unwilling to absorb large numbers of Jews, the Nazis decided on their final solution.[136]

In 1940, the first Jews were transported from Settin to Lublin. In December of that year, Grueber, who was classified as an Aryan, was arrested and placed in a concentration camp, where he remained until the end of the war. A few weeks later, Grueber's chief assistant, Pastor Werner Sylten, was also arrested and sent to Dachau, where he was murdered.[137] The humanitarian work, which had been carried by Grueber's office, thus came to an end.

The Role of the Deutsche Christen

The first reaction of the *Deutsche Christen* to the events of November 9 came from one of their provincial church councils. On November 30, the council issued a decree advising all its pastors not to administer any of the Church's sacraments to Jewish Christians.[138] This meant, in effect, that Jews were no longer recognized as communicants of the German Protestant Church in Thueringen.

On Febrary 10, 1939, the same province enacted a Church law, which simply said: "Jews cannot be members of the Thueringen Protestant Church." The law was signed by the Bishop of the Province, Martin Sasse.[139] Shortly thereafter, the other provinces passed similar laws.[140]

Following the decree that required all Jews who were six

years and older to wear the "Star of David,"[141] the Provincial
Church, office of Dresden, put out the following notice:

> Following the official introduction of the Star of David in
> the Reich it has become urgently necessary to place the
> following notice in all churches and church meeting
> rooms: "Jews prohibited."[142]

Although this notice originated at a provincial level and
apparently without the sanction of the Church ministry,
nothing was done to stop its implementation. Heinz Brunotte,
who was at the time an official of the Church ministry, gives
the following explanation:

> Ever since the introduction of the Star of David (and the
> first rumors of what was happening on the Eastern
> Front) a kind of deep-seated hopelessness, which was like
> a paralysis, had gripped the responsible Church depart-
> ments. One felt that, as a result of the brutality of the
> party and SS, it was impossible to control the unfolding
> of events and that, through protests, an already difficult
> situation for the life of the Church would worsen. Even
> from the Confessing Church, as late as autumn, no voice
> was to be heard.[143]

It was on November 13, 1933, that the *Deutsche Christen*
first made their offical demand for the introduction of the
Aryan Clause in the Church. The implementation of the
provisions of the clause would have meant expelling non-
Aryans from the Church as it was then constituted. This call
gave birth to a theological battle between the *Deutsche
Christen* and what eventually became the Confessing Church.
The battle raged for eight years, until December 22, 1941. On
that day, the Church Chancellery sent out the following order
to all administrative authorities of the German Protestant
Provincial Churches:

> The breakthrough of racial consciousness in our *Volk*,
> strengthened through the experience of war and the

relative measures of the political leadership have caused the exclusion of Jews from our community as Germans. This is an indisputable fact, which the German Protestant Church, as a servant of the Gospel . . . cannot ignore. In conjunction with the Spiritual Advisory Council of the German Protestant Church, we request the highest administrative authorities to take the necessary steps to prevent the baptized non-Aryans from participating in the church life of Germans.[144]

Bishop Marahrens of the Confessing Church (conservatives) was a member of the Spiritual Advisory Council that was a party to this pronouncement. The church historian Karl Kupisch, said:

There is not a more horrible church document than this order, not even from a pagan point of view.[145]

From the beginning of 1942, baptized Jews were no longer required to pay church tax, as was required of all Christians.[146] This step was taken to emphasize that Jews were no longer part of the German community—even in Church. Whatever was left of the Confessing Church remained silent. Bethge says:

When the final solution of the Jewish question was begun in the autumn of 1941, what was left of the Confessing Church was fully occupied with questions concerning its own existence, and there were only a few brave isolated actions.[147]

In July 1943, Bishop Marahrens wrote Hitler a letter in which he said:

In the name of God and in the name of the will of the German *Volk,* we urgently request the leadership of the Reich to prevent the persecution and extermination of many men and women in areas under German control which is carried out without the due process of law. Now that those non-Aryans who were under the control of the Germans have been eliminated, one must fear, as a result of isolated incidents, that the privileged non-Aryans who, until now were safe, are likely to become victims too.[148]

On December 20, 1943, in a letter to Hans Lammers, chief of the Reich Chancellery, and therefore one of those closest to Hitler, he said:

No one . . . can doubt that these Mischlingen (Jews of mixed blood) are faced with the similar fate that face full Jews—elimination.[149]

It is clear from these two letters that the bishop was not concerned with the fate of Jews as such, but with only those Jews who were married to Germans and their offspring.

Otto Elias points out that the bishop raised his voice for the first time in 1943, when the vast majority of German Jews had already been gassed in Auschwitz, Bergen-Belsen, and Treblinka—although he had full knowledge of the actions.[150] Other bishops of the Confessing Church (Conservatives) also knew of the mass deportations and gas chambers.[151] Brunotte says:

In 1941, when the advanced mass deportations became evident, the churches should have known that any kind of special treatment for non-Aryans Christians was pointless because it was too late.[152]

The bishop's letters were, therefore, the first and the last attempt to speak on behalf of the "privileged" Jews. According to Brunotte, the files of the Church Chancellery, where he was employed were closed about the middle of 1943 because:

With the deportation of the last German Jews to the extermination camps in the Eastern regions of Germany, the problem of caring for the Protestant non-Aryans disappeared.[153]

The Nazis arrested many pastors, and some of them were sent to concentration camps. However, not a single bishop was arrested. Walther Hofer concludes that was because the bishops had a large following and were held in high esteem within Germandom.[154] While this reason may be valid, it would appear that the failure of the bishops to oppose the Nazi policies toward the Jews made it unnecessary for the Nazis to persecute them. Hanns Kerrl may have influenced other leading Nazis when he said that the churches were useful to the Reich as long as they continued to ring their bells to celebrate German victories and as long as they continued to pray for the Fuehrer, *Volk* and fatherland.[155]

After the war Martin Niemoeller was asked why Hitler did not put him to death. His answer was:

He did not dare! He was afraid of the people, because he knew that would give way to too much public animosity.[156]

Niemoeller's reason was not unfounded. When Bishops Wurm and Marahrens were placed under house arrest by Mueller and Jaegger, it was the protests from their followers that finally secured their release. The question, therefore, is whether the Confessing Church was indeed afraid to come to the aid of the Jews, and, if so, why?

The Roman Catholics and the Nazis

Centuries before the Nazis came to power, the Roman Catholic Church had had its own running battle with the Jews. The Roman Catholic Church has a long history of meting out harsh treatment to the Jews for their refusal to embrace the Catholic faith. As early as the fourth century, the

Catholic Church passed canonical laws that discriminated against the Jews. Over the centuries, these laws discriminated against the Jews in areas of marriage, employment, professions, identification, religious practice, housing, and what can be generally called human rights. When Hitler, himself a Roman Catholic, came to power, he reminded the Catholics of their longstanding anti-Jewish tradition. Discussing the Jewish question with the Roman Catholic bishop of Osnabrueck, Berning, Hitler said:

> As for the Jews, I am just carrying on with the same policy which the Catholic church has adopted for fifteen hundred years, when it has regarded the Jews as dangerous and pushed them into ghettos etc., because it knew what the Jews were like. I don't put race above religion, but I do see the dangers in representatives of this race for Church and state, and perhaps I am doing Christianity a great service.[157]

Unfortunately it is not known what reply the bishop gave to Hitler, however, subsequent behavior of the Catholic hierarchy suggests that the bishop did not oppose Hitler. After all, Hitler was merely drawing the attention of the bishop to well-documented historical fact.

The interview was held in April 1933, and, in July of the same year, Hitler scored a major victory, when the Vatican, representing the entire Catholic Church, entered into a power-sharing agreement with the Nazis, known as the Concordat. The Concordat had three main advantages for the Nazis.

First, it made it much easier for them to argue that they were neither un-Christian or anti-Church.

Second, the Vatican gave full and unconditional recognition to the new Nazi state.

Third, both the powerful Catholic trade-union movement and the political Center Party ceased to be political factors.

Above all, the Nazis and the Catholic Church became

contractual partners in the new German Reich. The partnership was in the form of a pyramid with the Nazis at the top and the ordinary Catholic citizens at the base. The laity were thus subject to both the controls of the Nazis and those exerted by the Catholic Church. This is how the ordinary Catholic found himself supporting the enormous excesses of the Nazis.

There were, however, other important factors which made the marriage between the Catholics and the Nazis ideal. The traditional, excessive, and blind respect for authority among the Catholics made it easy for them to accept Nazi authority without questioning. The claim by the Nazis that they were out to destroy Communism—a hated foe of the Catholics—won them not only the admiration of the Catholics, but their almost total allegiance as well. There were also the strong elements of nationalism and patriotism among the Catholics so that, when the Nazis promised them not just Germany but the whole world, the enthusiasm was so high that "German Catholics and their bishops supported Hitler's war." [158]

Given the above picture, it is easy to understand why the Catholic Church was silent in the face of Nazi atrocities against the Jews. Like the Protestant Church, the Catholics were concerned with their own preservation and perpetuation—certainly not with the Gospel, which demanded justice for the oppressed and persecuted.

The Nazi persecution of the Jews was the first major test in modern times for the relevancy of the Catholic Church. Needless to say, it failed that test dismally. Like the rest of the Western Church, it proved to be more of a stumbling block than a source of help. Its hypocrisy was laid bare. Its preoccupation with such irrelevant issues as dogma and doctrine disqualified it from being a church. Until the advent of *apartheid,* its indifference to human suffering and its own contribution to that suffering was unparalleled in the history of mankind. There are those who will argue that the Church was not quite aware of all that was going on. Given the history of the Catholic Church in its relations with Jews, that argument is not plausible. Many of the anti-Jewish canonical laws that the Catholic Church passed were modernized and incorporated by the Nazis. There are others who say what happened forty years ago cannot be changed. That is true. But it is also true that what happened forty years ago can be repeated.

Naziism has found a new name and new home in South Africa. This is the second test for the Catholic as well as the Protestant churches. Will they act differently, or will history repeat itself?

4

The Nazi Stand on Christianity

The Stated Position

One of the first actions of the Nazi Party on coming to power in 1933 was to ban the Communist Party and to arrest its leadership and many members. As was mentioned previously this, together with their propaganda against Marxism, led many to believe that the Nazis were pro-Church and staunch supporters of the Christian faith.[1] This impression was reinforced when Hitler refused to identify himself with the anti-Christian views of some of his associates,[2] and further strengthened when he called for the unification of the twenty-eight Protestant provincial churches into a united German Church.

The leaders of all twenty-eight provincial churches agreed with the need for unification; they met and drew up a constitution, and the *Deutsche Evangelische Kirche* (German Protestant Church) was formed. But these same leaders were divided on the issue of administrative control of the newly formed Church, and two main factions developed: the *Deutsche Christen*, who favored Nazi control of the Church, and the "Confessing Church," which was opposed to government control.[3] There was a large number of pastors who supported neither side in the conflict and remained neutral.[4]

The leaders were also divided regarding the interpretation of the Nazi concept of "Positive Christianity," a term used in the section on Christianity in the Nazi Party program.[5] The Nazis were careful not to spell out what they meant by "Positive Christianity," thus gaining a favored position for themselves. Since the phrase was open to varied (even contradictory) interpretations among the different denominations— and within some denominations—in the midst of controversy, they could always claim neutrality. If they decided to intervene, they could claim they were doing so in the interest of the German *Volk*.

The *Deutsche Christen* were the first Church group to use the term "Positive Christianity." In their ten-point principles, they stated:

> We stand on the ground of positive Christianity. We profess an affirmative faith in Christ, fitting our race and being in accordance with the German Lutheran mind and heroic piety.[6]

They interpreted "Positive Christianity" as meaning Christianity free of all Jewish traces, especially the "Old Testament with its Jewish reward morality."[7] The Confessing Church rejected the idea of a Christianity that excluded the Old Testament.

The Nazis showed no direct interest either in theological matters or in those issues they considered relevant only to the internal life of the Church. Hitler never supported the idea that pastors should take a special oath of allegiance to him, nor did the Nazi Party insist that the Aryan Clause should be extended to include the churches. In 1938, therefore, the Nazis could boast that they had not interfered in the religious life of the churches.

> . . .The irrevocable truth is that religious life in Germany, under the protection of the National Socialist State, unfolds more freely and undisturbed. No form of Godlessness or blasphemy is tolerated, and the Churches as well as their religious affairs are secure, undisturbed,

and free of problems in a way that is unprecedented in history and almost unknown in any other country on earth.[8]

This claim probably referred only to the Roman Catholic Church and the Protestant Church, since, between the years 1933 and 1938, almost forty religious sects had been banned by the Nazis. These included such internationally known groups as the Jehovah's Witnesses, Pentecostals, and Seventh-Day Adventists. Some of the reasons given for the bannings included "endangering public morality" and "aims of the sect contradict the purposes of the National Socialist leaders." For a complete list, see John S. Conway's, *Nazi Persecution of the Churches 1933–1945,* pp. 371–374.

Religion and Politics

In 1935, an article in one of the Nazi publications drew the distinction between what was political and what was religious. According to the article,

Political is everything which in the earthly forms of organization, word, picture and demeanor, appears for the benefit of the *Volk,* even if it has the least meaning.
Religious is everything which in earthly form is incomprehensible like belief in heaven, eternity, and longing for things which are beyond the visible world.[9]

The Nazis insisted that the churches should play no active part in the political developments of the Reich. As long as the churches confined themselves to religious matters, their freedom would be guaranteed.[10] If there was tension between Church and state, it was because the churches had overstepped their religious boundaries and entered into the world of politics. The tension would end only if the churches stopped meddling in politics.[11]

To the majority of the Protestant clergy, this call for the

separation of religion and politics was neither new nor unwelcome. It was something that was basic to the Lutheran Tradition of "The Separate Kingdoms"—one earthly and the other heavenly. Jesus' call to "render unto Caesar what is Caesar's and unto God what is God's" could also be interpreted as meaning a separation between politics (Caesar) and religion (God).

The Confessing Church had called for a separation of Church and state in the Barmen Declaration. Point five reads:

> We reject the false doctrine that the state, over and above its special commission, should and could become the single and totalitarian order of human life, thus fulfilling the Church's vocation as well.
> We reject the false doctrine that the Church over and above its special commission, should and could appropriate the characteristics, the tasks, and the dignity of the state, thus itself becoming an organ of the state.[12]

This was a clear repudiation of the aims of the *Deutsche Christen* to make the Church "an organ of the state."

The commitment of the Confessing Church to the separation of Church and state is reflected in their protests against the Aryan Clause. They protested against, and resisted, the aryanization of the Protestant Church. However, there was no such protest or resistance when it came to the aryanization of other sectors of German life, for example, the civil service, the military and business. Otto Elias sums up their position in these words:

> The Confessing Church never officially spoke out against the Aryan Clause as such: The Church was either uninterested or it supported the measure outside of the Church.[13]

Since there were only thirty-five non-Aryan pastors who

could potentially be affected by the Aryan Clause out of a total of eighteen thousand Protestant pastors, the action of the Confessing Church was one of principle: Once the sacraments of baptism and ordination had been conferred, they could not be undone. Forcing non-Aryans out of the Protestant Church would have had the effect of undoing the sacraments. That was the argument of the Confessing Church.[14]

There were, however, a few voices within the Confessing Church calling for a stand on the Jewish question. These were in the minority and were reminded to keep politics and religion apart, lest the Confessing Church find itself in conflict with the state. Bishop Meiser, a prominent and powerful member of the Confessing Church, showed this concern when he expressed himself strongly against any discussion of the Jewish question, just two days before the Nuremberg Congress of the Nazis in September 1935. Speaking of a forthcoming Prussian Church Synod, Bishop Meiser said:

I would like to raise my voice against a self-inflicted martyrdom. I am worried about the forthcoming Prussian Synod if it wants to touch on such matters as, for example, the Jewish question.[15]

When the Confessing Church did discuss the Jewish question, it was emphasized that the question was not a political one, but rather theological:

The pronouncement of the Church on the Jewish question is based neither on political, economic, social or even incidental-personal considerations; it is based solely on God's Word which is above daily opinions. The only way to solve the Jewish question is through the conversion of Israel.[16]

The leadership in the Protestant Church, therefore, did not challenge the Nazis so long as they did not interfere in Church affairs.

The Nazis and the Protestant Church Conflict

The common view of both the Church and the state that politics and religion should be kept apart should have established an acceptable foundation for coexistence. However, the Nazis had their own interpretation of noninterference in church affairs. They understood it to mean no *direct* government control of the Church. They, therefore, encouraged and assisted their own supporters within the Church to play a more active and aggressive role. Through intrigue and manipulation, they were able to fill important positions within the church administration with these supporters. An example of intrigue was the replacement of Friedrich von Bodelschwing—(an anti-Nazi who had been elected Reich Bishop)—by Ludwig Mueller, Hitler's choice, and a member of the *Deutsche Christen.*

The constitution that all twenty-eight Church leaders signed, on July 11, 1933, was elevated to the level of state law[17] not just canon law. The constitution provided for Church elections to be held. The date of the elections was set for July 23, 1933.[18]

On July 19, the official Nazi mouthpiece, *Voelkische Beobachter,* published the following directive:

> Every party member who is a Protestant will vote on Sunday, the day of the Church elections. That simply goes without saying. It is also obvious that he will vote for the Movement of German Christians *(Bewegung Deutsche Christen).*[19]

On the night before the elections, Hitler made a radio broadcast in which he said:

> In the interest of the rebirth of the nation . . . I understandably wish that the Church elections, in their results, will support our new national and state policies. . . This, however, will not be guaranteed

through religious petrification but rather through the power of a living movement. I see this power in that part of the Protestant Church *Volk* that is primarily united and as part of the *Deutsche Christen,* is consciously on the side of the National Socialist State.[20]

Thus the *Deutsche Christen* were identified with the rebirth of the nation, with patriotism. They won more than two-thirds of the seats.

Bishop Mueller tried to establish his authority by taking drastic measures against all forms of opposition. Many pastors were suspended, including Niemoeller, who, however, ignored the suspension. Opposition to Mueller continued to grow, and, in 1934, a national *Reichsbruederrat* (Reich Council of Brethren) was formed. In August 1934, the *Reichsbruederrat* took a bold stand and declared that; "Obedience to this church regime (Mueller's) is disobedience to God."[21]

In order to demonstrate their defiance further, the *Reichsbruederrat,* which consisted only of pastors, joined hands with bishops who disapproved of the way Mueller was using dictatorial powers, to form a *"Vorlaufige Kirchenleitung"* (Provisional Church Administration). This demonstrated that they did not recognize Mueller and his administration. Mueller warned that the new organization was illegal, but he was ignored.

The authority of Mueller was further weakened by the fact that many of his decisions, especially the suspensions of those who disagreed with him, were successfully challenged in the courts of law. In order to curb this development, the Nazis declared that all legal matters of the Protestant Church had to be handled by the government department in the Ministry of Internal Affairs.[22]

The Nazis, realizing Mueller's ineffectiveness, established an Office of Church Affairs to supervise all Church matters. They hoped that this would help solve the conflict within the Protestant Church. Instead, the conflict was complicated by the split within the Confessing Church.

Hans Kerrl, as new Minister of Church Affairs, banned the *Vorlaufige Kirchenleitung,* but he too was defied.[23] On February 15, 1937, Hitler personally made the following announcement:

Following the failure of the Reich Church Commissions to unite the Church groups of the German Protestant Church, the Church should now, with full freedom, and in accordance with the regulations of the Church *Volk,* implement the new constitution and, therefore, bring about new order into the Church. I hereby authorize the Reich Minister for Church Affairs to prepare for an election of a general synod and to establish the necessary conditions for such an election.[24]

The Confessing Church feared that the election would once again be manipulated as had been the case in 1933. Therefore, together with other opponents of the *Deutsche Christen,* the Confessing Church printed leaflets informing the different congregations of the false teachings of the *Deutsche Christen.*[25] Otto Dibelius, General Superintendent and member of the Confessing Church, wrote directly to Hitler accusing the *Deutsche Christen* of being un-Christian.[26]

On June 25, 1937, the Nazis prohibited all forms of campaigning for the Church elections. The elections were never held. The concerted resistance of the Confessing Church resulted, for the first time, in a defeat for Hitler (since he had personally ordered the Church elections).[27] The success of the Confessing Church demonstrated their power within Germandom, and the extent to which the Nazis were dependent on the cooperation of the churches for the success of their policies. Hitler is on record for having explicitly said so.

. . .I need, for the building up of a great political movement, the Catholics of Bavaria just like the Protestants of Prussia.[28]

Instead of taking further action against the Confessing

Church as such, Kerrl concentrated on individual pastors. However, most of them received fines or light sentences for having committed such offenses as defying an order not to preach or hold a meeting or illegally distributing anti-*Deutsche Christen* literature.[29] Two prominent cases however, were more serious. One was the trial of Otto Dibelius, and the other that of Martin Niemoeller.

In August 1937, Dibelius was sued by Kerrl for defamation of character. The judges found Dibelius not guilty and acquitted him. Kerrl's efforts to have Dibelius rearrested and sent to a concentration camp were equally rebuffed by the judges.[30] This was a serious blow to a man who was a government minister and also had the backing of Hitler.

Martin Niemoeller's case was even more serious, since he was charged, among other things, with being a traitor. More important than the charge is what he said in his defense. Niemoeller noted that, since 1924, he had voted for the Nazi Party although, unlike his brother Wilhelm, he had not joined the party. He noted that Jews were "distasteful" and "foreign" to him. "But," he said, "Baptism cannot be replaced by a family tree." He went on:

We may not form God according to our own picture, an Aryan picture, but we have to accept him as He is: revealed to us in the Jew Jesus of Nazareth. This painful and difficult scandal must, for the sake of the Gospel, be accepted.[31]

Niemoeller's argument was purely theological. In essence he was repeating the position of the Confessing Church, namely that the Scriptures could not be altered to suit the wishes of the *Deutsche Christen* and that baptized Jews were an inseparable part of the Church. Niemoeller's defence reveals the dilemma of many Protestant Germans—being anti-Semitic on the one hand and having to defend the rights of baptized Jews on the other.[32]

Although Niemoeller won the case, he was immediately arrested and sent to a concentration camp on the personal orders of Hitler. According to his own evidence, he was not mistreated but he was not released from Dachau until the end of the war, in June, 1945.[33]

The Confessions of the Confessing Church

Although Germany surrendered on May 9, 1945, it took some time for all those who had been imprisoned by the Nazis to be freed. The fall of the Nazis also meant the end of the Nazi Office for Church Affairs. Bishop Wurm was one of those who tried to form a new leadership for the Protestant Church. He organized a conference of Church Leaders to be held in Treysa from August 27 to 31. Martin Niemoeller was sent the program on which his name appeared as preacher for the opening day, but he was not invited as a participant.

In a letter to Bishop Meiser, Niemoeller explained that he did not expect to be invited as a Church leader by Bishop Wurm.[34] He refused to preach at the conference, and, in his letter of refusal to Wurm, dated August 5, 1945, he said:

. . . especially because on the list of participants, except for my name, only that of Dr. Mensing from the circle of the Confessing Church, is listed. I could not but conclude that through the extremely unfortunate inclusion of my name, the impression should be given that I at least belong to the same circle of friends with those listed and that we work together. This is not the case. To determine the way the Church should go with "Neutrals" or even with positive representatives of Kerrl's Church Commissions-policy (for example Gerstenmeier) appears totally impossible for me especially because it would mean an end to all that the Protestant Church offered and lost in property and life in twelve years.[35]

It is clear from Niemoeller's letter that the Dahlemites did not consider the "Conservatives" part of the Confessing Church.

110

Before writing to Wurm, Niemoeller had written to Karl Barth on August 2, 1945, in which letter he refers to Wurm and his associates rather sarcastically, saying:

Just as there are no more Nazis in Germany, so are there no more *Deutsche Christen*; and just as no one ever had anything to do with Hitler, so also in the Church no one ever had anything to do with his [Church] measures.

In the same letter, Niemoeller informed Barth of the planned conference in Treysa.[36]

Fearing that the leadership of the Church would fall into the wrong hands, Niemoeller called a meeting of the Council of Brethren. The meeting took place in Frankfurt on August 12, 1945. In his opening remarks, Niemoeller said:

We know that in the developments of the last fifteen years the Church bears its measured part of the blame, and that we no longer can say: What do we have to do with it? We did not want it to be so. . . Now those who were party members are being dismissed from their positions, but those in the leadership of the Church who are also to be blamed for the fact that people who joined the party do not only want to keep their positions but want to decide on the future of the Church. How can the Church in future find believers in our people? It is an ignominy for the Church and a stumbling block for its future task if the deception of 1936 continues; if now the leadership of the Church should be in the hands of men who knew of nothing better to do than to be silent when they ought to have spoken out, and to be weak when they should have resisted.[37]

At this meeting, preparations were made for the conference that was to convene in Treysa a week later. It was suggested that Karl Barth, who was then living in Switzerland, should attend. The conference at Treysa revealed once more the gap between the group led by Wurm and the group led by Niemoeller. Although the war was over, the positions of the two sides remained as far apart as ever.

Bishop Wurm was the first to speak. He said:

If I were to be asked: What do you think the present task of the Church is, I could only say: It must feel itself in solidarity with our nation that is guilty and in misery and should preach the gospel from the point of view of vindication of the sinner. Solidarity with the guilt of the nation; for we also needed much time to completely see through the lies and we witnessed very faintheartedly.[38]

When Niemoeller's turn came to speak, his position was diametrically opposed to that of Wurm. He said:

I have to say something here which until now has not been said. . . Our present situation is . . .not in the first place the guilt of the nation or of the Nazis. . . No, the real guilt lies with the Church. The Church alone knew that the chosen path was leading to destruction and it did not warn our people; it did not expose the practiced injustices or when it did it was already too late. . . And here the Confessing Church carries a great measure of guilt. . . It did speak but then it soon got tired. That is what we have to tell our people and Christendom today.[39]

Karl Barth, who was a guest at Treysa, wrote of the conference:

To my surprise I found this Church—apart from the fact that the *Deutsche Christen* of 1933 now quite naturally had disappeared or gone underground or (in a few cases) had honestly been converted—roughly in the same structure, and groups and with the same divisions in which I saw it rushing to its destruction in 1933.[40]

At Treysa, it was clear that the German Protestant

Church was not united. The divisions that existed before and during the war were still present, if not wider. The question of admitting guilt seemed to be thorny. Yet it was this confession that Christendom expected. This is what Karl Barth told Martin Niemoeller in a letter he wrote to him in September 1945. Barth went on to suggest what points such a confession should include. These were:

> The Temporary Leadership of the Protestant Church in Germany recognizes and declares that the German nation found itself on the wrong path when, in 1933, it placed itself politically in the hands of Adolf Hitler.
> It recognizes and declares that the suffering which befell Europe and Germany as well was a result of this error.
> It recognizes and declares that the Protestant Church in Germany through its false talk and false silence shares the responsibility for this error.[41]

A meeting of the *Vorlaufige Kirchenleitung* was planned for October, and members of the Ecumenical Council were to be invited, including Visser't Hooft, who later helped arrange the Cottesloe Consultation in South Africa. Niemoeller wrote to Barth, assuring him that he fully agreed with him and that at the October conference in Stuttgart, he would see to it that "the *Kirchenleitung* makes a clear and unequivocal statement on the whole question of its guilt."[42] Barth had also requested Niemoeller to prevent the inclusion of such expressions as; "We were victims of demons and the devil," which, apparently, had become familiar excuses.

The bishops who were part of the *Kirchenleitung* did not know of the discussions that were going on between Barth and Niemoeller. The dates for the Stuttgart conference were set for October 17 to 19, 1945. On the evening of October 18, Martin Niemoeller preached a sermon based on the text of Jeremiah 14:7–11, in which he said:

It is not enough just to blame the Nazis. The Church

must also confess its guilt. Would the Nazis have been able to do what they did if the members of the Church were real Christians?

He went on to speak of the horrible suffering visited upon the people of Poland, Holland, Czechoslovakia, the Soviet Union, France, Norway, Greece, and other countries.[43]

The following day, the members of the Ecumenical Movement met with the *Kirchenleitung*. In that meeting Visser't Hooft said:

> In the Ecumenical Movement we need witness from the Protestant Church in Germany. We really need a spiritual reconstruction of the German people. For all of us in Europe that is a condition, *"sine qua non."*

In Niemoeller's reply, the formula of Karl Barth served as a basis. He said:

> We know that we, together with our people, followed the wrong path and therefore, that we as a Church are guilty of what became the fate of the whole world.[44]

That evening the *Kirchenleitung* met again to discuss the whole question of the Protestant Church. It is at that meeting that the *"Stuttgarter Schuldbekenntnis"* (the Stuttgart Confession of Guilt) was formulated. It took into consideration what had been said during the day and also Martin Niemoeller's speech in Treysa. Formulating a confession of guilt was not something that had been officially planned by the *Kirchenleitung*. It was the result of the behind-the-scenes work of Niemoeller and a few others, together with Barth's prodding. What was finally said, therefore, was the result of hard bargaining between the Dahlemites and the Conservatives. Since Niemoeller had already mentioned something about "guilt" during the day, it was no longer possible to ignore the question.

The final version that was read as the official statement on October 19, 1945, suggests a compromise between Niemoeller and Wurm.

> . . .We know ourselves to be one with our people in a great company of suffering and in a great solidarity of guilt. With great pain do we say: Through us endless suffering has been brought to many people and countries. . . We accuse ourselves for not witnessing more courageously, for not praying more faithfully, for not believing more joyously, and for not loving more ardently.[45]

The question that remained unclear was whether this confession was made in the name of the Church to be understood by both "man" (the world) and God or it was an expression of a small group within the Church. It did not take long before the positions were clarified.

For the confession to have any meaning, it would have to be echoed by the churches in Germany. On the annual day of "Confession and Prayer," in November 1945, Bishop Marahrens of Hannover said in his sermon:

> If this day of confession calls upon us to confess our guilt, then that is openly and rightly to be understood as a confession to God and not to men. In the past few weeks our congregations have been greatly troubled because (according to newspaper reports) it looks as though the Protestant Church now wants to solve a question that is tied up with so much bitterness. That the Church cannot do. It cannot be the task of the Church to solve political questions and questions of international law. The Church is incapable of comprehending the entanglement of guilt and fate.[46]

The "bitterness" mentioned by Marahrens was the widespread feeling in German Church circles that the Germans were not the only ones who were guilty, but that "the others" who bombed Germany and destroyed much property and many lives had to confess their guilt too.[47]

Martin Niemoeller was not surprised at the reaction of the German churches to the Stuttgart Declaration. In a speech in December 1945, he mentioned his fears:

It is quite thinkable that within the Church minds will be divided along the same lines as they were on the question of Barmen, because we in our churches have an understandable shyness when it comes to being understood politically, and when we are expected to act accordingly.[48]

With reference to the wording of the declaration itself, Niemoeller also wrote to Barth on November 20, 1945.

I would have liked to see a clear and decisive confession, but Meieser (Bishop) stood in the way. I hope the confession will serve the necessary purpose, although, unfortunately, one cannot say that today the whole Church is prepared to speak out this way. Within the Church there is still a great deal of work to be done.[49]

Those who expected a "spiritual renewal" within the German Protestant Church were to be sorely disappointed, including those who participated in the drafting of the declaration. In 1946, Niemoeller wrote Bishop Wurm a letter in which he said:

I must unfortunately confirm that, except for my lectures, as far as the congregations are concerned, the Stuttgart Declaration has simply remained a piece of paper. . . [50]

One of the few synods that identified with the Stuttgart Declaration was that of the province of Westfalen, to which

Martin Niemoeller's brother Wilhelm belonged. Their position was made clear at their meeting in Bethel, which took place from 16 to 20 July, 1946.[51] In a letter to his brother, Martin expressed his disappointment at the general attitude of the German Protestant Church:

> Your declaration on the "guilt question" is for me like balm on a broken heart. This is really the cardinal point in present-day Church affairs. I believe you have also done the ecumenical movement a great service because the whole of world-wide Christendom repeatedly asks whether the word from Stuttgart could have been truly meant when the echo from the German Church is missing.[52]

Karl Barth played a leading role in the drafting of the Barmen Declaration, hoping that it would serve as a basis for the churches to reject Naziism. He was proved wrong. He continued to the Stuttgart Declaration in the hope that it would serve as a basis for a new beginning in the Church life of Germany. In 1946 he sounded rather disappointed. In a lecture, he said:

> In spite of all the terrible things that have afflicted mankind in our time, in Europe there is still no Christian reawakening. There is no visible conversion of Europe's mankind. The blows came, the bombs fell, the courts of justice passed their terrible sentences, the people hid themselves, then got up and continued on their way as they had done before. I am not only talking about non-Christian, I am primarily talking about those who are well disposed toward Christianity.[53]

5

The South African Scene

The Attitude of the Protestant Churches to Race Relations: A Brief Historical Background

The establishment of Christianity in South Africa depended entirely on the work that was done by the different missionaries who came from Europe and America. Because these missionaries belonged to different denominations, besides preaching the Gospel, they were also engaged in the process of winning members for their particular denominations. The denominations were fairly well defined and distributed among the different countries of Europe and the continent of America: The Anglicans, Methodists, and Congregationalists came from England; the Presbyterians from Scotland; the Lutherans from Germany; the Catholics from France; the Dutch Calvinists from Holland; and the Baptists from America. From the earliest beginnings, therefore, denominationalism became an important factor in South African Christian life.[1]

The church that is commonly known as the Dutch Reformed Church has at least three independent churches under its umbrella.[2] The churches that originated in England and Scotland are commonly known as the English-speaking churches in South Africa.[3] These two, the Dutch Reformed

Church (DRC) and the English-speaking churches (ESC) are the most important Protestant groups of churches in South Africa in relation to *apartheid.*

In 1936, both groups together founded the Christian Council of South Africa, whose stated aim was to promote interchurch and interracial cooperation. However, the marriage did not last very long. In April 1941, the DRC withdrew its membership because of disagreement over the race question in South Africa. This disagreement included such issues as evangelism, education, social services, economics, politics, social contact, and equality.[4] In giving the reasons for the withdrawal, William Nicol, a DRC minister and also president of the Christian Council, said:

> The last reason for the failure was the deepest of all: our conflicting views on the right relations between White and Black. The English speaking missionary, especially the one born overseas, wishes to see as little difference as possible between the white man and the native. He does not hesitate to welcome the civilized native to his dining table. In many cases the native finds lodging for the night as an honoured guest among such white people. For us, on the other hand, the thought that we should use the same bathrooms and bathroom conveniences as even the most highly civilized native, is revolting. These principles run through all our conduct.[5]

The council continued to function without the participation of the DRC. For the DRC the separation meant that it could now pursue its racial policies without the need to discuss them with fellow-Christians.

The Attitude of the DRC to Apartheid

In the year 1829, the DRC had declared that the sharing of Holy Communion by the different races in the same church must be seen as an "immovable rule founded in the infallible Word of God."[6]

In the year 1857, however, the synod of the same church decided to erect separate church buildings for blacks and for whites, thus introducing segregation into the Church.[7] (The term "apartheid" did not exist at this time.)

The term "apartheid" first appeared in a book by a DRC theologian, G. Cronje, in 1942. In this book, the argument was put forward that God wills "apartheid" (separateness), as evidenced by the fact that He chose Israel as a special people. From this it can be deduced that God not only wanted separation, He wanted it to be total—that is, absolutely no mixing of the races.[8]

To support his argument, Cronje turned to the Scriptures. He cited a few passages for this purpose. These were:

Deuteronomy 38:8:

When the Most High gave the nations their inheritance, when He divided the sons of man, He fixed their bounds according to the numbers of the sons of God. . . .

Acts I:26:

From one single stock He not only created the whole human race so that they could occupy the entire earth but He decreed how long each nation should flourish and what the bounds of its territory should be.

A third citation was from Genesis II, the story of the Tower of Babel. According to Dutch theologians, sinful men tried to go against the Will of God, which is separateness (apartheid), by creating unity and homogeneity of the human race. God toppled the plan by causing confusion among the builders of the tower so that they ended up speaking different languages and, therefore, could no longer understand one another. He then divided the nations and distributed them all over the world.[9] In the practical situation of South Africa, this meant separating blacks from whites.

Cronje was not the only DRC theologian who found support for *apartheid* in the Scriptures. In 1940, P. J. Meyer wrote:

We Boer [Afrikaner] people entered into a covenant with God so as to maintain ourselves as God's people; to honour our separate calling as God's ordination, to fulfil it to the glory of God.[10]

The idea of being a called nation figures prominently in Afrikaner thinking and is used, as we shall see, to defend the privileged position of whites in South Africa.

Separateness was not possible if there was a mixture of blood, according to Afrikaner theologians, as is clear in their writings. G. Eloff states:

The maintenance of the Boers' tradition of racial purity must be protected at all costs and in every effective way as a sacred pledge entrusted to us by our predecessors as a part of God's plan for our people. Any movement, school or individual that offends against this tradition must be dealt with effectively by the authorities as a race-criminal.[11]

A few years later, Cronje echoed the same theme:

The more consistently the policy of *Apartheid* could be applied, the greater would be the security for the purity of our blood and the surer our unadulterated European racial survival.[12]

Every Afrikaner was urged to do his best to promote the idea of racial purity and *apartheid*. Cronje wrote:

The racial policy which we Afrikaners should promote

must be directed to the preservation of racial and cultural purity. This is because it is according to the Will of God and also because with the knowledge at our disposal it can be justified on practical grounds.[13]

Whether or not the Afrikaner churchmen were convinced that God had indeed called them, as they claimed, or whether they were simply reading into Scripture what they needed in order to defend racial supremacy, is difficult to establish. What is clear, however, is that they used other sources besides Scripture for support. In 1940, J. D. Vorster, who later became a leading figure in the DRC, cited Adolf Hitler as his authority. He told his congregation:

Hitler's *Mein Kampf* shows the way to greatness—the path of South Africa. Hitler gave the Germans a calling. He gave them a fanaticism which causes them to stand back for no one. We must follow his example because only by such a holy fanaticism can the Afrikaner nation achieve its calling.[14]

At the time this statement was made, Hitler was at the height of his glory. The Germans were beginning to believe that, indeed, they were about to experience the coming of the "Thousand Years' Reich." By the time the elections were held in South Africa, in 1948, the DRC had played its role by educating its flock about the need for *apartheid*.

Daniel Malan, in 1915, while he was still a pastor of one of the churches in the DRC, made the following statement:

The State controls the Church, and, conversely, the Church controls the State, for it is necessary for a man to become a leader in religious affairs before he can become of any political importance. As a result of this custom, the politicians are necessarily the most active Church members.[15]

The statement proved to be prophetic, at least for him

122

personally, since he became the first Afrikaner Nationalist Prime Minister in 1948 and introduced the policy and practice of *apartheid* to South Africa. Attention is called to the fact, contained in the remarks cited, that it is difficult to distinguish between the DRC and the Nationalist Party.

Afrikaner Assumption of Power

The "Programme of Principles," which the Nationalists used as a basic document for their 1948 election campaign, contained the following statement:

> As a basic principle of its attitude towards Natives and Coloureds, the Party recognizes that both are permanent parts of the country's population, under the trusteeship of the European race. It is strongly opposed to any attempt that might lead to the mixing of European and non-European blood. It also declares itself in favour of territorial and political segregation between Europeans and non-Europeans in general and in residential, and as far as practicable, in the industrial spheres.[16]

As soon as they came to power, the Nationalists embarked on a program that would transform *apartheid* from an ideology into a living reality. One must note that they actually carried out what they had for many years said they would do if elected to office.

Leslie Rubin, author of a brief commentary on *apartheid* legislation, states:

> Since the present Government came to power in South Africa in 1948, a vast body of legislative enactments has come into existence designed to give effect to the new policy of *apartheid*. Hundreds of laws have been passed by Parliament; thousands of regulations, proclamations and government notices have been issued under those laws. In addition there are numerous by-laws made by

the municipal councils of cities and towns throughout the country. All these combine to institute the legal apparatus which regulates the daily lives of more than four-fifths of the population of South Africa, that is, the 15 million non-Whites.[17]

The process for total *apartheid* continues. The laws, still being enacted in South Africa, contain the same elements that were found in the Nazi laws against the Jews: "racial purity," "self-preservation," "the Will of God." Whether the Afrikaner Nationalists will succeed where the Nazis failed is a question that goes beyond the limits of this study. Theological, moral, and humanitarian questions are raised by *apartheid*. The response of the churches to this challenge is now considered.

The Response of the DRC

In April 1950, the Federal Missionary Council of the DRC convened in Bloemfontein in order to define a "comprehensive Native policy." The conference stated that it considered all segregation a means of enhancing life and independence. It declared that:

The traditional fear of the Afrikaner of "equality" between Black and White had its origin in his antipathy to the idea of racial fusion.[18]

It went on record as opposing social equality and upholding the right of every nation to be itself and to endeavor to develop and elevate itself. *Apartheid* was defined as the process of development that seeks to lead each section of the people in the clearest and quickest way to its own destination under the gracious providence of God.[19]

The declarations of the DRC Conference drew an immediate response from the Nationalist government. The statements were so strongly in favor of *apartheid,* calling for it to be implemented "in the quickest way," that the government became alarmed. The Prime Minister issued a statement calling for patience, warning that *apartheid* could not be implemented in a hurry.[20]

Since the DRC wielded so much influence in Afrikanerdom, the government feared that, if the declarations were allowed to stand uncontested, pressure would be exerted on them for an immediate achievement of total *apartheid*. For political and practical reasons, this was not possible. It is interesting to note this public admonition did not weaken the strong links between the DRC and the Nationalist government.

The extent of DRC influence within Afrikanerdom can be assessed from the following statements:

The Dutch Reformed Church plays a major role in the life of South Africa because of its influence over Afrikaans-speaking South Africans at least two-thirds of whom support the Nationalist Party now in power.[21]

Writing on the same theme, Edgar Brookes says:

The Church (DRC) as a whole has supported *apartheid*. To the Afrikaner himself this has been a great factor in leading him to feel that his national policy is deeply rooted in morality and religion.[22]

And John de Gruchy elaborates by saying:

The Dutch Reformed Church with its million and a half members is quite clearly the dominant Church in terms of its access to the policy makers of the nation. Included within its ranks are most of the members of Parliament and of the provincial councils. Its members virtually control many of the town councils throughout the land. The vast majority of people employed by the Government in various capacities and institutions including the police and military, belong to the Dutch Reformed Church.[23]

In 1956, the DRC issued a policy statement on worship in which, *inter alia,* the following points were made:

a) The founding and development of independent indigenous churches for the purpose of evangelizing the Non-White races of South Africa was both necessary and in accordance with our understanding of the nature of the Church of the Lord Jesus on earth.

b) Since, under the pressure of circumstance, the historical development in the mission sphere throughout the centuries showed tendencies of un-Christian exclusiveness, thus impeding the realization of the true Christian fellowship between believers, this has happened not through ill-will towards the Non-Whites, nor with the approval of the official leadership of the Church, but must be seen as a result of uncontrollable circumstances and of general human weakness.

c) In each congregation, both mother and the indigenous daughter Churches reserve the right to regulate their membership according to the realistic demand of circumstances, and in accordance with the spirit of Christ; but at the same time it is also the Christian duty of the above mentioned Churches to educate their members for and in practice of a healthy Christian communion of believers, avoiding, however, any evil motives or annoying and willful demonstration.[24]

Of note, in the first paragraph of the statement is the complete reversal of the position on the sharing of Holy Communion as formulated by the Synod of 1829.[25]

It should also be noted, in paragraph two, that the statement suggests that the DRC hierarchy would prefer to hold mixed services, but "uncontrollable circumstances and general weakness" prevent this from taking place. This, of course, contradicts the resolution of the synod in 1950, which was extreme in its call for total *apartheid*. There is also no suggestion that the churches should work toward a United Church. The use of the terms "Mother Churches" (which are exclusively white) and "Daughter Churches" (whose membership is exclusively non-White) suggests compliance with the principles of the Nationalist Party, which call for blacks to be "under the Christian trusteeship of the European races."

This statement, justifying separate churches for the different racial groups, seems to have caught the eye of the government. A few months after its publication, the Nationalist government introduced a bill in Parliament aimed at legally extending *apartheid* into the churches. The bill finally became law and is euphemistically known as the "Church Clause."

The Response of the Dutch Reformed Church to Criticism

The position taken by the DRC on the question of *apartheid* led to criticism both from within the ranks of the DRC, and from outside.

The method of dealing with criticism from within has been to apply pressure to the critics so that they fall in line (as was done in the case of the ministers who tried to support the CI). Those who fail to do so are asked to resign or are expelled. Those who resign separate themselves from the family of Afrikanerdom, but the family remains united under strict discipline.

Like most churches worldwide, the DRC had joined Church-related organizations inside South Africa as well as international ones. The DRC also had very close links with the Dutch churches in Holland. When Church-related organizations challenged and criticized the DRC on its racial policies, especially its claim that it was merely carrying out

127

the will of God, the response of the DRC was to withdraw its membership from such organizations.[26]

In 1978, *Gereformeerde Kerken Nederland* (the Reformed Churches of the Netherlands) sent a delegation to South Africa to discuss the question of race relations in South Africa with the leadership of the DRC—their fraternal counterparts. On their return to Holland, members of the delegation made the following statements to the press.

Writing in *Vrij Nederland,* the Rev. Mak said:

> In Afrikanerdom there is no religion but an ideology—an ideology which permeates the whole being of the nation and about which the ministers preach. One naturally always looks for a miracle but I fear that violence will emerge from somewhere.

Writing in *Die Tyd,* another member of the delegation, Dr. Kruyswijk, said:

> The mighty and dominant Dutch Reformed Church is a brake on sound development in that country. This largest white Church is more hidebound than the Government on which it exercises a powerful influence. In South Africa it is still rather the Church than the State which stands in conflict with the Gospel.[27]

The third member of the delegation, Professor Ridderbos, said in *Elseviers magazine* that enlightened people within the Dutch Reformed Church feared to speak out because they felt powerless. He said the Moderature of the DRC "consists of the most hidebound people I have ever seen."[28]

In response, *Die Kerkbode* (official weekly of the DRC), said:

> The recent discussions between the delegates of the Reformed Churches in the Netherlands and the Moderature of our General Synod concluded without any posi-

tive results being achieved. . . .We should in fact have anticipated that the consultations would turn out unsatisfactorily, as indeed was the case. Our brethren from the Netherlands obviously never weighed the theological considerations behind the decision of our general Synod: "Under given circumstances and conditions, the New Testament leaves room for the organization of co-existence of different peoples in one country in the idiom of separate development." . . . Both groups found one another intractable and not open to conviction.[29]

The irreconcilable positions of the two groups led to the severance of relations in April 1978. Speaking of this break, a spokesman for the DRC said:

The sequence of events, involving the rupture of links with a Church with which we have had closest association and from which our Church has received sustenance in the theological idiom over the past century, is indeed a matter of sorrow. These developments become inevitable in our view as a result of the course pursued by the Church leadership in the *Gereformeerde Kerken Nederland* in recent years.[30]

A leading DRC theologian, Professor B. B. Keet, pointed out the isolation of the DRC as early as 1963. He said:

We of the Dutch Reformed Churches are standing quite alone in our interpretation of the Scriptures on the question of *apartheid*. We are not only standing against the convictions of other churches in South Africa, but we differ from the Reformed Churches of the world. All the Dutch Reformed Churches in this country stand for *apartheid* in the churches and in politics. . . . I think the Dutch Reformed Church leaders are very honest in their standpoint. But you can be very honest and yet be very wrong in your thinking.[31]

The DRC was so convinced of its God-given mission to be the bearer of light in Africa, that it considered all those opposed to its position on *apartheid,* to be misguided. It refused to reexamine its own stand and choosing, rather, to dismiss the criticism as unwarranted. Criticism, whether internal or external, could not be tolerated, since, as the argument went, "in *apartheid,* God's hand is at work." What strengthened the position of the DRC was the fact that the secular leaders spoke the same language as the Church leaders.

Daniel Malan, the first Afrikaner Nationalist Prime Minister (after the 1948 elections), spoke of Afrikanerdom as not being "the work of men but the work of God."[32] Another Prime Minister, Hendrik Verwoerd, referred to *apartheid* as willed by God and added:

It is the privilege of the leaders to be used by the Ruler of Nations and by their people as the vanguard in the fulfilment of His ideal [*apartheid*].[33]

Vervoerd's successor, John Vorster, continued the same theme when he said:

I believe that we still have a long way to go in the process of fulfilling our calling and that God who has so called us through His Grace, will not abandon us until we have completed our task.[34]

And finally, the National Party mouthpiece, *Die Transvaler,* declared:

God has summoned the white man and set him apart to build a separate nation in South Africa and to spread the Gospel of Jesus Christ among the Heathen. . . . To achieve this calling, the white man has been bidden to act as the guardian, master and spiritual leader of the black man. To do that, the white man has to have at his command the authority needed to uplift, Christianize and evangelize the black man; the purpose of this is that the black man who is still a child from the point of view of civilization, shall grow and develop in due course, in his own area, with his own language, according to the nature of his kind and in accordance with his own traditions. . . . We are in the process of setting the world an example since we know and believe that God wills it thus.[35]

The Response of the English-Speaking Churches

Unlike the Dutch Reformed Church, the four English-speaking churches under discussion, namely, the Anglican, Congregationalist, Methodist, and Presbyterian Churches, had neither a racial policy of their own, nor did they search the Scriptures for one. Prior to 1948, they concerned themselves primarily with missionary work among the blacks, specifically in the areas of education and health.[36]

Though these churches did not have a stated racial policy, they nevertheless practiced segregation in their schools, hospitals, seminaries—in all their institutions. This is pointed out by Bishop Reeves:

The observant visitor cannot fail to notice that the Church of South Africa is responsible for running segregated schools, hospitals and theological colleges. He will also see that the great majority of congregations are segregated even though it is true that many of them are segregated by accident and not by design. If such a visitor expresses surprise at this, he will probably be told that the law makes it impossible to integrate any institution under its control. But this is not by any means a complete answer, for the Church had control of these institutions long before the laws forbidding integration were passed, and did all too little to encourage them to become integrated.[37]

131

Until 1948, the churches had full control of their institutions, and the government did not interfere. With the coming of the Afrikaner Nationalist Party to power, however, the freedom hitherto enjoyed by the churches came to an end.

When it became clear that the Nationalist government was about to put *apartheid* into practice, leaders in the English-speaking churches became alarmed and began to issue public statements against *apartheid*. The Anglican Provincial Synod, which is the governing body of the Anglican Church, was among the first to issue such statements. At their conference held in 1948, they declared:

The conference is convinced that discrimination between men on grounds of race alone is inconsistent with the principles of Christ's religion. We urge that in every land men of every race should be encouraged to develop in accordance with their abilities. This involves fairness of opportunity in trades, and professions, in facilities for travelling and in the provision of housing, in education at all stages and in schemes of social welfare. Every Churchman should be assured of a cordial welcome in any Church of the Communion, and no one should be ineligible for any position in the Church by reason of his race or colour.[38]

The resolutions passed at the synod referred specifically to the *apartheid* legislation being enacted by the Afrikaner government, and included a warning regarding its final outcome:

This Synod believes that the effect of much recent legislation is likely to be the rigid division of the population into social classes with unequal rights, privileges and opportunities, and the relegation of the Non-Europeans to a position of permanent inferiority, and for this reason condemns this legislation as inconsistent with the respect of human personality that should be characteristic of a Christian society.[39]

132

In 1949, the four English-speaking churches, together with other denominations (except the Roman Catholic Church), met at Rosettenville, near Johannesburg, to discuss the situation that had arisen as a result of *apartheid* legislation. At the conference, the churches laid down the basic principles on which they were all agreed. These were:

1. God has created all men in his image. Consequently, beyond all differences remains the essential unity.
2. Individuals who have progressed from a primitive social structure to one more advanced should share in the responsibilities and rights of their new status.
3. The real need for South Africa is not *apartheid* but unity.
4. Citizenship involves participation in responsible government. The franchise should be accorded to all capable of exercising it.
5. Every child should have the opportunity of receiving the best education that the community can give and for which the child has the capacity.
6. Every man has the right to work in that sphere in which he can make the best use of his abilities for the common good.[40]

In a letter dated March 6, 1957, the Anglican bishops addressed themselves specifically to the "Church Clause."[41] The bishops wrote directly to the Prime Minister, even though the Church Clause came under the jurisdiction of the Minister of Native Affairs, because they considered it a matter that affected the entire membership of the Church and not limited merely to the "Natives." The bishops said:

The Church cannot recognize the right of an official of the Secular Government to determine whether or where a member of the Church of any race (who is not serving a sentence which restricts his freedom of movement) shall discharge his religious duty of participation in public worship or to give instructions to the minister

133

of any congregation as to whom he shall admit to membership of that congregation.

The letter ended with both a plea and a threat:

We, therefore, appeal to you, Sir, not to put us in a position in which we have to choose between obeying our conscience and obeying the law of the land.[42]

In 1960, the Synod of the Presbyterian Church issued a statement. It read:

We re-affirm the historical position of our Church. There is no barrier on the grounds of colour or race to attendance at worship or to membership in any congregation, but we follow the reformation principle of the right to worship in one's mother tongue and the freedom to develop forms of worship appropriate to different cultural backgrounds. Language and residence have led to the formation of separate congregations, but members of all races meet together in Presbytery and General Assembly. We believe this arrangement, for practical purposes, to be conformable to the will of God, and acceptable to our members of all racial groups. We must nonetheless be constantly alert that this natural division does not produce real alienation between groups within the Church.[43]

At first reading of these statements, it would seem that the churches took a strong stand against *apartheid,* and that this should have had some influence on the Nationalist government. They pointed out that *apartheid* was inconsistent with Christ's principles; they urged equality of rights and opportunity in all aspects of life; they spoke against limitation of travel and for the rights of citizenship—in particular the right to vote; they warned against the final outcome of legalized racial discrimination, namely, a rigid class system, with Afrikaners and other whites a privileged class, while blacks and other non-Europeans would be denied basic human rights. The Anglican Church was even courageous enough to threaten to defy the government if it interfered with freedom of worship.

The question must be asked then: If these statements reflect the actual position of the churches, and reflect it accurately, how was it possible for the Nationalist government to succeed in establishing *apartheid* in South Africa, and why is it still the law of the land today?

Some possible reasons for this apparent paradox have been advanced by persons attempting to analyze the situation. Bishop Ambrose Reeves, writing in 1962, points to one reason—the fact that racial discrimination existed within the English-speaking churches long before any legislation against blacks was enacted.[44]

When the Minister of the Interior, Theophilus Donges, introduced the bill in Parliament that finally became the Prohibition of Mixed Marriages Act, he stated that the Dutch Reformed Church had requested the measure. That was no surprise, since they had already established their theological rationale for *apartheid*. In the debate that took place before its passage, Margaret Ballinger, a member of Parliament who opposed the bill, spoke to this claim of Church support for it, saying "neither the Anglican nor the Roman Catholic Church will recognize the state's right to interfere with the Sacrament of Marriage."[45] Whether Ballinger was expressing her own opinion or whether she had been informed by Church officials that such a law would be defied is not certain. What is certain, however, is that the bill became law and was *implemented without any opposition from the churches.*[46]

Another factor was the weakness of the statements themselves. Although the principles drawn up at Rosettenville were intended to demonstrate differences in attitude between the Nationalist government and the churches, they were so broad there was ample room for flexibility in applying them as norms for action, and consequently they did not provide a sense of direction to Christians.

In like manner, although the Presbyterian statement

claimed that its members were free to worship in any congregation, it admitted that "for practical purposes," segregation existed in its churches.

The "practical purposes" were, of course, the need to obey the "Group Areas Act of 1950" (which divided residential areas according to race),[47] and the "Pass Laws" (which require a black person to have a permit in order to enter a white area).[48] What the statement neglected to mention is that all the denominations had contributed to racial separation in worship by building churches in the separate residential areas. They could, of course, use the "Reformation principle" cited in their statement to support this policy.

Another reason why the Church statements did not influence the government's commitment to *apartheid* is the lack of unity within the churches and the disagreement on the question of *apartheid*. There was a gap existing on this question between Church leaders and the membership, and also differences of opinion within the hierarchy itself. Leslie Cawood describes the situation this way.

The statements and resolutions . . . made by the leaders and higher councils of the different churches . . . do not necessarily reflect the opinion of the majority of the members, and especially the white members of the Churches. Some Church leaders have met with strong resistance from the white members when they have tried to improve understanding between the races by encouraging them to meet for worship and fellowship. Letters which appeared in the press following a series of newspaper articles in 1963 on the Church and the Race problem made it abundantly clear that there are many ordinary Church members who hold racial views diametrically opposed to those expressed in official statements by their Churches.[49]

Colin and Margaret Legum make a similar observation. They say:

One of the saddest features of the English language

Church in South Africa is that its hierarchy so often speaks for a small minority of its members. The political climate might have been very different if the attitudes of the English speaking Christians had been those of the leaders like the former Archbishop of Cape Town, Dr. Joost de Blank; the former bishop of Johannesburg, the Rt. Rev. Ambrose Reeves; The Bishop of Natal, the Rt. Rev. Vernon Inman; and the Roman Catholic Archbishop of Durban, Monsignor Denis E. Hurley. But these men do not talk for all the hierarchy, let alone for their Synods and members. They have spoken as much against the entrenched prejudices of their own flock as against the official upholders of the policy of *apartheid*.[50]

An additional reason was the fact that the primary concern of the churches was with the Church Clause, and with government interference in the area of worship, and yet worship, in the economy of *apartheid* occupies a very minor position. In passing a law to regulate attendance at church services along racial lines, the Nationalists were merely demonstrating in the political arena the claims they had made regarding racial separation, namely, that it is the "Will of God." If God wills that the races should be separate, then the last place He would expect His Will to be disregarded would be in His own house, the Church.

Although the law remains on the statutes, there is no evidence of any minister or church official being prosecuted for allowing mixed services or mixed meetings in the churches.[51] However, as Alan Paton points out (if somewhat indirectly) in his foreword to *The Church Struggle in South Africa,* the law barring mixed church services is, in actuality, operative. He says:

> In fact, the Minister of Plural Relations* had announced that the government will not require permits for one day gatherings, but only for those that continue longer, which means those that continue overnight. This provi-

*Formerly Minister of Native Affairs.

137

sion has, to me, an unmistakable sexual connotation,* whether conscious or unconscious.[52]

Paton further notes, that the Church Clause has never been directly invoked because the government was "astonished by Church reaction."[53] They had expected approval of their legislation since it merely affirmed legally what was already in practice, and also because they had considerable support among the leaders in the English-speaking churches.

In summary, the statements of the English-speaking churches were too broadly phrased to have impact in the social or political arenas. The disunity within the churches made for a lack of commitment to the principles as they were articulated by the hierarchy; thus the statements had no impact even in the religious domain—they gave no moral guidance to the church membership. The lack of unity within the churches also made it impossible for them to agree on any united action against the racial legislation and the Afrikaner Nationalist government was well aware of this, since it had many supporters among church officials. But perhaps the strongest reason for the total disregard of Church statements by the government was the knowledge of the racial discrimination existing within the churches. The Afrikaner government could very easily ignore the statements, knowing them to be the facade they were.

There are those, however, who have not ignored the deeper question, namely, that concerning the duty of the church to uphold justice and the rights of human beings in a situation of oppression. There are those who criticize the Church for defaulting in its duty at this crucial time in the history of South Africa. Bishop Ambrose Reeves is one of these persons. He writes:

Today, I believe that the crucial point for the Church in

---

* An apparent reference to the Immorality Act.

South Africa came with the passing of the Prohibition of Mixed Marriages Act, No. 55 of 1949, by which all marriages between Whites and Non-Whites are prohibited. From that date all such marriages are void, and any marriage officer performing such a marriage is liable to a fine. Perhaps at that time the churches concerned did not realize the far reaching implications of this particular piece of legislation. Certainly at that moment all the churches missed the opportunity of taking their stand on an issue of major theological and moral significance.[54]

This criticism was leveled against the churches by Bishop Reeves in 1962, thirteen years after the passage of the law cited. It is hardly necessary to point out that eighteen additional years have passed—and *apartheid* is still the law of the land.

The term *"apartheid"* may have been new to the Afrikaner vocabulary in the 1940s, but racial discrimination was not new in South Africa. The Nationalist Party in their election campaign of 1948 gave *apartheid* an ideology; the Dutch Reformed Church gave it a theology; and the Afrikaner Nationalist government enacted laws that gave it legal status. But the soil of South Africa was fertile for these racial seeds to take root and grow, and the English-speaking churches did nothing to prevent that growth.

The Confessions of the English-Speaking Churches

One of the greatest weaknesses of the ESC is their inability to translate word into action. Desmond Adendorff, writing in the *Pro Veritate Supplement,* confirms this:

The highest ecclesiastical courts and many leaders of the English-speaking Churches have also declared that the ideology and policies of the State are condemned by

139

fundamental Christian principles, though these Churches often do little really to live by these pronouncements on the congregational level.[55]

This inability has led, on several occasions to public breast-beating. The Anglicans have said:

... [The Provincial Synod] recognizes that the Church has not in practice been always faithful to her own principle and has allowed herself to be infected by the racial prejudices prevalent in the world around her. It, therefore, calls upon all members of the Church to re-examine their racial attitudes in the light of the Christian Gospel, that in every parish witness may be borne to the equal standing of all churchmen before God, and to their brotherhood one with another in Christ.[56]

The Anglican bishops were not the only ones to admit that good-sounding resolutions have not been put into practice. At least one of the bishops admits that the problem is not just with the membership, but even more with the hierarchy. He says:

Too often, unfortunately, the deeds of [white] Christians speak so loudly that Africans cannot hear their words. Further, official church utterances often have little effect on those in power because those who are criticised know that much of the practice of the Church in its own life is at variance with its profession.[57]

The Presbyterians in a synodal statement admitted that the Church has not been able to effect change in South Africa. This confession, made by the Rev. Robert Orr, a delegate to the synod reads:

In previous years your committee [Church and Nation] has tried, in its own stumbling fashion, to indicate some

of the positive things Christians may do, considering all
the circumstances. We have also done our best to study
legislation and make clear its implications for the Christian. To the best of our knowledge, these statements and
recommendations, piously noted by the Assembly, have
had less effect than the rattling of tin cans tied to a cat's
tail. In fact, we are worried that they have soothed the
conscience of Church-members, who can point to them
and say "There you are—that is what my Church thinks"
and then go back to their reading of the Sunday paper.[58]

The Congregational Church of South Africa has also
confessed that the Church has not lived up to its own teaching:

The Assembly acknowledges in humble repentance that
the United Congregational Church of Southern Africa
has not always upheld and practiced the fundamental
principles of the teaching of Christ it has advocated. Our
spiritual unity in the Church has often been a facade
hiding the division and hurt in our *real* life outside the
Church.[59]

Eberhard Bethge, a former member of the Confessing
Church in Germany, visited South Africa in 1975 and, on his
return to Germany, made the following observation:

Racism and the realities of *apartheid* have a long history
in South Africa. And the Churches have been implicated
in them not as victims but as accomplices, sanctioning
and supporting them.[60]

In addition to admitting past failures, there have also been
warnings to the churches regarding the future:

. . .But we need to realize that the old South African
adage *"More is 'n day"* [tomorrow is yet another day] no
longer holds any water. I doubt if there will be any other

141

day of peace and good-will in the near future unless we, as a Church come to grips with the evil forces which separate us.[61]

It seems clear that within the leadership of the ESC there is awareness of the evils of *apartheid* and that the ESC reject *apartheid* theoretically. In trying to explain the reasons for the gap between what the ESC say and what they practice, John de Gruchy has said:

In more recent years, the English-speaking Churches have become more aware of these gaps between resolutions and resolve, between work and deed and have sought ways of overcoming the inherent problems. But it remains true that white members are usually opposed to change or else apathetic. The problem lies at a deeper level than simply the question of race relations. It is wrapped up in political uncertainties and *fears* for the future.[62]

At a conference of English-speaking South Africans held at Grahamstown in 1974, the question of fear among them was mentioned:

Behind the facade of our impressive material success, what do we find? A great deal of cynicism and shoulder-shrugging, bitterness and resentment at Afrikaner power; disillusionment at Britain's diminished world-stature; *fear* of, and guilt towards our [sic]blacks; and a habit of buck-passing and scapegoat hunting.[63]

What this fear is all about is not spelled out. The DRC has referred to *apartheid* as a response to the Afrikaner's fear of miscegenation. The question must be asked whether the fear of the ESC is not this same fear of miscegenation so clearly expressed by the Afrikaners. Is the continued support for the "Prohibition of the Mixed Marriages Act" a sign that the fear is not limited to the Afrikaners but runs through white South Africa?

There is considerable feeling in South Africa, primarily among the clergy in the English-speaking churches that, although many resolutions have been passed against *apartheid,* the members in the ESC are unlikely to act on them. John de Gruchy says:

> Thus, the struggle of the Church requires a servanthood-spirituality more demanding than most white Christians seem ready to adopt; it requires a spirituality which combines a reliance upon the power of God's Spirit with a whole hearted effort to do God's will in the world through that power.[64]

This feeling almost of impotence has led the ESC to look more and more to the "Church struggle" in Germany for a solution. In the same statement above, de Gruchy adds that:

> In the past, Bonhoeffer pointed to this need when he called the Church in Germany to both prayer and righteous action.[65]

What de Gruchy does not add is that the Church in Germany ignored Bonhoeffer's call. Further, some of his closest associates within the Church found him too radical when he called the Church to defend the rights of the Jews, regardless of whether they were baptized or not.

The search for a solution in the experiences of the Confessing Church is based on what Bethge called "hazy notions about the Confessing Church." That the notions are indeed hazy can be seen in a report published by "The Study Project on Christianity in *Apartheid* Society."[66] In comparing the situation of the Protestant churches in South Africa with that of the churches under Naziism, the reports say:

> The Church may have to intervene if there is a strong

move towards further totalitarianism. The lesson to be learned from Nazi Germany is that the Church is the only effective institution for combating a totalitarian regime. The efforts of trade unions, newspapers, universities, opposition parties are of little avail. Hitler succeeded against all of these but never succeeded in "breaking" the Church to his will.[67]

Hitler's own words can be used to refute this claim that the Church in Germany had been effective against Naziism and that Hitler had not succeeded in breaking it to his will. This is how he described the Church's resistance:

I promise you that, if I wished to, I could destroy the Church in a few years; it is hollow and rotten and false through and through. One push and the whole structure would collapse. . . .[68]

If it is recalled that Hitler did not hesitate to destroy any form of opposition "to his will"—he ruthlessly banned the Communist and Social Democratic parties, and banned all religious sects he did not approve of—then it will be realized that this was no empty threat. Far more important, however, is that the Protestant church never gave Hitler any cause for him to break it to his will. The Protestant church—including the Confessing Church—supported Hitler's policies. This is at least mentioned in the confession made by the leaders on October 19, 1945, in Stuttgart. With a few exceptions, the churches in Germany never admitted that they had been wrong in supporting the Nazis.

It must also be remembered that Karl Barth, who was not a German but a Swiss, was the author of the Barmen Declaration, which, by its own admission, the Confessing Church never put into practice.

It was again Karl Barth who was instrumental in the drafting of the "Stuttgart Declaration." That, too, remained a piece of paper. There is no evidence that the German Protestant Churches were opposed to the Nazi policies other than as they affected internal Church affairs. The Church's support for the Nazis was clear even to a visitor in Germany as the following report indicates:

There is almost unanimity [among churchmen] in standing by Hitler. Many reasons for it appear. They have confidence in him. They feel the need of a strong hand upon the nation. They believe in his sincerity and in his unselfish interest in nation and people. More than one Churchman emphasized Hitler's personal integrity and his belief in a moral character for the State, his success in breaking down classes and his developing unity among them ... It was interesting to hear a lifelong National Liberal like Walter Simons, former President of the Republic and former Chief Justice of the Supreme Court express confidence in Hitler, adding that "National Socialism, with all its errors, has saved us from Bolshevism." There you have the main ground for Christian support of Hitler or of National Socialism or of both.[69]

The Afrikaner Nationalists have pointed to Communism as being the greatest danger facing South Africa. Their propaganda to this effect, supported by that of the DRC, has been aimed at creating a fear of Communism and the acceptance of *apartheid* as the only viable alternative to a Communist state.[70] Judging by the overwhelming victory of the Nationalists in the election of 1977, it can only be concluded that the English-speaking churches have accepted this line of thinking, and one cannot help but agree with Eberhard Bethge when he accuses the churches in South Africa (all of them) of being accomplices in *apartheid*.[71] Their statements condemning *apartheid,* therefore, in the words of Robert Orr, *are* actually less effective than "the rattling of tin cans tied to a cat's tail."[72] This gap between word and deed, as John de Gruchy points out, "has been exploited by the government as blatant hypocrisy.[73]

The Roman Catholic Church

Unlike the four English-speaking churches mentioned above, the Roman Catholic Church is neither a member of the World Council of Churches, nor a member of the South African Council of Churches, nor a signatory to the Cottesloe Statement. Nevertheless, the Roman Catholic Church has produced its share of statements on the question of apartheid. They include the following: In 1957 the Catholic Church said:

> There must be a gradual change: gradual, for no other kind of change is compatible with the maintenance of order, without which there is no society, no government, no justice, no common good. But change must come, for otherwise our country faces a disastrous future. That change could be initiated immediately if the ingenuity and energy now expended on apartheid were devoted to making South Africa a happy country for all its citizens. The time is short. The need is urgent. Those penalized by apartheid must be given concrete evidence of change before it is too late. This involves the elaboration of a sensible and just policy enabling any person, irrespective of race, to qualify for the enjoyment of full civil rights. . . .[74]

The bishops addressed themselves to their flock in the following words:

> To our beloved Catholic people of the white race, we have a special word to say. The practice of segregation, though officially not recognized in our churches, characterizes nevertheless many of our church societies, our schools, seminaries, convents, hospitals, and the social life of our people. In the light of Christ's teaching, this cannot be tolerated forever. The time has come to practice more vigorously the change of heart and practice that the law of Christ demands. We are hypocrites if we condemn

146

apartheid in South African society and condone it in our own institutions.[75]

It is more than twenty years since these statements were made, and still apartheid is the way of life in south Africa.

Six years after these statements were made, one of those who participated in their formulation, Archibishop Denis Hurley of Durban, made the following observation:

The [Roman Catholic] Church's biggest effort so far in re-educating its members has amounted to the publication of statements on the racial question by the bishops. The statements are rather theoretical but very much in keeping with what has been the trend up till recently in the Catholic Church when it is faced with a problem.

It has been inclined to issue a theoretical statement on the assumption that the members of the Church would spontaneously make the necessary practical applications. There is an obvious weakness in the system and the trend today is to insist far more on the practical education of Church members in the attitudes necessary to solve the problem. The more psychological and practical methods are found in Church groups which aim at giving their members the practical ability of applying Christianity to the circumstances in which they live.[76]

From the foregoing one must conclude that the position of the Roman Catholic Church on what should be done about apartheid is very similar to the one of the English-speaking churches. The breast-beating is also similar. However, the statement made by Bishop Hurley in 1977, which seems to include all the churches in South Africa that are opposed to apartheid, is more than breast-beating. It borders on resignation. He says:

The churches have been in the habit of issuing statements, declarations and pastoral letters on the racial

147

situation in South Africa in the hope that they would effect change. They have effected very little change. It is clear that the kind of Christian teaching, witness and action needed to effect changes in South Africa requires much more than the average white church leader, teacher or worker is capable of offering. It requires something approaching heroism in the matter of conversion and dedication. Mediocrity is insufficient but, unfortunately, mediocrity is the rule, as it usually is in human affairs.[77]

Earlier, Bishop Hurley posed this question:

The Christian standard is a terrifying one. And even as we take it upon ourselves to suggest where our brothers of the Dutch Reformed Churches may have fallen short of it, we dare not judge and condemn, for in the same circumstances, would we have done better? [78]

He concludes:

In the light of the behavior of other Churches in South Africa, we would not. For these Churches, too, have been hamstrung by their inability to break out of theory into practice. They have not suffered from an inadequate theory. They have just suffered from a paralysing incapacity to translate the right theory into practice.[79]

The question these statements by Denis Hurley and others raise [80] is whether or not the English-speaking churches, together with the Roman Catholic Church, will ever be able to translate their theories into practice.

6

The Afrikaner Nationalist Stand on Christianity

The Stated Position

On June 3, 1941, the Nationalist Party meeting at Bloemfontein drew up a "Programme of Principles," which became the
party's policy document. Section 1:1 reads:

> The Party acknowledges the sovereignty and guidance of
> God in the destiny of countries and seeks the develop-
> ment of our nation's life along Christian-National lines,
> with due regard to the individual's freedom of conscience
> and religion.[1]

Without spelling out exactly what was meant by "Christian-
National," the document did provide a few examples of what
was expected and not expected. On education, the document
said:

> The Party considers it the duty of the authorities to
> supervise education and ensure that every child receives
> instruction in accordance with its talents and oppor-
> tunities and based on healthy educational and national
> principles. It thus urges that in carrying out this duty

the Christian-National basis of the state should be taken fully into account as well as the right of the parent to determine in which direction such education should be given as regards the ethical and religious development of the child.[2]

On public morality, the document said:

The Party recognizes the duty of the authorities to respect and preserve Sunday as a day of rest in the public sphere, to oppose all unChristian practices in the national life, and to maintain a high moral code at the same time, taking into consideration the freedom of the individual citizen in his own sphere.[3]

Thus stated, the principles were bound to have an appeal that stretched beyond party lines. The stress on the need for a Christian education as well as the need for "a high moral code" made it unnecessary, in the public mind, to demand a clarification of what was meant by "Christian-National."

If the "Programme of Principles" did not spell out clearly what was meant by "Christian-National," other documents that are closely linked with the Nationalist Party give some indication of what the Afrikaners understand by "Christian-National." An example of this is the document that deals with Christian National Education (C.N.E.). The document was issued in February 1948, and the policy stated therein was approved by "the whole Afrikanerdom." Even though C.N.E. is not the official policy of the government, "it exercises a strong and pervasive influence in the country."[4]

In the C.N.E. document, "Christian" is defined as a view of life and the world "based on Holy Scripture and formulated in the Articles of Faith of our three Afrikaans Churches."[5] "National" is understood as "love of everything that is our own, with special reference to our country, our language, our history and our culture."[6]

The idea of *exclusiveness* comes out clearly because, even

though Holy Scripture is cited, it is interpreted as formulated in the Articles of Faith of the DRC. This interpretation, as we have seen, is essentially different from that given by other denominations. In fact, the difference is readily admitted by leading DRC theologians. One of them, B. C. Keet has said:

> We of the Dutch Reformed Churches are standing quite alone in our interpretation of the Scriptures on the question of *apartheid*. We are not only standing against the convictions of other churches in South Africa, but we differ from the Reformed Churches of the world. All the Dutch Reformed Churches in this country stand for *apartheid* in Churches and in politics . . . .[7]

"National" not only implies that South Africa belongs to the Afrikaners alone, but explicitly excludes all those in South Africa whose language, history, and culture are different from those of the Afrikaners.

Politics and Religion

The policies of the Afrikaner Nationalists have been met with both positive and negative responses from the churches. The response from the DRC has always been positive, which is not surprising, since the DRC finds *apartheid* consistent with the Will of God. In South Africa, therefore, the DRC is unique as a church in that it nurtures one political movement and is in turn nurtured by that political movement—the Nationalist Party. Together, the DRC and the Nationalist Party are two members of one family—Afrikanerdom.

The English-speaking churches, on the other hand, have followed a policy of selective opposition to *apartheid*. The stand of the churches on the question of mixed services shows that when the interests of the Church were directly affected, they were not afraid to threaten the government, nor to break the law, if necessary. However, when the ESC have been called upon to defend the rights of blacks in the social, economic, and political spheres, the most they have done is to pass resolutions; and the resolutions have never been backed by action.

Other Church-related organizations have been critical of the Nationalist government. In 1968, the South African Christian Council (SACC) issued a document, "The Message to the People of South Africa," in which government policy toward blacks came under sharp attack.[8] The document has been compared to the Barmen Declaration, but they are not actually similar. "The Message," as it is called, is a rejection of *apartheid,* whereas the Barmen Declaration was not a rejection of Naziism, but only a rejection of *Deutsche Christen* theology.

"The Message" did draw a response from the South African Prime Minister, John Vorster. In a speech given a few weeks after its publication, he warned against those "who wish to disrupt the order in South Africa under the cloak of religion."[9] This was absurd, since "The Message" was by no means a call to defy South Africa's discriminatory laws, simply because the SACC was a small organization of Church people with no influence, not even that found in the denominational churches.

Response of the Afrikaners to Criticism

Within the English-speaking churches, most of the opposition has come from the Anglican clergy, and almost exclusively from expatriate bishops and priests. Notable among these courageous men are: Father Trevor Huddleston, the Reverend Michael Scott, and the Right Reverend Ambrose Reeves.[10] When the government took measures to silence them, there was no protest either from their congregations or from fellow-clergy. This lack of protest probably encouraged the government in its dealing with other dissidents within the churches.

The fact that most of those within the Church who have been critical of *apartheid* were not South African citizens has given some credence to the widely held view that it is not just the DRC that approves of *apartheid* but the ESC as well. There may be theological differences between the two groups, but otherwise there is agreement as far as the policy itself is concerned. Pointing to recent evidence to support this view, David Bosch says:

> The November 1977 National Party landslide victory at the polls is not imaginable without massive support from members of the English-speaking churches.[11]

In that election, the Afrikaners won their highest number of seats in the thirty-year history of *apartheid* rule.

Within the DRC there has always been support for tough action against those who speak out against *apartheid*. The approval of the banning of the Christian Institute in 1977 was in keeping with this DRC policy. The reason given by the government for banning the Christian Institute was "its persistent incitement which could have led to violence."[12] What form this "incitement" took was never explained. The Minister of Justice, whose office was responsible for the banning, received valuable support for his action in an article in *DRC Africa News,* the official paper of the Church:

> You may note that the Minister was careful not to say that the banned organizations were actually engaged in revolutionary activities or violence but that they were, through their actions and pronouncements, fostering a spirit of polarization between White and non-White which could lead to violence.[13]

The article does not say what these "actions and pronouncements" were. It is also significant that none of those involved in the banned organizations was given the opportunity to face charges in a court of law.

It will be recalled that in 1966 the DRC theologian Professor A. D. Pont accused the Christian Institute of spreading propaganda in the churches and that such propaganda suited Communism admirably. When the Christian Institute was finally banned eleven years later, the DRC welcomed the ban and recalled that:

As far back as 1966 the General Synod declared that the Christian Institute "is an organization which endeavours to disturb the good order in the Church and sow dissent among Church members." These were prophetic words which have tragically been fulfilled.[14]

7

The Consolidation of Afrikaner Power

Sharpeville

The enforcement of the pass laws referred to in chapter 2 led to a demonstration in Sharpeville, a small town with a large black population. On March 21, 1960, a demonstration was held against the pass laws and other South African repressive measures. Over sixty blacks were shot to death by the South African police, and over two hundred blacks were injured, some seriously. After the killings, the government declared a state of emergency, arrested thousands of blacks, and declared their organizations illegal.[1]

There was a worldwide outcry against the actions of the South African government. As a result, nine leading members of the DRC, including Rev. J. D. Vorster (who, in 1940, called on the Afrikaners to follow the "example" of Hitler), protested "the besmirching of [their] country, people and Church by untrue and slanted information." In defending *apartheid* they said:

> The Church has also accepted that this policy *[apartheid]*, especially in its initial stages, would necessarily cause a certain amount of disruption and personal hardship, for example, in connection with the clearing of slums. The whole pass system must be seen in this light.[2]

At the time of Sharpeville in 1960, both the English-speaking churches and the DRC were members of the World Council of Churches. Because of the lack of remorse on the part of the DRC, Joost de Blank, Anglican Archbishop of Cape Town, wrote to the General Secretary of the World Council of Churches saying:

> The future of Christianity in this country demands our complete dissociation from the Dutch attitude. . . . Either they must be expelled or we shall be compelled to withdraw (from the WCC).[3]

The Cottesloe Consultation

In an effort to avoid a serious confrontation between the DRC and the ESC, the World Council of Churches helped to arrange a conference of South African Church leaders at Cottesloe in South Africa. The conference was held from December 7 to 14 and included both black and white Church leaders as well as representatives from the World Council of Churches. The subject under discussion was *apartheid* and the Church's responsibility, especially in light of the events at Sharpeville. After deliberating for a week, the leaders issued a statement that said, in part:

> We recognize that all racial groups who permanently inhabit our country are a part of our total population and we regard them as indigenous. Members of all these groups have an equal right to make their contribution towards the enrichment of the life of their country, and to share in the ensuing responsibilities, rewards and privileges. No one who believes in Jesus Christ may be excluded from any Church on the grounds of his colour or race. The spiritual unity among all men who are in Christ must find visible expression in acts of common worship and witness and in fellowship and consultation on matters of common concern.[4]

156

The report, which was given the official title "Cottesloe Consultation Report," dealt a great deal with the question of freedom of worship and stressed that Church membership should not be decided on the basis of race. This emphasis reflected the position of the English-speaking churches, but not that of the DRC.

There was agreement on the need to reject all unjust discrimination, but disagreement on the basic issues of *apartheid*. The disagreement divided the conference along expected lines: Those supporting the basic principles of *apartheid* were from the DRC and those opposed were from the English-speaking churches.[5]

Although this was a conference of Church leaders representing various denominations, it had no power to implement the resolutions. When the report was presented to the various synods of the churches, the synods of the English-speaking churches accepted it, while those of the DRC rejected it. Charging that the World Council of Churches had been unfairly critical of South Africa, the DRC withdrew its membership from the world body.[6] If there had been any hope for genuine cooperation between the two white Church groups on the question of solving *apartheid,* that hope died at Cottesloe. As de Gruchy has pointed out:

> To many, it now seemed as if the only way forward for cooperation between Christians of various Churches was through personal participation in a new kind of ecumenical thrust not tied to denominational structures.[7]

In August 1963, individuals from different denominations and from different racial groups, came together to form the Christian Institute of Southern Africa (CI). A detailed examination of the CI is beyond the limits of this book, although a few comments are appropriate.

The Christian Institute of Southern Africa (CI)

The Christian Institute was an organization that had no

157

denominational affiliation. It was both interdenominational and interracial, but it was not a church.

When it was formed, Beyers Naude, who was a DRC pastor and editor of an interchurch monthly magazine, *Pro Veritate,* became its director. In the words of Naude, the CI was intended to become a "Confessing Movement" similar to the Confessing Church in Germany during Hitler's time, but adapted to the South African situation.[8] The German Church experience is said to have influenced the founding of the Christian Institute, as de Gruchy points out:

Indeed, the CI was profoundly influenced by the German Church struggle in its basic orientation to the state and to the Churches and in its understanding of the Lordship of Christ.[9]

Beyers Naude explained that the shootings at Sharpeville in 1960 had changed his life. He said:

The tense months that followed Sharpeville brought long and earnest discussions among Churchmen. It was then that the full implications of traditional race policies were borne in on me.[10]

Having been forced to resign his position as pastor of a local DRC because of his role in the CI, he preached a farewell sermon to his congregation in which he said:

It is a strange phenomenon that Christian men accepted the Word of God in theory but made it powerless in practice. Like the false prophets in Jeremiah's time, they gave the nation the false assurance that no disaster could touch them as long as the Temple was in their midst. They called "peace, peace" when Jeremiah warned it was not true peace. Are there not also national traditions which cannot stand up to the honest test of Scripture, but which we place alongside or above the Word?[11]

The DRC was opposed to Beyers's decision to direct the CI. Apart from leaving the "Afrikaner family" he was joining a multiracial organization—the very thought of which was "revolting" to the Afrikaners. As Colin and Margaret Legum noted:

The fate of the Reverend Beyers Naude and his family as a result of his action is the fate of every dissenter of prominence in the Church: social ostracism, reinforced by public attack.[12]

And Naude himself agreed:

The Afrikaner who deviates is apt to be labelled a traitor, to be accused of falling for the "bribes of the English," a sell-out of his people and a political renegade.[13]

These remarks were not just speculation but were based on a thorough knowledge of the DRC by a man who was once part of its hierarchy. Indeed, the Christian Institute immediately came under the attack of the DRC. A leading professor of theology at Pretoria University accused the CI and the magazine *Pro Veritate* of being under the influence of Communists:

It is not far fetched to allege that the Christian Institute and the Journal, *Pro Veritate,* are nothing but liberalist stepping stones from which propaganda which suits Communism admirably are carried into our Churches.[14]

The seriousness of this charge becomes clear when it is remembered that the "Suppression of Communism Act, No. 44 of 1950," with its almost yearly amendments, gives the government unlimited powers to deal with anybody or any organization that is suspected of being influenced by Communism.

Having been denounced and rejected by his fellow-Afrikaners and his own DRC, Naude sought support from the English-speaking churches. Though these churches were more sympathetic to Naude, they turned out to be a disappointment.

Here in the English-speaking Churches he gained some encouragement, but Naude soon discovered that White English support was not much greater than Afrikaner support when it came to fundamental social change. As a result he grew increasingly disenchanted with most Whites and attempted to become more directly involved with Blacks in their struggle.[15]

The fact that Naude was able to keep the Christian Institute functioning at all is because it received financial support from abroad.[16] However, without strong support from within the white churches, the task of bringing about fundamental change would seem to be hopeless.

Beyers Naude had turned to the English-speaking churches for support and cooperation because he had been encouraged by their statements on *apartheid*, particularly those issued after Sharpeville. For example, the Methodist Church introduced, in 1960, a program of education based on the understanding that "the Church is an Inclusive Church— a church for all races." Their preoccupation was still with the right to worship at a church of one's choice rather than with "fundamental social change."

The program made provision for the exchange of visits among the various Church organizations such as women's auxiliaries, Women's *Manyanos* (Prayer Groups), local preachers' guilds and men's leagues. The idea was to encourage better understanding within the Methodist community. There was also a suggestion for pulpit exchange so that black Methodist ministers could serve whites and white ministers serve blacks. Finally, the program made provision for study groups to study race relations as well as racial legislation.[17]

The program was started because of the events at Sharpeville. Since this was twelve years after the first "racial legislation" had been passed, and since back in 1957 the Methodist Church had rejected the "Church Clause," it is difficult to see why it was necessary to "study racial legislation."

In 1962, the Assembly of the Presbyterian Church passed its own resolutions, which had to do with the internal life of the Presbyterian Church. The resolutions read:

a) The Assembly strongly urges ministers and sessions to increase and strengthen multi-racial contacts, not only for the purpose of worship, but also for discussion, mutual understanding, and joint service;

b) instructs Presbyteries to organize ministerial retreats and conferences for office bearers and youth, on a multi-racial basis.[18]

The first part of the resolutions, which could have maximum impact within the life of the Church, since it would affect the greatest number of people, is very mildly worded. "Ministers and sessions" are merely "urged" to increase multiracial contacts, but, where relatively few people are involved and where opportunities for contact are few, the resolution is stronger; it "instructs" the Presbyteries to bring about multiracial contact.

The Assembly (governing body) of the Congregational Church welcomed the Cottesloe Report and passed the following resolution on race relations in South Africa:

We strongly support every effort for the holding of a multi-racial consultation to plan for better relationships and happier conditions, rights, and privileges for all peoples of this land.

This Assembly expresses its gratitude to the World Council of Churches for arranging the Cottesloe Con-

161

sultation as a creative contribution to the solution of the many problems of a multi-racial society such as exists in South Africa. Though we ourselves might have made a more far reaching statement, we are grateful to God for the measure of agreement attained and pray that the process of consultation between the Churches begun at Cottesloe may continue at all levels.[19]

There was also protest against the restrictions placed on the freedom of movement where blacks were concerned. The assembly said:

The Congregational Union of South Africa believes that all law-abiding inhabitants of a country have the inalienable right to freedom of movement, association and domicile within its borders.[20]

In 1963, The Synod of the Anglican Bishops reaffirmed the stated position of the Anglican Church in these words:

In these circumstances, it seems necessary to the Bishops of the Church of the Province of South Africa, now meeting in Bloemfontein, to reaffirm their unanimity in proclaiming their conviction that the Church must openly and fearlessly condemn all that it believes to be evil and false in the social, political or economic life of any nation and, wherever the claims of obedience to the State and God are in conflict, it is to God that our obedience must be given.[21]

It will be recalled that the loopholes in the Prohibition of Mixed Marriages Act and the Immorality Act had been closed by additional legislation. These were further tightened in 1968, and the same procedure was followed for the Population Registration Act in 1969 and 1970.[22] With the passage of the Bantu Homelands Citizenship Act, No. 26 of 1970, and the Amendment of the Bantu Laws Amendment Act, No. 70 of

1974, the legal machinery to deny blacks their South African citizenship was established, and Bantu homelands were created.

The problems created by forcibly moving blacks from their homes to distant "Homelands" artificially created by the government, in pursuance of its policy of *apartheid,* are summed up in statements by the English-speaking churches.

A resolution passed by the Assembly of the Presbyterian Church reads thus:

> The Assembly expresses its great concern at the continuing process of removing the rights of Africans to live and work in urban areas and compelling them to move to so-called "Homelands," where very few can find work and a decent living.
>
> It expresses grave concern at the forcible removal of so many to rural dumping grounds like Sada, Thornhill, and Glenmore, in the Ciskei, and Tin Town in Kwazulu where they live in inhuman conditions of unemployment, malnutrition, sickness and despair. It condemns this as a denial of Christian principles that is inevitably provoking bitterness and deep hostility between Black and White in South Africa and increasing the danger of armed conflict between them. It implores the Government to do something about places like Sada, where it is reported that four to six people are dying of malnutrition every week. It calls on the Government to phase out the entire oppressive Pass Law and Influx Control system, and instructs that the substance of this clause be conveyed to the relevant authorities and made known to the members of the Presbyterian Church of Southern Africa.[23]

The creation of the Bantu homelands on 13 percent of the total land area of South Africa, and the ultimate removal of 80 percent of South Africa's population to these homelands, will mark, for the Afrikaner Nationalist, a triumph for their policy of *apartheid*. The hardships described above by the Presbyterian Church would probably be dismissed by the DRC as a necessary "amount of disruption and personal hardship."

8

Apartheid's External Support Systems

The Role of the Western Churches

The Christian Church prides itself for being "a universal church," an upholder of morality, and "the voice of the voiceless." This means that it is not an inward-looking church but one that is concerned about the welfare of human beings, wherever they may be, and one that is involved on the side of justice. While it is beyond dispute that the Western Church did not do all in its power to save the Jews from their terrible persecution, it is not quite clear whether the Western Church outside Germany knowingly participated actively in the persecution of the Jews. Now that Naziism has been transferred to South Africa, we need to examine what role, if any, the Western Church is playing.

Since the introduction of *apartheid* in South Africa in 1948, the Western Church has shown a growing interest in the affairs of that country. Indeed, the *question* of *apartheid* has been, and continues to be, a major topic of discussion at Church conferences, synods, meetings, and church-sponsored seminars. It is safe to say that every major Western denomination has condemned *apartheid*. The number of church resolutions calling for action against *apartheid* is so large that if 1 percent of them were implemented, *apartheid* would cease to be. This has not happened because there remains a huge gap between what the Church says and what it does. The responsibility for this blatant hypocrisy must be borne entirely by the church leadership. There are several obvious reasons why the leadership is to blame.

First, *apartheid* is the greatest evil facing mankind today. To deny an entire race its humanity on scriptural grounds calls for uncompromising opposition first and foremost from the Church. That opposition can only be effective if the leadership in the Western Church takes the lead in educating their flock in word and in deed. Instead of being the champions of justice here and now, the vast majority of the leaders in the Western Church have distinguished themselves by pretending to know everything about heaven while turning a deaf ear and a blind eye to the needs of their neighbors. If the Church leaders made a concerted effort to educate their congregations about the evils of *apartheid,* they would set in motion a process that would certainly lead to the destruction of that evil. Where church leaders have demonstrated uncompromising antiapartheid commitment, the congregations have been supportive.

Second, the refusal on the part of the church leadership to take drastic action against *apartheid* is not motivated by ignorance of the South African situation. Indeed it is the result of careful analysis and decisions. As we shall show in the next section, *apartheid* depends to a large extent on foreign investments and bank loans. The blacks of South Africa have called for the withdrawal of these investments and a stop to all loans. Many churches have passed resolutions calling for these measures to be supported. However, the resolutions have never been implemented. The blacks of South Africa have also asked all churches and church organizations to withdraw their funds from banks that give loans to South Africa and place them in banks that have no dealings with South Africa. They have also asked them to sell their stocks in companies that are adamant in continuing their investments in South Africa. With a few exceptions, the Western churches have refused to take any meaningful action. The reason is that, when put together, the Western churches form the largest and wealthiest single multinational corporation in the world. Because this "corporation" has its accounts in banks that give loans to *apartheid* South Africa and holds stock in corporations that through their investments have become the backbone of the world's most evil system, the Western Church leaders have become active supporters of *apartheid,* and they know it. The resolutions against *apartheid* are a smokescreen designed to deceive their flock into believing that the leaders are determined to do something about *apartheid.* It must also be remembered that the vast majority of the multinational corporations are led by people who call themselves Christians. Most of them sit in the front pews of their churches and are among the biggest financial contributors to their churches. This, they can afford, since part of what they "give" to the church is money that rightly belongs to the underpaid black workers of South Africa. The leadership in the Western Church dares not challenge the exploitative economic policies of the corporations these people represent for fear that they will lose their large contributions. As long as the leadership supports resolutions but does nothing about taking action, the contributions will not be endangered. But the resolutions have become demonic in that they raise false hopes in the blacks of South Africa who are suffering and looking for support primarily from the Western Church. Viewed from this angle, the Western Church is, by far, worse than the German Church, which did not raise its voice in support of the persecuted Jews. At least the Jews had no false hopes. The leadership in the Western Church today, on the question of *apartheid,* is guilty of both hypocrisy and deception. To condemn an evil verbally and at the same time support fully the instruments that perpetuate the evil is, by definition, un-Christian.

Third, there are those leaders in the Western Church who openly support *apartheid.* This confirms the existence of Fascists within the Christian leadership. It is no coincidence that the West German Lutheran Church leadership excels in its support. First of all, the white Lutheran Church in South Africa is an ardent supporter of *apartheid*. It is also a matter of historical record that the same church in Germany supported Naziism enthusiastically. The Western Church leaders who support *apartheid* are always quick in lecturing black South Africans on their situation. They are also the most ardent supporters of South African propaganda, claiming that the black people's struggle for liberation, freedom, and human dignity is nothing but a "Communist plot." That they are insulting the oppressed blacks of South Africa does not in the least bother them. This is the same group that does everything in its power to frustrate the World Council of Churches' Programme to Combat Racism—a programme intended in part to help the victims of *apartheid*. By refusing to finance the programme, these Western leaders demonstrate their support for the continuation of *apartheid*. Paradoxically, it is the churches from the Socialist countries that give their full support for the programme. To be sure, there is a worldwide anti-*apartheid* movement. But the movement is not led, nor is it enthusiastically supported, by the Church. It is ordinary people who are doing all the anti-*apartheid* work, while the leadership in the Western Church is, at best, silent and, at worst, hypocritical. Students at Western higher institutions of education have done a most commendable job in trying to get their institutions to stop supporting corporations and banks that are financing *apartheid*. The Church leadership has not even bothered to give them the support they so obviously deserve. On the contrary, the Western Church leadership hides behind the demonic view, which has been invented by the exploitative multinational corporations, that divestment and the stopping of loans to South Africa "will hurt the blacks." The Western Church leadership is well aware of the fact that it is the black South Africans who are calling for these measures.

Much of the decline so noticeable in the Western Church is due to its own failure to be prophetic, to support the oppressed, and to be one with those who are engaged in the liberation struggle. It is also due to an uncritical support for capitalism to the extent that Christianity and capitalism have become one.

This unholy marriage between Christianity and capitalism is the best example of just how divorced the Western Church is from the original Christian Church. Since Communism is a system based on the idea that property is owned by the community as a whole, it follows that the early Christian Church in Jerusalem practiced Communism as opposed to capitalism. Those who think the opposite is true should read again and again the Book of the Acts of the Apostles.

Finally, the decline is due to the practice of a Christianity of convenience.

That the Church has to struggle and suffer with those who struggle and suffer has long been forgotten in the West. These are the same ills that afflicted the German Church. They have been inherited by the vast majority of Western Church leaders.

The Role of the Transnational Corporations

South Africa is endowed with one of the world's richest deposits of natural resources. Except for oil, every natural resource that is necessary for industrial development is available in South Africa. This fact alone makes South Africa attractive to foreign investors. But investors will not risk their capital unless the climate in the country they wish to invest in is favorable. It is this factor that is most important to investors.

The Nats, who are in need of foreign capital, have gone to great lengths to make the investment climate favorable. Through the multiplicity of interlocking oppressive laws, they have been able to provide a huge reservoir of captive, cheap, black labor. With no right to vote, to join free trade unions, to sell their labor competitively, to choose their place of employment, to choose the type of employment, to change the area of employment, to move about freely in search of employment, to negotiate wages and conditions of employment, and to strike if necessary, the black labor force in South Africa—which is by far the largest labor force—is a labor force of slaves. On the other side of the coin is a well-armed and -trained police and military force, which is there to take care of any labor unrest. Thus, South Africa provides "an ideal" investment climate.

This ideal climate was severely tested in 1960. Indeed, after the massacre at Sharpeville referred to above, foreign capital began to leave the country, and frightened investors held back. As a result, the economy began to slump, and the country was faced with imminent economic collapse. Even the Nats were so frightened that they suspended the hated, oppressive, and dehumanizing "pass laws" in an effort to attract crucial foreign capital. Even this—by South African standards—drastic act did not restore confidence. The Finance Minister failed in his efforts to attract capital. It was not until Harry Oppenheimer, the South African mining magnate, approached American banks for a loan for one of his companies that things began to change. Only after receiving this loan was confidence reestablished, and capital began to flow back to South Africa. Once capital began to find its way back to South Africa, the hated "pass laws" were once again enforced with renewed brutality and continue to be the Nats' chief weapon against blacks to this day. Since 1960, there has been an acceleration in the amount of foreign investments in South Africa. This has been accompanied by an intensification of repression and a steep rise in poverty among the blacks. Amnesty International summarizes the situation thus:

> Just as the benefits of economic growth have not "trick-led down" to the black population, the projected increase in social and political rights has failed to materialize. In fact, economic abundance has been accompanied by an intensification of political repression. Thousands of blacks have been imprisoned under an increasing number of South African security laws—statutes so com-

prehensive that activities likely "to endanger the maintenance of law and order" can be construed as terrorism and punished by imprisonment or death. Between 1950 and 1978, more than 1,300 people were banned by the Minister of Justice. A "banned" person may not belong to certain organizations, attend meetings or social gatherings, speak publicly, or be quoted in print. In 1976 alone, more than 40 banning orders were served, many of them against trade unionists, journalists, and activists in the growing Black Consciousness Movement. In a sweeping Government clamp-down on 19 October 1977, 18 black organizations were banned including the *World,* the largest black newspaper, and leading black organizations such as the Black People's Convention and the South African Students' Association (SASO). More than 50 black leaders were arrested and an unknown number banned.[1]

The role of the transnational corporations in South Africa has been described by the African National Congress in the following terms:

Singly and collectively the Transnational Corporations' operations in South Africa constitute the foundations of the barbarous tyranny of white domination and exploitation in South Africa. The bloodshed, want, and deprivation imposed on the black people by the white minority racist regime emanate from the boardrooms of the Transnational Corporations in Johannesburg, London, Washington, Bonn, Paris, Rome, Tokyo and other capitals of imperialism.[2]

The main reason why these corporations invest in South Africa is the high rate of return they receive, which is made possible by paying slave wages to blacks who, by law, can do nothing to change that situation. Thus the transnational corporations are guilty of financing and perpetuating

171

apartheid, just as the German corporations supported and financed Naziism and the Holocaust.

Although mention is often made of the role of the transnational corporations, it has to be emphasized that these corporations are run by individuals and groups of individuals who claim to be good, decent, law-abiding citizens. None of them would ever agree that their involvement in South Africa is motivated by nothing else but greed—the desire to maximize profits, regardless of the human suffering involved in the process. Indeed, the standard argument used by the bosses of these corporations is that they are in South Africa to "help bring an end to *apartheid*" and that, if they were to divest, "the blacks would suffer most." In other words the monstrous transnational corporations would want the people they exploit and oppress to believe that they are, in fact, their liberators! They would also like to be seen as philanthropic organizations working for the benefit of the downtrodden. Nothing of course is further from the truth. The transnational corporations are, and have always been, in South Africa at least, monsters.

Following the Soweto massacre, in 1976, when the South African police and army murdered young black schoolchildren in cold blood, maimed thousands of them, and drove thousands more into exile, the transnational corporations did not even respond as they had in 1960 when they withdrew their investments. In 1976, they demonstrated clearly that they had fully accepted the conditions of investing in South Africa, namely, unqualified support for the brutal oppression of the black people, for only under such conditions could their profits be maximized. While this attitude was welcomed by the Nats, it did not go unchallenged in the home countries of these corporations. There was strong reaction on university campuses, from trade unions, and from church groups in Europe and North America, where the corporations claimed that they were motivated by Christian ideals. The calls for divestment grew in quality and quantity. The big lie of the corporations became naked for all to see. They had to find a way out. The way they invented was the so-called "industrial codes of conduct" whose real title should be "The Transnational Corporations' Right to Support *Apartheid*." Basically these codes deal with conditions of service for the blacks who are employed by the corporations. The reasoning behind them is that if applied they will prove to be the panacea for the black victims of *apartheid*. They are supposed to be the cure for *apartheid*. The madness and utter stupidity in this approach, if at all it is seriously meant, becomes obvious when one realizes that the transnational corporations employ less than 1 percent of the South African black population. Even if they were to pay these blacks the same wages as whites, how would that change the nonhuman status of the 24 million blacks? The codes are silent on the political rights of blacks; they say nothing about the hated "pass laws"; they do not address the dehumanizing migrant labor system and influx control, on which the profits of the corporations depend; they are conspicuously silent on all the repressive laws that make *apartheid* work. To add to this, the codes are merely suggestions, which cannot be enforced. Even the few corporations that have accepted them have not put them into practice. This, however, can only surprise the naive. The codes were never intended to be put into practice. They were and remain a cunning propaganda device to keep the opponents of *apartheid* in Europe, North America, and Japan silent, by misleading them into believing that the corporations are on the side of the oppressed in South Africa. If the corporations invest in South Africa because they are philanthropists, why do they not show their concern for the citizens of their own countries, especially since unemployment is such a problem in their own countries? They must admit that they cause unemployment in their own countries in order to invest where the laws allow them to exploit and so maximize profits. The transnational corporations can never devise "codes of conduct," because they are inherently immoral. They exploit and oppress the black South Africans and at the same time oppress the citizens of their own countries by deliberately denying them job opportunities, thereby dehumanizing them by making them recipients of

173

handouts instead of earning a decent living. To cover up their inhuman actions, they employ such tactics as make Josef Goebbels, the Nazi propaganda genius, look like a saint!

Finally, a word must be said about the type of activity the transnational corporations are involved in. Research has conclusively shown that the corporations are heavily involved in the building up of South Africa's military-industrial complex. After the 1960 massacre, the Nats increased their military expenditure dramatically so that the expenditure now stands at more than $2 billion, a monumental sum for South Africa. A study by Elizabeth Schmidt concludes that:

> The dramatic increase in defense expenditures stimulated a new influx of foreign capital into the South African economy. The white minority regime was interested in bolstering its security system with sophisticated new trucks, tanks, computers and electronic equipment. Foreign companies rushed to meet the demand. Rather than discourage foreign investment, the repressive South African military apparatus actually encouraged it.[3]

The weapons manufactured with the active participation of the corporations enable South Africa to occupy Namibia illegally; keep the black population in South Africa under bondage; and make it possible for South Africa to commit acts of aggression against her black neighboring states of Angola, Mozambique, Botswana, Lesotho, Swaziland, Zambia, and Zimbabwe, where thousands of innocent and defenseless men, women, and children have been murdered in cold blood by white South Africa for no other reason except that they are black and that, therefore, their lives count for nothing. It is the transnational corporations that supply all the goods and technology which make this aggression and murder possible.

Inside South Africa the Nats use vehicles built by the corporations to enable their police and army to terrorize the black population. The computers enable the government to enforce the pass laws, to control the movement of blacks and to keep them under general surveillance. South Africa's nuclear weapons programme is almost entirely dependent on the transnational corporations. On the whole, the transnational corporations have enabled white South Africa to reach the highest standard of living in the world, while reducing the blacks to a level of poverty hitherto unknown. The attitude of all the transnational corporations doing business with South Africa is reflected in a General Motors "secret" memorandum. In that memorandum, the chairman of General Motors wrote:

> It is apparent to us that manufacturing plants involved in such basic industries as petroleum production and refining, mining primary metals, transportation, and machinery—industries which generate the lifeblood of any economy—also assume equally strategic importance in time of emergency. Any of our plants can be converted to war production as clearly demonstrated in the United States in 1941.[4]

The time of emergency referred to is the uprising of blacks against their oppressors. When that time comes, the document says General Motors will act to "meet imposed requirements, *e.g.,* trucks and commercial vehicles. . . ." The company would cooperate with the Nats, who would establish "a military presence on the property" and "control all aspects of security . . . regulate output and coordinate the entire industrial effort." The company would also encourage its white employees to "volunteer to join a local commando unit. . . ."[5] which would be fighting to crush the black struggle for freedom. One has to point out that General Motors is one of the corporations that signed the so-called "code of conduct."

The struggle for the total liberation of the black oppressed people of South Africa will end in the victory of the oppressed. This, the transnational corporations must be constantly reminded of. The Nats may seem invincible now, but that should not surprise anyone with an elementary knowledge of history. After all, the Nazis did not only *seem* invincible. They said they were, and they actually believed it. All tyrants and terrorists are mightily armed and apparently strong. In reality, however, they are weak and live in constant fear and anxiety. That is why in the end they are always defeated. The Nats will be no exception. After the inevitable fall of the Nats, the corporations will still want to do business with the legitimate government of the new nation. Whether or not that will be possible will depend entirely on the behavior of the corporations now.

The oppressed of South Africa have repeatedly said in no uncertain terms that the corporations must get out of South Africa and the banks should give no more loans to the Nats. This is not a negotiable request but a firm demand. Failure to comply will have serious consequences in future. The blacks of South Africa have not asked the corporations for any advice; they have not asked them for their opinions; they have not asked for codes of conduct. There is only one resounding demand: OUT OF SOUTH AFRICA.

Economic boycotts can be an extremely powerful weapon if properly applied. When the German Jews called on the nations of the world to boycott Germany economically, the effects were severe on the German economy, and this led to calls from the Nazi hierarchy, especially from those officials who had something to do with the economy, for the Nazi Party to modify its treatment of Jews. The Nazis also mounted a massive international campaign that aimed at deceiving the world about the true nature and aims of Naziism. It is worth noting that not all the corporations and governments supported the boycott. For many, it remained "business as usual" with the Nazis, until the war made normal business transactions impossible.

The Nats in South Africa are extremely worried about the effects of a boycott on their economy and their standard of living. Like the Nazis, they have embarked on a massive international campaign aimed at deceiving the world. Anyone who advocates boycotts and economic sanctions in South Africa is sent to jail for five years.[5] If the Nats did not fear the effects of an economic boycott, they would not resort to such

176

draconic measures. (The maximum sentence is death.)

The Role of Western Governments

Before we examine the role played by Western governments in the present-day South African situation, a few
observations about the Western governments' role during the
Nazi persecution of the Jews are necessary.

One of the direct results of the Nazi persecution of the
Jews was the creation of a large Jewish refugee problem.
Many Jews escaped for their lives from Germany and sought
refuge in countries that were willing to extend a helping hand
in time of desperate need. It has been mentioned above that
those Jews who sought refuge in South Africa were made
unwelcome by the Nats who, of course, were one with the
Nazis. But, even in countries where Naziism was verbally
condemned, Jewish refugees were not welcome. Several authors point this fact out. Arthur Morse, for example, blames
the American system of allowing only a restricted number of
persecuted Jews into the United States on anti-Semitism,
which, he says, was to be found at the highest levels of the
State Department.[6]

Henry Feingold comes to a similar conclusion when he
says:

On those occasions during the holocaust years when
mass rescue appeared possible, it required of the nations
a passionate commitment to save lives. Such a commitment did not exist in the Roosevelt administration.[7]

Another author, David Wyman agrees with this assess-
ment but adds that the American people share part of the
blame because they did not follow up their condemnation of
Naziism with practical help for the victims, for example, by
supporting measures that would have made it easier for the
refugees to enter America.[8]

Britain showed no great sympathy for the Jews either.

The government seemed unwilling to offend the Nazis, and the general public showed no sympathy either.[9] A conference held at Evian-les-Bains failed to solve the problem of Jewish refugees primarily because those Western countries that were in a position to help were unwilling to do so.

As we turn to the South African scene, we are struck by the fact that many international conferences have been called to discuss *apartheid*, and the number of resolutions condemning that wicked system can hardly be improved upon. Every such international conference has ended with a call to an end to that pernicious policy and appeals to the international community to take steps that would result in the rehumanization of the blacks in South Africa.

Nowhere has this call been stronger and clearer than at the United Nations. At the General Assembly of that body in New York, the vast majority of the nations of the world have consistently voted in favor of ending *apartheid* and have recommended specific action to be taken against the Nats in order to compel them to take two important measures: (1) To give up their illegal occupation of Namibia and to place that territory under the UN—its rightful jurisdiction—and (2) End *apartheid*. The General Assembly has recommended that, should South Africa refuse to comply, economic sanctions should be applied against her by the nations of the world that are opposed to Naziism, regardless of the name it may bear.

When the question of applying sanctions against South Africa, because of her persistent and arrogant ignoring of the UN resolutions, has come before the Security Council for implementation, the governments of Britain, France, and the United States have persistently vetoed any such action against the Nats. They have used their veto power in order to protect their investments in South Africa, investments that yield large profits, which large profits are a direct result of the exploitation and oppression of blacks. These governments are heavily supported by West Germany, Canada, and Japan in particular, also for the same reason of high profits.

The governments of Britain, France, Canada, West Germany, and the United States have also collaborated with the Nats in keeping the people of Namibia under subjugation and exploiting the country's wealth. Although Namibia is the responsibility of the entire United Nations, these five countries have unilatarally usurped the authority of the UN and have entered into agreements with South Africa that are designed to keep the Nats in power and, therefore, in control of Namibia so that they may continue to be the watchmen of Western investments that are a clear violation of UN resolutions.

The Nats have unleashed a reign of terror hitherto unknown in Namibia. It is ironic that countries that ostensibly fought Naziism in Germany—excluding of course West Germany itself—are now the main supporters of Naziism, which is called *apartheid* in South Africa. In this regard, the relations of East Germany on the one hand, and of West Germany on the other, are of special interest.

One cannot overlook the fact that the government of West Germany is one of *apartheid* South Africa's staunchest supporters, diplomatically, economically, politically, morally, and militarily. It is mainly West German scientists who have developed South Africa's nuclear programme. Over three hundred West German corporations have South African connections. Most of these were staunch supporters of Hitler's Nazi Germany and policies. Most of them exploited cheap Jewish labor exactly as they exploit cheap black labor in South Africa today. The strong ties that existed between the Nazis and the Nats in the late thirties and early forties have been solidified and the Pretoria/Bonn axis is stronger than it ever was. This is not surprising, since many of Hitler's former supporters sit in the West German Bundestag (Parliament). This was once pointed out by Herbert Wehner, chief whip of the Social Democratic Party in West Germany, when he said that most of Hitler's former supporters in the Bundestag were the older members of the Christian Democrats and Christian Socialists in post-1949 West Germany. Although the different political parties represented in the Bundestag differ in their rhetoric as far as support for *apartheid* is concerned, there is no difference as far as their practical support for South African Naziism is concerned. And that is what counts.

On the other hand, The German Democrat Republic (East Germany) has taken a decisive anti-*apartheid* position, which is not limited to verbal condemnation of that evil, but finds concrete expression in practical support for those forces that are working for the destruction of *apartheid*. Apart from the support given by East German delegations at international conferences, at home, the East German public is officially well informed about the atrocities of the apartheid system. At banks and other institutions, containers marked *"anti-apartheid"* are prominently displayed on counters so that the ordinary East German citizen can make a direct financial contribution toward the important fight against *apartheid*. Thus, the ordinary citizen in East Germany actively participates with the oppressed black South Africans in their struggle for freedom. Beyond that, the East German government is unwavering in its practical support for the oppressed of South Africa. This should come as no real surprise since the founders of the German Democratic Republic were themselves persecuted by the Nazis because of their opposition to Naziism.

The Western governments mentioned above argue against imposing sanctions against South Africa on the grounds that they will not work. Yet all of them, including Japan, recently imposed sanctions against Iran!

These governments are guilty on at least three fronts:

They have sought to hoodwink Africans and their supporters into believing that they are on the side of the oppressed in South Africa and, therefore, are strenuously working for an end to *apartheid*. At the same time they have persistently frustrated any effort to bring an end to *apartheid*. They have unashamedly defended South Africa at international conferences, thus providing South Africa with the moral and diplomatic support she needs to carry out her evil policies.

Western governments have knowingly distorted the facts

about the terror of the Afrikaner regime against blacks. They have actively participated in South African propaganda the aim of which is to deceive the world by camouflaging the inhuman *apartheid* system in such "acceptable" terms as "separate development," "plural democracy," and "good neighborliness." It is this kind of support that has encouraged South Africa to refuse to take any resolution against *apartheid* seriously and instead to engage the whole world in a game of delaying tactics and diplomatic charade. Whenever the Nats make statements about "change" in South Africa, these are magnified in the West, despite the total lack of any evidence to support such claims.

Western governments, particularly those mentioned above, have deliberately insulted the oppressed blacks of South Africa and their supporters by claiming that sanctions against the Nats will hurt the blacks more than anyone else. They pretend to be concerned about the welfare of the oppressed when, in fact, they are the direct cause of that oppression. Further, they are in effect saying to the blacks that they are stupid and incapable of differentiating between their long-term interests and self-destruction. They pretend they are unaware of the fact that the blacks of South Africa want the multinational corporations, which they regard as monsters, out of South Africa.

While the Nazis were committing their unprecedented atrocities, they claimed that the greatest danger facing the world of their day was Communism. The governments mentioned above have joined the Nats in their effort to divert world attention from the real evil—which is *apartheid*—to some imaginary "communist threat." Hitler must be turning and smiling in his grave as he hears his foul inventions officially espoused by those who once claimed they were opposed to Naziism.

The Role of International Fascism

The search for ways of justifying oppression and exploitation in South Africa has led to a new fallacy in the West.

181

There is now talk that Western countries must support oppressive regimes as long as those regimes are friendly to the West. The practice, of course, is not new. What is new is the arguments for such action.

It has been pointed out above that the reason why *apartheid* has survived for so long and is thriving is that it has the full backing of most of the Western governments, multinational corporations, and the Western Church. These, however, are institutions, whose leadership changes from time to time. Since 1948, the leadership in all these institutions has certainly changed several times. Yet the support for *apartheid* has been persistent and consistent. On the crucial question of taking meaningful action against the Nats—action that would spell an end to *apartheid*—the Nats have enjoyed, and continue to enjoy, dedicated Western support. This support is well distributed among the centers of influence in the West, namely, in government, in business, in the Church, in the military, in cultural circles, and in the media. One can thus speak of an international brotherhood of Fascists, who are dedicated to the maintenance of *apartheid*.

One cannot ignore the fact that the Nats spend hundreds of millions of dollars in Western countries for the sole purpose of identifying *apartheid* supporters and sympathizers and drafting them into their well-organized and financed ring of international advocates of *apartheid*. Apart from the lucrative financial rewards, these advocates are invited to South Africa by the Afrikaner regime where they are lavishly entertained and briefed on how to sell *apartheid* in their respective countries. Part of their assignment is to recruit emigrants from Western countries. Needless to say, no black person may emigrate to South Africa. Whites who emigrate to South Africa must be prepared to support *apartheid*. *Apartheid,* therefore, is no longer the ideology of a few misguided Afrikaners. It is now the sum total of all that is evil in the Western political, economic, and social spheres. *Apartheid* offers everything that a Fascist can hope for, and more.

To be sure, most Western countries have laws that make

it difficult for Fascists to act out their Fascism freely and legally. Laws, however, do not convert human beings. In today's world, South Africa is unique in that it offers Fascists the legal framework to exercise their Fascism to the fullest. South Africa, therefore has become a haven for Fascists, an international playground, the center of the international brotherhood of Fascists. Anyone who is white, who is a citizen of a Western country, and who hates people who are not white can emigrate to South Africa, where hatred of nonwhites is the legal policy of the land. So also, one who believes that whites are inherently superior to blacks will be very comfortable in South Africa. For those who believe in slavery and exploitation, in South Africa there is a mass of blacks who are legally slaves. For the sadist, one who loves to torture and murder, South Africa legally offers unlimited opportunities and a ready supply of blacks. For those who delight in oppressing others and those who find satisfaction in causing human pain, misery, and suffering, the Nats have passed laws that make such practices, against blacks, the acceptable South African way of life for whites. And for those Western Christians who believe in a Christianity of convenience—verbal condemnation of, but practical support for evil—the South African white churches will never bother their consciences. On the contrary, they will find all the support they need to make them feel comfortable. Should anyone dare to question their actions, all they need do is to declare, as the Nazis did, that they are "anti-Communist."

Despite the machinations of the Western countries mentioned above, despite their overt and covert support for the hideous *apartheid* ideology, despite their unrelenting efforts to discredit the just liberation struggle of the oppressed black people of South Africa, and despite their collusion with the Nats to make Naziism succeed in South Africa, *apartheid* will, in time, be totally destroyed. In the end good must, and will, always triumph over evil. It is only a question of time.

9

The Final Solution: Bantustans

Of all the stages of Nazi persecution of the Jews, the "Final Solution" has been given the most exposure. This is understandable since, in the Final Solution, we are presented with a degree of human hatred no human or known language can fully describe. The Holocaust has been so thoroughly dealt with by so many authors that it needs no elaboration here. One needs only to point out that, before the actual Holocaust, the Nazis had spoken of the need for "separate development" for the Jews and for the Germans. They planned on shipping all the Jews to a "Homeland" which, according to their plans, was to be Madagascar. Further, before the actual Final Solution, the Nazis concentrated the Jews in ghettoes and camps. They starved them. They exploited them economically, and finally they exterminated them. The actual extermination was the end of a long process in which government, the Church, and business formed an unholy alliance against the Jews.

While all this was happening, the Nats were openly backing the Nazis. Most of the statements in support of Naziism were made by leading Nats between 1940 and 1943, when the Nazi persecution of the Jews was at its peak. But, even prior to that, the Nats made no secret of their anti-Semitism. As early as 1937, when Jews were leaving Germany in search of safe havens, some of them went to South Africa. Afrikaner organizations such as the "Greyshirts" organized demonstrations to protest the arrival of persecuted Jews in South Africa. The demonstrations had the backing of the Afrikaner leadership, as is evidenced by the statement made by F.C. Erasmus, who later became Minister of Justice when the Afrikaners came to power. He said:

> My party is glad to give expression to the sincere appreciation of the useful work done by the Greyshirts in one important aspect, viz. that they have very pertinently drawn the attention of the people to the Jewish problem. . . .We consider that a service has here been done to the nation which deserves recognition and perpetuation.[1]

Another Afrikaner organization, known as the "South African Gentile National Socialist Movement," openly declared that its aim was to destroy:

> . . .the perversive influence of the Jews in economics, culture, religion, ethics, and statecraft and to re-establish European Aryan control in South Africa for the welfare of the Christian peoples of South Africa.[2]

The fact that Nazis were dealt a blow before their grand dreams of a world dominated by Aryans could be realized has not deterred the Nats from relentlessly pursuing their program the objective of which is identical to that of the Nazis. The target of the Nats is indeed not the Jews but the blacks, especially those of South Africa. The program has been modified to suit the present world and South African conditions, where blacks outnumber whites five to one. Despite the special South African conditions, there can be no doubt that the Nats, like their Nazi masters and teachers, are making preparations that, however, in their calculations, will make the mass murder of blacks swifter and simpler than the Nazi methods.

Instead of the gas chambers, the Nats have created Bantustans, euphemistically known as "homelands," where millions of blacks are destined to perish through a variety of carefully planned methods.

The present population of South Africa is about 28 million. Of this number, only 4 million are white. The land is arbitrarily divided in such a way that 87 percent of it belongs to the 4 million whites, and the 24 million blacks *may* live on the 13 percent at the pleasure of the Nats. They can be moved at any time. Since the Nats came to power in 1948, over 4 million blacks have actually been arbitrarily and forcibly deported from areas where their ancestors once lived to overcrowded, distant Bantustans. Their homes have been bulldozed to the ground, and their property has been confiscated. They have been moved to areas lacking basic amenities such as shelter, water, food, not to mention schools and clinics. The Bantustans are the dumping ground for the blacks, particularly the elderly, the sick, and the dying. They are designed to serve four main purposes, all of which are part of white South Africa's Final Solution to the "black peril."

First, like the Jewish labor camps that preceded the extermination, they serve as reservoirs of unlimited cheap black labor for the white-owned mines, industries, and farms—the pillars of white power, profit, and privilege. Blacks are drafted into the white areas, where they are forced to work and live apart from their families for eleven months of the year. What they earn is insufficient to support their families. The Bantustans have been strategically fragmented into little pockets all around white South Africa's farms and industries. Apart from being overcrowded, they are situated on land that is impoverished, badly eroded, lacking in resources, and without prospect of ever being developed. All this is not an accident but part of a carefully worked out plan, and its execution is reminiscent of the mass deportation of Jews from their homes to distant labor camps that served the carefully worked out plan of the Nazis of reducing Jews into cheap labor units.

Second, the Nats have been criticized for the hardships and suffering they have deliberately caused blacks. Sensitive tourists, foreign journalists, and visitors have been appalled by the poverty of blacks in a land flowing with milk and honey. The Nats have responded by deporting the blacks from those areas where they are visible and have banished them to distant parts of the country inaccessible to the ordinary tourist, journalist, or visitor. Having done that, the Nats can easily say that the blacks have their "homelands," where they have all the rights according to "international law" such as "independence" and "self-determination." As far as propaganda goes, the Nats surpass the Nazis—having learned from them. Through these mass deportations of blacks, the Nats hope finally to achieve their dream of "a totally white South Africa" in which blacks will officially be "temporary sojourners." It is a wicked scheme designed to keep the blacks, the real owners of South Africa, in a state of perpetual servitude. The Nazis were so obsessed with an Aryan Germany that, in 1942, they declared that Germany was "free of Jews."

Third, the fact that blacks outnumber white South Africans five to one poses a problem of large numbers. The Bantustans are an attempt by the Nats in the words of one of them, "to keep the numbers of the blacks down."[3] They are doing this by creating conditions in the Bantustans that result in widespread starvation, diseases and large-scale deaths. It is all a deliberate policy "to keep the numbers of blacks down." South Africa produces and exports more food than any other country on the continent of Africa. Almost all the food produced is from the 87 percent of the white-occupied land. The irony of it all is that the food is produced with the use of cheap black labor that includes forced prison labor and child labor. The blacks who work on these farms live under subhuman conditions. Their families on the Bantustans die of starvation. South Africa has the highest black-infant-mortality rate on the continent. Children die from hunger and food-related diseases such as malnutrition, gastroenteritis, and TB. While it may be true that there are no gas chambers in the Bantustans, the Bantustans themselves are starvation

187

and disease chambers where, since the Nats came to power in 1948, millions of blacks, young and old, have been systematically and deliberately allowed to die by a "Christian government," in order to finally achieve the goal of a "white South Africa."

The Nazis were usually careful to deport the Jews to areas far removed from where the Aryans lived. As a result, most Germans to this day claim that they did not know what was being done to the Jews. The Nats are operating along the same principles. However, white South Africa cannot claim ignorance of the fact that blacks are being systematically and officially murdered, in the Bantustans especially, but also in the black ghettoes around the white cities, the other reservoirs of cheap black labor. It will be recalled too that, as Jews were dying from starvation and disease in the ghettoes and labor and concentration camps, the Nazis were busy painting a glorious picture of their policies and blaming "international Jewry" for propaganda against the "German *Volk*." While that was going on, the Nats were busy taking notes as they waited for their turn to do to the blacks what the Nazis did to the Jews, namely to exterminate systematically what they consider to be "subhuman."

Fourth, if starvation, disease, exploitation, and death in the ghettoes and Bantustans do not silence the blacks forever, then the plans of the Nats provide for the unlimited use of force against them. Such action is planned to be swift and effective. Both the Bantustans and the ghettoes are isolated from, yet completely surrounded by white South Africa. This makes them ideal military targets. South Africa's nuclear program, thanks to Western assistance, is designed to provide small nuclear bombs that can do havoc to the black areas without affecting white South Africa. Thus, South Africa's "Final Solution," in its last stage, is meant to be completed in minutes rather than years—a great improvement on the Nazi methods! The Nats will then declare South Africa "free of blacks."

No one should underestimate or doubt the willingness,

desire, and capability of the Nats to commit atrocities against the blacks, atrocities that could be far worse than the Nazis committed against the Jews. The use of unprovoked, naked force and brutality against blacks in South Africa is part of the culture of the Nats. Every day in South Africa, blacks die brutal deaths caused by the instruments of Afrikaner power for no other reason than that they are black and expendable.

As recently as June 1976, when young black school-children aged between seven and eighteen years, demonstrated peacefully against an inferior education and the daily humiliation and oppression they and their parents suffered at the hands of white South Africa, the Nats responded by shooting to death more than two thousand, injuring more than four thousand, and terrorizing into exile more than six thousand young boys and girls. Many of those brutally murdered were buried secretly in mass graves. A clear demonstration of what the Nats think of the lives of blacks is their ordering police and soldiers to shoot and kill black mourners as they stood in prayer at the gravesides of their murdered loved ones. The police and soldiers were carrying out a longstanding order, which is: "When dealing with blacks, shoot first and ask questions later."[4]

While the name of Steve Biko made international headlines when he was brutally murdered by the Afrikaner police after being subjected to incredible torture, his case was by no means an exception. Black opponents of *apartheid* are arrested and tortured on a daily basis in South Africa. The Nats do not hesitate to murder their opponents.[5] Whereas the Nats may differ from the Nazis, in their methods, the philosophy, objectives, and goals remain identical.

10

The Resistance Movement

Oppression breeds resistance. Resistance finally leads to victory over oppression. The nature of resistance is determined by the nature and degree of oppression. Resistance can be expressed through demonstrations against injustice, through strikes, through boycotts, and through the ballot box by voting an unpopular regime out of power. However, a particular regime bent on maintaining exclusive power forever may decide to give itself power to prevent any of the forms of resistance mentioned above from taking place. Such action does not stop resistance. It simply drives it underground and in the end helps to make it more deadly.

Whenever the question of resistance in Nazi Germany comes up, the date of July 20, 1944, is almost inevitably mentioned. That was the day on which the last attempt to assassinate Hitler, and thus overthrow the Nazi regime, was made by some of those who had a long record of opposition to Naziism.

To be sure, resistance to Naziism did not start on July 20, 1944. Opposition to the Nazis started even before they actually came to power in 1933. The first thing the Nazis did when they came to power was to take measures to silence the opposition by banning such political organizations as the Social Democrats and the Communists. These bannings, however, did not spell an end to the opposition to Naziism. As the inhumanity of the Nazis intensified, men and women from all walks of life made their contributions toward resisting Hitler.

At no point was there a mass movement against Hitler. Such a movement would have required extensive organization, and Hitler's totalitarian state was quick to accuse its opponents of treason and of being unpatriotic. Having been so accused, they faced certain death.

One of the great plans to topple Hitler was worked out in the summer of 1938. It was anticipated by leading German military men that Hitler would order the invasion of Czechoslovakia. The plan was to court-martial Hitler if he carried his plans out. However, at the conference in Munich, Chamberlain of Britain gave Hitler the green light, despite his knowledge of the plan to topple Hitler. This was a triumph for Hitler, whose popularity among the German *Volk* reached unprecedented heights. Concerning the lost opportunity to stop the Nazis, Walther Hofer concludes:

> This action plan of late summer 1938, was the only one which had any chance of success, and if it had succeeded it would have marked the turning point of events, without much loss of blood.[1]

As it turned out, Hitler was appeased, and the result was the loss of some 30 million lives in the Second World War and destruction of vast property.

The outbreak of the Second World War helped to consolidate Hitler's power and his standing among the German people. He became their messiah, especially in the early stages when the military victories seemed endless, and the chances of a world ruled by Germany seemed brighter. Under such conditions, any talk of opposing the Nazis seemed doomed. However, the atrocities of the Nazis, coupled with their military reverses, once again encouraged resistance, which finally led to the assassination attempt in 1944. After the attempt, those responsible were summarily executed, and, as a result of the brutality of the Nazis against their critics, the resistance movement within Germany suffered a serious setback. However, by then, resistance to Naziism was no longer an internal German affair. Practically the whole world, with the noted exception of Japan, was involved in massive resistance against Naziism. The only people who remained steadfastly loyal to the Nazi cause, from its inception in 1919 to its fall in 1945, were the Afrikaner Nats, the present-day rulers of South Africa.

In South Africa, black resistance against white domination was not born when the Nats introduced apartheid in 1948. Black resistance against foreign domination goes back to the 17th century. Everywhere where people have been colonized, they have been economically exploited, politically oppressed, and racially discriminated against. These are the universal distinguishing marks of colonialism. It has already been pointed out that oppression, exploitation, and discrimination breed resistance. Black South Africans are not an exception to this rule.

Since the first white settlers from Europe came to South Africa on April 6, 1652, one can talk of the resistance movement in South Africa as having started on that day. Throughout the centuries, black South Africans have resisted white domination and oppression in various ways, which have included wars, demonstrations, boycotts, and strikes. The form of resistance has always been dictated by the nature of oppression.

An example of this was the formation of the African National Congress in 1912. At the end of the Anglo-Boer War, which was fought between the Dutch—who by then called themselves Afrikaners—and the British. The issue was whose colony South Africa should be, and a peace treaty, signed in 1902, gave Britain, the victor, control over South Africa. A clause that barred blacks from being members of Parliament was included in the treaty. In 1910, Britain granted South Africa self-rule, and once again blacks were conveniently left out of the negotiations. Refusing to be voiceless, the blacks formed their political mouthpiece in 1912. The purpose was to oppose increasingly discriminatory legislation, which was being passed by an English-speaking government. At that time, the Afrikaners were in opposition and virtually remained that way, except for a brief period when they formed a short-lived coalition with the English-speaking government, which broke up because the Afrikaners supported the Nazis and wanted South Africa either to fight on the side of the Nazis or to remain neutral. The blacks, through their movement, the African National Congress, supported the Allies and fought the Nazis. It is also worth pointing out that, in the West, there are many voices in official circles that refer to the African National Congress as "a Communist-inspired organization." There are two reasons for this. One is chronic ignorance, and the other is a deliberate distortion of facts. By the time the Russian Revolution took place, in 1917, the African National Congress was already five years old and was busy organizing blacks to resist white domination and oppression. That struggle continues.

Apartheid has been deliberately watered down in the Western media and presented to the public as "a policy of *racial separation*." While it is true that "racial separation" was practiced in various degrees almost from the time the first Europeans set foot in South Africa in 1652, to refer to *apartheid* as "a policy of racial separation" is both ignorant and dishonest. The practice of racial separation that was common in South Africa was based on prejudice and the kind of racism practiced by Britain wherever she has colonized peoples. This kind of racial discrimination ended in South Africa in 1948 while it continued in places where Britain remained in control, especially in countries with a sizeable British population, such as in Southern and Northern Rhodesia as well as in Kenya. In South Africa, racial discrimination was replaced by *apartheid*.

The year 1948, therefore, is a watershed in South African race relations. With the coming of the Nats to power in that year, having won a so-called "election" in which 80 percent of the population was excluded because they were black, the Nats were free to introduce into South Africa a new ideology which was based on the premise that blacks were inherently inferior to whites and that this inferior status was ordained by God and, therefore, could never be changed. If such was the Will of God, it was only logical for the Nats, as elected representatives of their God-fearing Afrikaner *Volk,* to pass such laws as would reflect the Will of God in the daily experiences of blacks. At the same time, the laws had the effect of brainwashing white South Africans into believing that the blacks were indeed inferior through God's Will, and, therefore, treating them as human beings would be going against God's Will—a powerful and convincing argument in Christian, God-fearing white South Africa! With the white electorate so convinced, it became an easy matter for the Nats to embark on a program of repressive legislation, which, in its extensiveness and degree of inhumanity toward blacks, is unprecedented in the history of the world. South African legislation against blacks now exceeds Nazi legislation against the Jews, both in volume and in its brutal application against blacks. To say *apartheid* is "a policy of racial separation" is as ludicrous as saying that Naziism was a policy of racial separation. Given a chance, the Nats are bent on doing to the blacks what the Nazis did to the Jews. Despite their denials, the Western backers of *apartheid* know this.

Black South Africans have not taken this oppression and dehumanization lying down. But, as their resistance grew, so did the brutality of the Nats intensify. The brutality reached a new high in 1960 when peacefully demonstrating black men, women, and children were brutally murdered and seriously injured by the police of the Nats' regime. To add insult to injury, the Nats banned the African National Congress as well as the Pan Africanist Congress, which had been formed in 1958. All resistance to *apartheid* was declared illegal, and the *apartheid* laws were further tightened to make South Africa, as far as the treatment of blacks was concerned, a police state, which it has continued to be to this day. The resistance movement was therefore driven underground at the same time as the police state's repressive machinery was placed on maximum alert. In 1964, part of the underground leadership of the African National Congress, which included Nelson Mandela, was arrested and sentenced to life imprisonment, which means, in Afrikaner terminology, never leaving prison alive. That leadership is now behind bars on Robben Island, a heavily guarded concentration camp for black opponents of *apartheid,* just off the western coast of South Africa. Though he has been imprisoned for almost twenty years now, Nelson Mandela remains the undisputed hero of black South Africans and the unifying symbol of their resistance. Since their arrest and imprisonment in 1964, thousands of other black South Africans have been arrested, banned, placed under house arrest, tortured, murdered, or driven into exile for their opposition to *apartheid.* Those so persecuted include children as young as five years old! Those in exile are engaged in a program of winning international support for the struggle against *apartheid.* Despite the unconditional support the Nats enjoy from the governments of Britain, France, Canada, West Germany, and the United States in particular, as well as from churches and business circles in these countries, the support for the liberation struggle among the ordinary citizens of these countries is also growing. While there is a very clear and visible alliance of supporters of *apartheid,* there is a less visible alliance of international forces against *apartheid.* This alliance has been deliberately and conveniently ignored by the Western media.

There is no doubt that if the Western media performed its function of giving factual information to the public, the respectability and support the Nats enjoy in the Western world would be greatly reduced and limited to die-hard Fascists. But the Western public is deliberately kept in the dark and consciously misinformed about the monstrous operations of the Nats against the voiceless black South Africans. It is the same Western media that succeeded in making the name of Idi Amin infamous throughout the Western world.

While the stated reason was to expose the excesses of Amin, the real demonic intention was to present Amin as a typical African leader in order to discredit all Africans, especially their leaders, and lend weight to the racist assertion that "Africans are incapable of governing themselves." Everyone knows—except those who delight in being deceived—that the Uganda of Amin can never, by any stretch of imagination, be compared to the brutal South Africa of the Nats. The inhumanity of the Nats is acceptable in the West in part because the Nats are white and those who suffer are black. It is only the Christian West that supports evil if it is committed by "friends" and condemns it if it is committed by "enemies."

Mention must also be made of the fact that it is the West that overthrew the legally elected government of Uganda under the leadership of Dr. Milton Obote. Obote refused to be a paid, corrupt puppet of the West, ready to sell his country and his people for a few pieces of silver.

To be sure, there are many governments in the world today that can be accused of tyranny. But the tyranny of the Nats is unique in today's world in that it is racial tyranny—a small white minority legally terrorizing a huge black majority. The only other example of racial tyranny we have in recent history is Naziism—the forerunner of *apartheid*.

Mention must also be made of the fact that there has always been a small remnant of white South Africans who have been part of the liberation struggle. The price they have paid for being out of step with white South Africa's legal and cultural standards of oppression, terrorism, exploitation, and racism has been very high indeed. These standards, the Nats constantly repeat, are the "standards of Western civilization and Christianity." The number of white South Africans who have joined the resistance movement is still small and the growth rate is slow—not unlike the experience of the German Resistance Movement during the Nazi era. Many more white South Africans simply turn their backs on *apartheid* and

196

emigrate to safer havens. The few who have joined the struggle against *apartheid* are the converts who clearly see *apartheid* for what it is, namely, an evil. On the other hand, the advocates, supporters, and adherents of *apartheid* represent the powers of darkness. They have plotted a path that leads to suffering, destruction, and death.

The resistance movement, which is the sum total of all the individuals, groups, and organizations world-wide that are in different ways engaged in the struggle against *apartheid* is the only viable alternative to *apartheid* and the sole guarantor of freedom and justice in South Africa, progress and stability in Africa and, therefore, world peace.

The lines, therefore, are clearly drawn. On one side are the forces that are dedicated to the overthrow of the evil *apartheid* system. On the other side are forces that seek to maintain *apartheid*. On the question of *apartheid* there can be no neutrality. Those who claim to be neutral are camouflaging their endorsement of and active support for *apartheid*. To claim neutrality in the face of evil is evil.

11

The Future

It is now over thirty years since the Nats imported Naziism, which they have given the name *"apartheid,"* into South Africa. Through a carefully planned and executed system of interlocking laws, they have reduced the blacks to a status that effectively excludes them from the human race. Through their well-organized propaganda machinery, they have won supporters for *apartheid* primarily within the power centers of Western Europe, particularly in Britain, Canada, France, West Germany, and the United States. Viewed in its proper perspective, therefore, *apartheid* is not just a monstrous ideology of the Nats. It has become an adopted child of the Western capitalist system—adopted for the express purpose of being the watchdog of the Western investments in South Africa. The Western centers of power have, by their support for *apartheid,* let it be explicitly known that, when the choice has to be made between profit and people, as is the case in South Africa, people are irrelevant and expendable. This conviction finds its practical expression in the neutron bomb, which is designed to destroy human life while leaving buildings (capital) intact.

South African propaganda is unashamedly echoed in the West by people who are basically supporters of the Nats. Most of them, after spending a week or two in South Africa as guests of the Nats, return to their respective countries as "experts on Africa," mainly to inform their listeners that "there is change in South Africa." While it is true that there are some Western scholars who have made studies of some African countries, there is not a single Western person who is an "expert on African affairs." The claim is preposterous.

It is these so-called "experts" who lecture us, the victims of *apartheid,* on who are our friends and who are our enemies. They want to tell us what our problems are. They are tireless in their efforts to make Africans a fulcrum in their struggle with the "Communist" nations. While they are directly involved in perpetuating our oppression, they seek to convince us that by oppressing us they are actually concerned with our welfare. The amazing thing is that, although they are "experts," the African psyche has persistently eluded them.

The "experts" need to be reminded that what counts for the oppressed blacks in South Africa are not words, not glorious-sounding promises. What counts are deeds and deeds only. A few pages of elementary African history should help the "experts" understand that the blacks of Africa in general know too well that it is the Fascists who enslaved Africans and not the Communists. It is the Fascists who colonized them and not the Communists. It is the Fascists who exploit them today and not the Communists. It is the Fascists who commit acts of aggression in black Southern African states of Botswana, Lesotho, Swaziland, Mozambique, Namibia, Angola, Zimbabwe, Tanzania, and Zambia, but certainly not the Communists. Conversely, it is the "Communists" who have helped Africans liberate themselves from the yoke of colonialism, exploitation, and oppression. Without them, most of Africa would still be in the claws of Western imperialists. These are facts which neither propaganda nor rhetoric nor Western "history" can alter. The leaders of a liberation struggle in Africa are subjected to abuse and ridicule in Western circles. They are usually referred to as terrorists, murderers, powers of darkness, and Communist agents. The outcome of all this abuse is that in liberation circles—and

199

those are the only circles that count—these labels are regarded as the greatest honor for a freedom fighter. In liberation circles, nothing is more honorable than to be called a "Communist" by a Fascist. This is the highest award for a freedom fighter. Its recipients include such distinguished African heroes as President Samora Machel of Mozambique and Prime Minister Robert Mugabe of Zimbabwe.

To those who now go about claiming that the Nats are bringing about progressive change in the situation of the dehumanized blacks, one has to pose the question: "What apartheid laws, which in the last thirty years have reduced blacks to subhuman beings, have been repealed by the Nats?" The answer is none. The struggle of black people in South Africa over the last thirty years has nothing to do with "civil rights." It is a struggle to regain our humanity and our land—a rehumanization struggle; a struggle for nationhood.

No words can aptly describe the feelings of those who live under the degrading, dehumanizing, hideous *apartheid* system. No human language is equipped to describe the inhumanity of *apartheid*. It is one thing to empathize with victims of injustice. It is quite another to experience *apartheid*. Those who sit in their comfortable armchairs in Western capitals, having academic discussions about change in South Africa must be reminded that only the blacks, who have been oppressed, dehumanized, brutalized—mentally, physically, and spiritually—will be able to tell when change does come. It is only the voice of the voiceless that is authentic.

That voice can only be heard in the silence of the black South African whose door to his shack in the ghetto has been smashed open in the middle of the night by police who have arrested him because he has no pass, and shipped him out to work as forced labor on a white man's farm; or from the millions who have been forcibly moved from their homes to distant Bantustans, where they have faced starvation, disease, and death; or the wife who sits alone with her children for eleven months in the year or for two or even three years

200

while her husband toils for slave wages in a white-owned mine; or the mother who helplessly watches yet another of her young ones die of starvation, not because there is scarcity of food in South Africa but only because the white regime in power has determined that the starving of blacks is the best way "to keep their numbers down"; or the black parents who cannot send their child to school because their child must pay tuition whereas a white child receives free education; or the millions of blacks who cannot vote because the law forbids it because of their color, something they can do nothing about; or the student who cannot choose a career because blacks may only study what the white regime allows them; or the young black school graduate whose chances of finding a job are limited by the influx control that determines where he or she can look for work; or the millions of blacks who cannot own property in their own land; or the frustrated young adult who cannot marry the partner of his or her choice because the white regime does not permit free choice as far as marriage partners are concerned; the father who cannot attend the funeral of his child in the Bantustan because he will lose his job in white-ruled South Africa; the same man who gets paid one-twentieth of a white man's salary because, according to the principles of apartheid, blacks must legally earn only a fraction of what whites earn; or the parents in Soweto and other black ghettoes who, on returning from work learn that their six-year-old child has been shot dead by the police; or their neighbors who find that their three children have "disappeared"—been murdered and buried in secret by the police; or the young black student leader who is hanging by his thumbs from the ceiling of the white police torture chamber for refusing to admit that South African black students are "Communists"; or the black journalist who is banned for publishing Afrikaner atrocities against blacks; or the teacher who is placed under house arrest, incommunicado, for saying that black education is inferior to white education; or those blacks shot by the police while at the graveside burying other black victims of police brutality; or those blacks sentenced to life imprisonment for daring to oppose *apartheid;* or the young black children in wheelchairs, maimed, and paralyzed by the bullets of the *apartheid* police for peacefully protesting against white-imposed inferior education; or the thousands of black youngsters driven into exile by the intolerable ruthlessness of *apartheid;* or the black Christians in a church holding a memorial service who are attacked by police and have to run for their lives; and, above all, the black Christian who is told by the white Christian Church that he is created in the image of God and, at the same time, that he is subhuman. For over thirty years, this is what blacks in South Africa have experienced under *apartheid.* This is what *apartheid* is in 1982. No outsider can lecture to black South Africans about "change." When change does come, we will be the first ones to let the world know!

This picture of apartheid has led the United Nations to label *apartheid* "a crime against humanity." It must, therefore, follow that the Nats and their supporters are criminals, just as the German Nazis were. This crime against humanity is manifested in three ways.

First, the reign of terror that the Nats have unleashed against blacks is only comparable to the Nazi crimes. It is constitutional crime that is enshrined in law, supported by the Church and business and is visible—clearly identifiable—by its dehumanization of blacks and its brutality spelled out above.

Second, the Nats have committed a crime against white South Africa. It is one that is only indirectly enshrined in law. In its application, it is not brutal. It is invisible, insidious, and, therefore, more damaging than naked force. The Nats have brainwashed white South Africans into believing that they are inherently superior to blacks, and, therefore, that it is morally right and benevolent to treat blacks as a subhuman species. White South Africans are nurtured this way from the cradle to the grave. They are taught this at home; they hear it at church; at school; they see it on the streets and at their places of work, and the vast majority of them finally accept it as a fact. The very high standard of living that *apartheid* bestows on white South Africans—one of the highest standards of living in the world—has made them swallow the Afrikaner propaganda that they are "the chosen of God." The Nats have placed white South Africans in prisons without walls or heavy iron doors. By teaching them to dehumanize blacks, they have actually dehumanized whites. By teaching whites to treat blacks inhumanly, they have made whites less than human in their behavior. By making whites conscious of imaginary racial superiority, they have impaired their human conscience. By making them substitute evil for good and good for evil, they have made them immoral. While inflicting heavy physical damage to blacks, the Nats have inflicted heavy mental damage to white South Africans.

Third, the artificial and illusionary balkanization of South Africa into pockets of "National States" (13 percent of the land is *allocated* to blacks who comprise 87 percent of the population) is one of the most expensive illusions of our time.

The resultant waste in human and material resources is incalculable. About 95 percent of the time spent in the all-white parliament is wasted on devising oppressive legislation against blacks instead of legislation designed to improve the lot of all South Africans. A huge slice of the budget is wasted on financing *apartheid* (which is doomed to failure) instead of improving the standard of living of all South Africans.

South Africa has the human and material resources that can transform the lives of all her people. Collectively, South Africans can play a significant role in the development of the whole of Southern Africa. Together with the other African states, South Africa can make important contributions to the future development, prosperity, and stability of the entire African continent. A South Africa free of *apartheid* can take her proper place in the world community and contribute her fair share to the betterment of the entire human family. Because of apartheid, she remains a pariah, and rightly so.

It must be remembered that if Albert Einstein had been born in a Bantustan, the chances are that he would have died before reaching the age of five years. If he had lived to be an adult he would not have become a physicist. The *apartheid* education laws would have seen to that. If Christian Barnard, the famous white South African heart specialist had been black, *apartheid* would have prevented him from making any contribution to medical science. If Gary Player, the internationally celebrated white South African golfer, had been black, he would have ended up a caddie. Who knows what contributions Steve Biko would have made in a society free of *apartheid*? What about Albert Lutuli, the black South African statesman, leader of the African National Congress and first African Nobel Peace Prize winner, who was banned by the Nats and died under mysterious circumstances? What about the hundreds of black great, brave men rotting on Robben Island because of their opposition to apartheid? What about the millions of brains that have been legally wasted because they were in heads whose skin cover was black? The world is all the poorer because of *apartheid* and that is why "*apartheid* is a crime against humanity."

Western supporters of *apartheid* have been tireless in their efforts to delude the world into believing that they are working strenuously to bring an end to that evil. This is a plain ruse. The truth of the matter is that, despite their pretenses, the power centers in the West are the bulwark of *apartheid. Apartheid* can never be overcome by negotiation, just as Naziism could never have been overcome by negotiations. To deny this fact is to indulge in fantasy. Fascists, by their very nature, have no respect for diplomacy, persuasion, negotiation or compromise. For them, these are signs of weakness. South Africa's intrigues, charades, and shifting positions on the independence of Namibia, the territory she illegally occupies, is a clear demonstration of the true nature of Fascism. Since *apartheid* is a crime against humanity, the way to deal with the Nats is by declaring an international moral war against them. That war cannot consist of words as in the last thirty years, but in practical steps, the pressure of which must be aimed at bringing the evil men in Pretoria to their knees and the creation in South Africa of a totally new and rehumanized society. The South Africa of the Nats has been called a pariah many times by the international community. Now, that community, which is abhorred by *apartheid*, must take the following steps without further debate:

Governments

Give full and unconditional support to the UN resolutions, which call for punitive action against the Nats. Until now, the Nats have been richly rewarded, especially by Western governments, for their crimes against humanity. That in itself is a subhuman act.

Systematically scale down diplomatic representation until all ties are cut. The argument that the maintenance of diplomatic relations will help end *apartheid* is a Western ploy capable of deceiving only those who wish to be deceived. The Nats fear isolation; hence their massive propaganda machinery. The overwhelming majority of Third World and Socialist countries have no such relations with the Nats. The culprits are the Western countries. They must learn from history. Oppression cannot last for ever.

Ban all communication links with the Nats.

Stop all cooperation in the military, nuclear, and security fields with the Nats. Impose a severe penalty on all those responsible for supplying arms and military personnel to the Nats. For all this, the Nats depend entirely on Western support.

Give full recognition to the Liberation Movement, which is dedicated to the destruction of *apartheid* and the establishment of a new society in South Africa. Give full assistance to the victims of *apartheid*, to refugees, and to those who may seek asylum. If the West had acted with compassion in the early days of Naziism, many innocent lives would have been saved, and the whole course of Naziism might have been altered to the benefit of the entire world.

Western nations are on record for having banned trade with countries they consider their adversaries. The argument that sanctions and boycotts will not work is hollow.

Ban all *apartheid* propaganda, especially from schools, colleges, and religious institutions. Promote the dissemination of information that exposes the evil *apartheid* system. Socialist and Third World countries are doing a splendid job in this area. Western governments on the other hand have distinguished themselves by being apologists for *apartheid* or by being the chief instruments of *apartheid* propaganda outside the borders of South Africa.

Multinational Corporations and Banks

Stop all further investment in, and bank loans to, the *apartheid* regime.

Set up the machinery for systematically withdrawing existing investments in South Africa. The withdrawal must be completed within a set time frame. The Nats depend heavily on foreign investments and loans for their *apartheid* system to function, just as the Nazis depended on German industry and banks for Naziism to succeed. The claim by Western investors and financiers that divestment will be disastrous for the blacks is demonic in that it suggests that they have the welfare of blacks at heart, when in actuality they are helping to consolidate oppressive *apartheid* for their own benefit and are using cheap black labor in order to maximize their own profits at the expense of blacks who have been reduced to nonpersons. Advising the multinational corporations to divest is actually a favor to them. Many German corporations supported the Nazi effort by employing cheap Jewish labor. Many of those corporations are doing to blacks in South Africa what they did to Jews in Germany, namely, treating them as slaves. They have been joined by corporations from Britain, France, Canada, and the United States. At the end of the war, the corporations that had exploited the Jews were made to pay compensation to the victims or their relatives. Thus an international precedent was set, and rightly so. Those who use their money to support and perpetuate crimes against humanity are themselves guilty of criminal acts. The multinational corporations are exploiting blacks in South Africa. They are also furthering the aims of *apartheid,* and they know it. While it may seem profitable to invest in South Africa and to give loans to the Nats, in actual fact a huge debt is being accumulated by the corporations and banks, one that, someday, in keeping with international law and practice, they will surely have to repay. They will not be able to say: "We did not know." Today's arrogance will be tomorrow's disaster.

The corporations and banks must cut all commercial and other ties with the *apartheid* regime. They must neither export anything to, or import anything from, *apartheid* South Africa. They should strengthen their ties with other Third World countries. Instead of financing oppression, they should lend their support to those forces that are engaged in a struggle to rid South Africa of *apartheid.* If they do that, then their withdrawal from South Africa will be temporary. They will, in future, be able to do business with a free South Africa. They remain in South Africa now at their own peril, for those who are not part of the struggle for justice and humanity now will never be allowed to share in the fruits of victory, which fruits are certain. The view, prevalent in Western business circles, that corporations need pay no attention to the suffering they are causing blacks in South Africa because any future black government will be too eager to conduct business as usual with the West, is, to say the least, dangerously erroneous.

Trade Unions

Instruct union members not to handle any cargo going to or coming from South Africa.

Withdraw all union funds from banks that do business

with the evil *apartheid* regime, and sell all stock in companies that continue to support and finance *apartheid*.

Encourage all union members to boycott all South African products.

Artists and Sportsmen

Impose an unconditional ban on all appearances in South Africa until all the vestiges of *apartheid* have disappeared from the surface of the earth. It must be remembered that the Nats consider not just black South Africans to be subhuman but all people whose skin color is not white, regardless of their citizenship, character, ability, achievement, or qualifications. On the other hand, a white skin color qualifies a person for a superhuman status, whether one is a monster or an imbecile. So obsessed are the Nats with skin color that, whenever it has suited the objectives of *apartheid* propaganda, foreign blacks and other nonwhites have been allowed to visit South Africa, not as they are, but as "honorary whites." They are allowed to live in "international hotels" and use facilities reserved for "whites only" in South Africa. Unknown to these visitors, the linen and utensils they use are marked in such a way that they are reserved for non-white visitors only. After they leave, their rooms are thoroughly fumigated! This applies particularly to sportsmen and entertainers. The promoters, who are interested only in the money they can make, often make the ludicrous and false assertion that contact with South African sportsmen and artists breaks down barriers and will finally bring down *apartheid*. These are the statements of ruthless, greedy men, who will stop at nothing to make money. The truth is that the Nats consider black artists and sportsmen to be exactly what the Nazis considered Jesse Owens, the black American star athlete to be: subhuman!

Educational Institutions

Each educational institution must reserve a certain number of places for the victims of *apartheid*. These must be free and advertised as a contribution to the gallant struggle the oppressed people of South Africa are waging against the vicious *apartheid* system.

The fact of *apartheid* must be kept alive on all campuses by programs that deal with South Africa, which should include seminars, courses, and lectures. All *apartheid* propaganda should be banned. However, the supporters and defenders of *apartheid* should be invited to debate their points with representatives of the liberation movement so that the students can hear "both sides" of the story and have an opportunity to field their questions. All this should be part of a carefully prepared program and not just a whim. The aim should be to enlighten the students, who tomorrow must bear their parents' sins.

Withdraw funds from banks that give loans to South Africa while arrogantly defending the indefensible.

Sell all stock in corporations that, by their involvement in South African business, are guilty of criminal acts against the black people of South Africa.

Initiate programs aimed at boycotting all South African products.

Churches

If corporations and banks refuse to cut their economic ties with the evil *apartheid* regime, the churches must, without any hesitation, unilaterally sever all connections with these institutions. By virtue of their being the national conscience and moral yardstick, it is impossible for churches to be involved with institutions that are the mainstay of the world's most evil regime since the days of Hitler. Churches, if they are what they claim to be, must, by their actions, always and unequivocally, be on the side of the poor, the suffering, the oppressed, the victims of injustice. If they are what they claim to be, then it must logically follow that they cannot, even for one moment, consciously participate in perpetuating evil either by their silence, or by their excuses, or by accepting blood money—which is what investments in, and loans to, South Africa yield.

The leadership in the Western Church must vociferously expose the lies of the multinational corporations and banks when they claim that they are in South Africa for the benefit of the blacks.

The leadership of the Western Church must declare its unconditional support for the liberation movement in South Africa, both in word and in deed. That support must be heard in sermons, read in Church publications and seen in the Church programs initiated for the express purpose of destroying *apartheid*. The Church's commitment to the destruction of the horrendous *apartheid* ideology and practice must be total, unconditional, and nonnegotiable. And this commitment must clearly and boldly manifest itself, even if and when those who run the multinational corporations take their pocketbooks and leave the church in disgust.

We are told that for the past thirty years, our brothers and sisters in the Western churches have been constantly reminded by their leaders to pray for the victims of *apartheid*. We are grateful for this concern. However, we, the victims of *apartheid,* would be failing in our duty if we did not point out to our Western Christian brothers and sisters that the time has now come for them to pray for themselves rather than for us. They must do so in order that they may muster the strength and the courage to practice what they preach, and above all, to put into practice what the Gospel calls for. They need to pray for themselves so that their faith may shift from the "Almighty Dollar"[1] to Almighty God, where it rightly belongs. Once their faith finds its proper home it will be easy for them to sell their stocks in corporations that invest in *apartheid* and reap blood money for them. It will go without saying that, as Christians, they cannot keep their money in banks that use it to finance *apartheid,* which is a total denial of all that Christianity stands for. These actions may cause some inconvenience and even some pain, but then that is what Christianity in practice is all about. It is the opposite of the

Christianity of Convenience, so prevalent in the West today. It must be emphasized that unless the Church is actively involved in the struggle for human dignity as it is expressed in social, economic, and political justice here and now, it is not a Christian Church. It can only be called a cultural and class church and, therefore, irrelevant.

These steps are the very least that the victims of *apartheid* expect from the international community. It must be stressed that many countries in the Third World as well as the Socialist countries are already making their positive contributions toward the destruction of the South African version of Naziism, which is *apartheid*. The efforts of these nations are greatly weakened by the massive economic, political, diplomatic, military, and moral support that most of the Western nations give to the evil *apartheid* regime. It must be emphasized that Western support for the Nats will in no way alter the outcome of the just struggle against *apartheid*. All that this support does is delay the final victory. It can never prevent it. It is too late for that. Conversely, Western support for the liberation struggle will not in and of itself destroy *apartheid*. What it will do is remove the bastions of *apartheid* and, therefore, make it easier and quicker for the foes of *apartheid* to destroy it completely.

There are many voices today that claim that the Jews did not let the world know the true situation in Germany until it was too late. There are voices today that are accusing the Jewish leadership in Argentina for not speaking out against alleged anti-Semitism in that country. We do not wish these accusations to be leveled against us. We also want to make it difficult for the West to claim ignorance when the blacks take over in South Africa and ask the West to account for its support for *apartheid*.

As Western leaders continue to turn a deaf ear and a blind eye to the cries of the oppressed in South Africa, we must remind them that the blacks are the future rulers of their own country. Nothing can alter that fact. In spite of the Nats' being the strongest military power on the continent of

211

Africa; despite their having the most advanced war planes, tanks, warships, and guns—thanks to the corporations in Britain, Canada, France, West Germany, and the United States, their chief suppliers, the Nats cannot keep the blacks under subjugation forever. This is not because the blacks have better "Communist weapons." It is because the South African soldiers who must fight for the Nats have a bad conscience, like most of white South Africa. In order to win a war, those who are fighting must be totally convinced that their cause is just. There lies the invincible strength. And this is the strength that the blacks have. If the blacks did not have this strength, white South Africa would be sleeping peacefully every night. As it is, whites in South Africa have no peace of mind because, despite all the brainwashing the Nats have done and despite all the efforts to justify the unjustifiable, *apartheid* remains a malignant tumor on the conscience of white South Africa. Malignant tumors are deadly. That is why white South Africa will lose in the not-too-distant future.

Unfortunately for white South Africans, they have been led to believe that they have two main enemies; the blacks and the Communists. In reality, white South Africans do have two deadly enemies: their present Western backers and themselves.

Though the Nazis were militarily defeated in 1945, their dream did not die with their defeat. They merely found a new home in the South Africa of the Nats, which came into being in 1948. This is no wild speculation. In their speeches, the Nats have said it eloquently. In their laws, they have spelled it out unambiguously. In their actions, they have demonstrated it superbly. *Apartheid* is the South African version of Naziism.

In the eyes of the *apartheid* regime and its Western backers, all those who are working for the overthrow of *apartheid* are "radicals," "lovers of violence," "terrorists," and "pawns of Communism." All this is false, and they know it. The Nats are on a disaster course, just as the Nazis were. We speak out and act not out of hatred and a desire for revenge against white South Africans. We do so out of concern for them and their children and also because of our total commitment to peace.

However, we know too well that there can never be peace without justice. Injustice breeds destruction. That is why we must warn white South Africans of the wrath to come.

May they never say: "We did not know."

Notes

Chapter 1

1. Quoted in Hans Kohn. *The Mind of Germany.* New York: Charles Scribner's Sons, 1960, p. 81.

2. Johann Gottlieb Fichte. *Reden an die Deutsche Nation.* Leipzig: Philip Reclam, 1808, pp. 240–248.

3. Christian Lassen. *Indische Altertumskunde.* Bonn: Moller, 1851, pp. 22–24.

4. Arthur de Gobineau. *Essays on the Inequality of the Human Races.* London: Heinemann, 1915, pp. 34–39.

5. Houston Stewart Chamberlain. *Foundations of the 19th Century.* Barnes and Noble, 1968, pp. 14–23.

6. Quoted in H. G. Adler. *The Jews in Germany.* Notre Dame: University of Notre Dame Press, 1969, p. 41.

7. Paul de Legarde. *Mitteilungen, Vol. II* Goettingen: Vanderbilt, 1887, pp. 345–380.

8. Wilhlem Marr. *Der Sieg des Judentums ueber das Germanentums.* Berlin: Union, 1873, pp. 33–35.

9. Adolf Stoecker. "What We Demand of Modern Jewry," *Messing.* Berlin. Vol. II, Nr. 4, pp. 278–287.

10. Heinrich von Treitschke. "Unsere Aussichten." in J. Boehlich (ed.) *Der Berliner Antisemitismusstreit.* Heft 3, Berlin, 1880, p. 113.

11. J. Reventlow. *Judas Kampf und Niederlage in Deutschland.* Berlin: Union, 1902, pp. 342–344.

12. Lucy S. Dawidowicz. *The War Against the Jews 1933–1945.* New York: Holt, Reinhart and Winston, 1975, p. 43.

13. Adolf Hitler. *Mein Kampf.* Muenchen: Frz. Eher Nachf. G.M.B.H., 1972, p. 184.

14. Alfred Rosenberg (Hrsg) *Das Parteiprogramm. Wesen, Grudsaetze und Ziele der NSAP.* 21. Aufl., Muenchen, 1941, pp. 15ff.

15. Lucy Dawidowicz, op. cit. p. 60.

16. *Ibid.* pp. 60–61.

17. E. Schaefer. "Die Judenfrage und Wir," in *Studienhefte zur Judenfrage.* hrg. v. Gerhard Jasper. Heft I. Dresden, 1925, p. 12.

18. H. Kirchner. *Ibid.* p. 7.

19. Ino Arndt. *Die Judenfrage im Licht der Evangelischen Sonntagsblaet-*

ter von 1918–33. Phil. Diss. (unveroefeffentlicht) Tuebingen, 1960, p. 220.

20. Rolf Italiaander, *Die Neuen Maenner Afrikas.* Econ-Verlag, Duesseldorf 1960, p. 175.

21. Walther Hofer, *Dr Nationalozialismus. Dokumente 1933-1945.* Fischer Taschenbuch Verlag. Frankfurt am Main, 1977, p. 28.

22. Adolf Hitler, op. cit. p. 198.

23. Hans Guenther, *The Racial Elements of European History,* Methuen & Co., London, 1927, pp. 191-192.

24. RGBI, No. 100, 1935, p. 1146.

25. Rosenberg, op. cit. p.6.

26. H.B. Fantham & A. Porter, "Notes on Some Cases of Racial Admixture in South Africa." S.A. Journal of Science, Vol. 24, pp. 476-485, 1927.

27. A speech in Parliament. See *Hansard,* 1940, Vol. 40, col.2070.

28. The Afrikaner's Programme of Principles was drawn up in June 1941 and compares well with the Nazis' "Programme" referred to above.

29. G. Eloff, *Rasse en Rassensermenging: Die Boerevolk gesian van die Rasseleer,* Bloemfontein: Nasionale Pes. 1942, p. 14.

30. G. Cronje, *Tuisfe vir die Nageslag,* Stellenbosch: Nasionale, 1945, p. 11

31. See ProVeritate Supplement, July, 1971, p.4. The statement was made in 1952.

32. *Ibid.* p.3.

33. *Ibid.*

34. S.W. Pienaar (ed). *Glo in U Volk: D.F. Malan as Redenaar, 1908-1954,* Cape Town: Tafelberg Uitgewers Beperk, 1964. pp. 235-236.

35. Cf. *Journal of Theology for Southern Africa, Vol. 19,* June 1977, p.25

36. *Ibid.* p.26.

37. The Nazi Party Programme. See Note 21 above. pp. 28-32.

38. *Suedafrica Bericht,* 26 September 1940; AA-Bonn Pol. xf. 240626.

39. *Die Transvaler,* October 4, 1937.

40. *Ibid.* October 7, 1941.

41. *Voelkische Beobachter,* April 14, 1928.

42. *The Star,* October 31 1941. See Hepple, pp.213-215.

43. *Ibid.*

44. N'dumbe A. Kum'a, *Relations Between Nazi Germany and South Africa,* UN Notes and Documents. No.12/76 p.16.

45. B. Schoeman, *"The Future of Africanerdom"* in *Die Transvaler,* 6 November, 1940.

46. D.F. Malen, *Die Nationale Party,* Stellenbosch: TUB, 1941, p.6.

47. William Vatcher, jr., *White Laager,* New York, Praeger, 1965, p.66.

48. Cf. The Cape Times 1940. See Brian Bunting. *The Rise of the South African* Reich. Middlesex: Penguin Books, 1964.

49. D.F. Malan, p.6.

Chapter 2

1. A. Kum'a N'dumbe, p. 16.

2. Alfred Rosenberg, *Partei der Freiheit,* "Sonderausgabe des Deutschen Nachrichtenburos GMBH" 2Jg. Berlin, 1935, p.6.

3. Hans Guenther, *The Racial Elements of European History,* Methuen and Co.: London, 1927, pp. 191-·92.

4. Josef Wulf, Die *Nuernberger Gesetze,* Berlin: Arani, 1948, P.6

5. Philip Tobias, *The Meaning of Race,* Johannesburg: South African Institute of Race Relations, 1972, p.29.

6. *Reichsgesetzblatt,* Nr. 100, 1935, p. 1146.

7. Quoted in Walter Hofer, p.285.

8. *RGBI* N. 100, 1935, p. 1146.

9. *Wiener Library Bulletin,* XVI/3 (July 1962), pp. 52-fi3.

10. *GCGR* Nr. 33 (Note III/33, Rol 128, Frame 2654114).

11. Leon Poliakov/Josef Wulf, *Das Dritte Reich und seine Diener,* Berlin: Arani, 1956, p. 225f.

12. *RGBI,* Teil I, 15 September 1935, p. 1146.

13. *Ibid.*

14. Rosenberg, p. 6.

15. "Programme of Principles of the Nationalist Party." See Gwendolen Carter, *The Politics of Inequality,* New York: Octagon Books, New York, 1977, p. 467.

16. House of Assembly Debates (Hansard) Vol. 69, Col. 9065–9071.

17. *Ibid.*

18. D.F. Malan, *Apartheid. South Africa's Answer to a Major Problem.* State Information Office, Pretoria, 1954, p.6.

19. *Ibid.*

20. The *Star,* 18 January, 1961. Quoted by Phillip Tobias, *"The Meaning of Race,"* p.32.

21. The *Star,* 24 November, 1959, in Phillip Tobias, p. 33.

22. Muriel Horrell, *Laws Affecting Race Relations in South Africa, 1948-·976,* Institute of Race Relations, Johannesburg, 1978, pp. 373–374.

23. Leo Marquard, *The Peoples and Policies of South Africa,* Oxford University Press, Cape Town, London, New York, 1960, p. 69.

24. Phillip Tobias, p. 33.

25. Hansard, 1950, Vol.70, Col. 9.

26. *Ibid.*

27. G. Eloff, *Rasse en Rassevermenging: Die Boerevolk gesien,* van die Rasseleer, Bloemfontein: Nasionale, 1942, p. 20.

28. Leo Marquard, p. 68.

29. Gwendolen Carter, *The Politics of Inequality: South Africa Since 1948,* New York: Octagon Books, 1977, p. 81.

30. In 1910, the Union of South Africa was formed. It comprised the Cape Province, Natal, the Orange Free State, and the Transvaal. Only in the Cape Province did Africans have the right to vote. In 1936 this right was abolished by the Hertzog government.

31. *Hansard,* Vol. 16, Col. 6215–16, 1959.

32. Gwendolen Carter, p. 469.

33. *Die Transvaler,* November 7, 1947, in W.H. Vatcher, Jr., p. 156.

34. Supra, footnote 27 in chapter 1.

35. *Hansard,* E.G. Jansen (Minister of Native Affairs), Vol. 12, 1950, Col. 4703.

36. *Laws Affecting Race Relations in South Africa,* p. 40.

37. *Hansard,* H.F. Verwoerd, Vol. 14, 1964, Col. 68.

38. *Ibid.*

39. Leslie Rubin, *Apartheid in Practice.* UN Publication, New York, 1971, p.5.

40. *RGBI Teil I,* April 25, 1933, S. 225.

41. Non-Aryan children who either had one German grandparent or whose parents had fought in the First World War, were exempted from this law.

42. *Erlass des Reichsministers fuer Erziehung und Unterricht ueber d. Schulbesuch juedisher Kinder v. 15.* November 1938 (*Amtsblatt,* Seite 520).

43. Raul Hilberg, p. 112.

44. Hansard, Vol. 83, Sept. 1953, Col. 3575–4129.

45. Hansard, Vol. 24, May 1959, Col. 2304–2927.

46. Muriel Horrell, p. 326.

47. Daniel Malan, p. 6.

48. Edgar Brookes, p. 51.

49. *RGBI* Teil I, April 7, 1933, p. 175ff.

50. Joachim Gauger (ed.), *Chronic der Kirchenwirren;* I. Teil (Gotthard Briefe, 138 bis 145. Brief), Elberfeld, 1934. p.II.

51. Dieter Schwarz, *Die Grosse Luege des politischen Katholizismus, (Artikelreihe im Schwarzen Korps)* Berlin, 1938, p.40.

52. Wilhelm Corsten, *Koelner Aktenstuecke,* Koeln, 1949, p. 63.

53. *Bischoefliches Ordianariat. Dokumente.* Berlin, 1948, p.92f.

54. The Group Areas Act, No. 41 of 1950 divided all residential areas in urban areas into racial zones. The Native Laws Amendment Act of 1952 requires that blacks must have permits to enter an urban area. These measures practically ruled out mixed services except in a few exceptional cases. There was, therefore, a little or no need to enforce the "Church Clause."

55. Statement by Christian Council, April, 1957.

56. *Die Transvaler,* February 27, 1957, p.3.

57. Cf. *Pseudo Gospels in South Africa,* A report published in Johannesburg, 1968, p. 34.

58. Margaret Bellinger, *From Union to Apartheid,* p.264.

59. Prime Minister, John Vorster. Speech reported in the *Cape Times,* March 3, 1971, p.4.

60. *RGBI* Teil I, September 9, 1933, p. 713.

61. *Voelkische Beobachter,* 51 Nr. 318 Vol. 14, Nov. 1938 P. I Col. 4.

62. Order of the President of the *Reichkulturkamer,* Nov. 12, 1938.

63. Decree of the Minister of Transport, Dec. 30, 1939 Document NG-3995.

64. Gestapo Directive, L-15 October 24, 1941.

65. *Ibid.*

66. These measures are sometimes known as "petty apartheid," although contravention can have serious consequences. In some areas of South Africa, particularly in the large cities that are frequented by foreigners, some of these measures have been modified—not by the government directly, but by municipalities. The aim is to lessen international criticism of *apartheid.* In most cases the government has gone along with the changes. But these are privileges. The laws remain on the Statute Book and can be imposed whenever the government decides to do so.

67. Edgar Brookes, p. 89.

68. The Gestapo directive of October 24, 1941, cited by Raul Hilberg, p. 5.

69. *RGBI* Teil l, July 6, 1938, p. 823.

70. *RGBI* Teil I, July 25, 1938, p. 969.

71. Raul Hilberg. p.84.

72. Hansard, 1956, Vol. 82, Col. 2355–2401.

73. Muriel Horrell, p. 226.

74 Nursing Act, No. 69 of 1957. Hansard Vol. 37, Col. 3547.

75. Muriel Horrell, p. 372ff.

76. *RGBI* Teil I, Oct. 3, 1941, p. 887, and Oct. 31, 1941, p. 681.

77. *RGBI* Teil I, Oct. 3, 1941, p. 675.

78. *Ibid.*

79. Raul Hilberg. p. 100.

80. Hansard, 1953, Vol. 82, Col. 870. In 1979 the Minister of Labour gave permission for some black trade unions to be registered. This is a privilege which can be revoked at the minister's pleasure. The registered trade unions are a minority.

81. A. De Kock, Industrial Laws of South Africa, Cape Town: Juta, 1965, 2nd Ed., p. 506.

82. Section I (i) of the Industrial Acts.

83. Bantu Laws Amendment Act, 1970.

84. Hansard, 1953, Vol. 82, Col. 1622.

85. Hansard, 1959, Vol. 12, Col. 4252.

86. *RGBI* Teil I, December 3, 1938, p. 1709.

87. *RGBI* Teil I, January 1, 1939, p. 837.

88. *RGBI* Teil I, December 31, 1938, p. 2017.

89. Hansard, 1950, Vol. 73, Col. 7446.

90. Hansard, 1952, Vol. 10, Cols. 3449, 3522, 3524.

91. Hansard, 1954, Vol. 9, Col. 3204.

92. Bruno Blau, *Das Ausnahmerecht fuer d. Juden in d. Europaischen Laendern,* 1933–1945. New York, 1952, pp. 15–29.

94. Gwendolen Carter, p. 81.

95. Population Registration and Identity Documents Amendment Act, No. 36 of 1973.

96. Walther Hofer, *Nationalsozialismus Dokumente 1933–1945.* Fischer Taschenbuch Verlag, Frankfurt/Main, 1957, p. 271.

97. Phillip Tobias, pp. 31–32.

98. *RGBI* Teil I, Nr. 1, 2 and 4, July 23, 1938, p. 922.

99. Muriel Horrell, pp. 174–175.

100. Leo Marquard, p. 122.

101. Muriel Horrell, et al., *A Survey of Race Relations in South Africa.* Johannesburg: South African Institute of Race Relations, 1976, p. 99. See also Leslie Rubin, pp. 16–17; also Julian R. Friedman, "Basic Facts on the Republic of South Africa and the Policy of *Apartheid,*" *Notes and Documents,* No. 8/77, New York: United Nations, April, 1977, pp. 44–47.

102. Instructions from the *Reichspolizei,* Sept. 1, 1939. See Bruno blau, p. 75.

103. *RGBL* Teil I, Nr. 2 (b), September, 1939, p. 547.

104. Raul Hilberg, p. 145.

105. *Ibid.*, p. 149.

106. *Ibid.*, p. 145.

107. Muriel Horrell. p. 172ff.

108. *Ibid.*

109. John Dugard, *Human Rights and the South African Legal Order.* Princeton: Princeton University Press, 1978, p. 78.

110. RGBI X S.293, Mai 1933; RGBI. I S. 479 Juli 1933; RGBI.1933 Nov. S.797ff.

111. Suppression of Communism Act, No. 44 of 1950, as amended, section 1. See also Government Notice 2017, 18 September 1953. Also Prisons Act, No. 8, of 1959. Also Riotous Assemblies Act, No. 17 1956, section 3. Also General Law Amendment Act, No. 93 of 1962, section 44. Also Publications and Entertainment Act, No. 26 of 1963 section 8(1) or section 3 of Act, No. 85 of 1969.

112. See Richard Lapchick, *The Politics of Race and International Sport: A Comparison of South Africa and Nazi Germany.* An address prepared for the World Conference for Action against Apartheid, Lagos, Nigeria, 22-26 August 1977. Available at the United Nations' Centre Against Apartheid.

113. *Ibid.* p. 1

114. *Ibid.* pp. 6-7.

115. *Ibid.* p. 1.

116. Cf. Walther Hofer. pp. 289-290.

117. Suppression of Communism Act, No. 44 of 1950 as Amended. Also Terrorism Act, No. 83 of 1967.

118. RGBI, I, 1097. July 4, 1939.

119. Urban Bantu Councils Act, No. 79 of 1961 and Community Councils Act, No. 125, of 1977.

120. Cf. Raul Hilberg, p.45.

121. Assembly Hansard 3 of 1962, Col. 850 and Hansard 14 of 1962 col. 4769-71.

Chapter 3

1. Martin Broszat, *Der Staat Hitlers. Band 9. Muenchen: Deutsche Taschenbuch Verlag,* 1969, p. 285.

2. *Das Parteiprogram,* Punkt 24.

3. Alfred Rosenberg (ed.), *Das Parteiprogramm. Wesen, Grundsaetze und Ziele der NSDAP, 21 Aufl.,* Muenchen: Parteidrueckerei, 1941, S. 15ff.

4. *Ibid.*

5. Martin Broszat, p. 286.

6. Friedrich Zipfel. *Kirchenkampf in Deutschland 1933–45. Statistiken fuer Berlin.* Berlin, Walter de Gruyter, 1965, pp. 18ff.

7. Martin Broszat, p. 100.

8. *RGBI I,* p. 293. Mai 1933.

9. *RGBI I,* Nr. 25 p. 141. Maerz 1933.

10. Walter Hofer: *Der Nationalsozialismus. Dokumente 1933–1945,* p. 46.

11. *Voelkischer Beobachter (Sueddeutsche Ausgabe), 46 Vol.* Nr. 88, March 29, 1933, p. l cols. 4–6.

12. Wilhelm Niemoellers Bielefelder Archiv. Akte B 2'301.

13. *RGBI I,* April, 1933, p. 175.

14. Martin Broszat. p. 286.

15. Hans Buchheim. *Glaubenskrise im Dritten Reich.* Stuttgart: Gruenewald, 1953, p. 89f.

16. Martin Broszat. p. 287.

17. The *Deutsche Christen* produced a ten-point program that, among other things called for a Reichs Church, one that would be a Church for Aryans only. Wilhelm Niemoeller claims that Joachim Hossenfelder was the author of the program. See Wilhelm Niemoeller: Ist die Judenfrage Bewaeltigt Dortmund, Mai, 1968, p. 7.

18. *Stenographic Report of the Deliberations of the German Reichstag, Vol. 45.* Session of 23rd March, 1933. Humbolt University Library.

19. Friedrich Zipfel. *Kirchenkampf in Deutschland 1933–45,* p. 33.

20. *Ibid.* p. 34. See also Broszat, p. 287.

21. *Ibid.*

22. Reprinted in *Kirchliches Jahrbuch fuer die Evangelische Kirche in Deutschland 1933–44,* ed. J. Beckmann, Guetersloh, 1948, p. 13.

23. *RGBI I,* p. 471, The Constitution provided for the election of church officers including the Reichs bishop.

24. For collaboration between the Nazis and the Deutsche Christen, see: Klaus Scholder, *Die Kirchen und das Dritte Reich,* p. 560ff. Also Friedrich Zipfel, *Kirchen Kampf in Deutschland 1933 – 45,* p. 30ff.

25. In October 1933, there were thirty-five "non-Aryan" Pastors in the German Protestant Church. *(Deutsches Pfarrerblatt.* Okt. 1933, p. 60ff.) The church in Saxony applied the Aryan paragraph on Sept. 16, 1933 (Kirchl. ges. und VO. Bl. Nr. 2 v. 22.9. 1933). Some provincial churches resisted the application of this measure; see Heinrich Hermelink, *Kirche im Kampf.* Tuebingen, Stuttgart, 1950, p. 52.

26. Friedrich Zipfel, p. 40.

27. Although the opponents of the *Deutsche Christen* stood for a free Church, they at the same time emphasized that the Church had to remain unconditionally loyal to the state. See "Aufruf und Richtlinie" in *Junge Kirche* 1, 1933, p. 43f.

28. Documentation: *Ein NS-Funktionaer zum Niemoeller-Prozess. Vierteljahrhefte fuer Zeitgeschichte,* 4. Jg. 1956, S. 313.

29. Joachim Gauger (ed.), *Chronik der Kirchenwirren Teil 1,* Elberfeld, 1934, p. 111.

30. Joachim Gauger, *Die Kirchliche Aufgaben des Notbundes,* Elberfeld, 1933, p. 103.

31. Dietrich Schmidt, *Die Bekentnisse des Jahres 1933,* Goettingen, 1934, p. 97.

32. Dietrich Schmidt, p. 97f.

33. Wilhelm Niemoeller, *Die Evangelische Kirche im 3. Reich,* Bielefeld, 1956, p. 112.

34. Dietrich Bonhoeffer, *Gesammelte Schriften Bd. 1 Oekumene,* Briefe, Aufsaetze, Dokumente, 1928–42, Hrsg. Eberhard Bethge. Chr. Kaiser Verlag Muenchen, 1965, S. 37.

35. Dietrich Bonhoeffer, *Gesammelte Schriften Bd. II 1933–34,* Hrsg. E. Bethge, Muenchen, S. 44ff.

36. *Ibid.* S. 50.
37. *Ibid.* S. 48.
38. *Ibid.* S. 126.
39. *Ibid.* S. 128.
40. Dietrich Bonhoeffer, *Gesammelte Schriften,* p. 132.
41. *Ibid.* pp. 86–87.
42. Eberhard Bethge, *Dietrich Bonhoeffer, Man of Vision; Man of Courage,* Harper and Row, Publishers, New York, 1970, p. 254.
43. *Jungekirche. Heft 1 Jahrgang* 1933, S. 5.
44. The acceptance of one constitution for a unified Reich Church, by all twenty-eight provincial churches was seen by the Nazis and Church leaders as a major victory. The election of Ludwig Mueller as Reichs Bishop was a second victory. See Martin Broszat, p. 286; also Walther Hofer, p. 120.
45. W. Niemoeller, (note 1–19) pp. 63–64.
46. Joachim Beckmann, (Hrsg) *Kirchliches Jahrbuch fuer die Ev. Kirche in Deutschland,* Guetersloh, 1948, S. 32f.
47. See Eberhard Bethge, *Dietrich Bonhoeffer,* p. 29.
48. *Ibid.* The final paragraph of the six-point declaration reads thus: The Confessional Synod of the German Protestant Church declares that the acceptance of these truths and the rejection of false teachings forms the indispensable theological foundation of the German Protestant Church as the union of Confessing Churches. Hofer. pp. 143–144.
49. Heinrich Zipfel, p. 50.
50. *Kirchliches Jahrbuch,* p. 70.
51. *Gesetzblatt der Deutsche Evangelische Kirche* v. 10.8.34.
52. Joachim Gauger, *Chronik der Kirchenwirren,* 2. Teil S. 283–285.
53. Friedrich Zipfel, *Kirchenkampf,* p. 50.
54. *Ibid.*
55. John S. Conway, *The Nazi Persecution of the Churches, 1933–1945,* p. 100.
56. *Ibid.*
57. Wilhelm Niemoeller, *Die Zweite Bekenntnissynode der Deutschen Evangelischen Kirche zu Dahlem,* Goettingen, 1958.
58. *Ibid.*
59. Zipfel, p. 52.
60. *Ibid.*
61. Broszat, p. 291.
62. Zipfel, p. 53.
63. Joachim Beckmann, S. 83.
64. Zipfel, p. 53.
65. *Ibid.*
66. *Junge Kirche* 2. Teil, Jahrang, 1934, S. 334.
67. *Bundesarchiv Schumacher Akten* (BA, Sch) Berlin, Akte 244/1/163.
68. *Kirchliches Jahrbuch,* (Ch. II/11), p. 94.
69. *RGBI* Teil I. 1935, S. 1029 and also *Gesetzblatt der Deutschen Evangelischen Kirche,* (GB1DEK, 1935, p. 83.
70. *RGBI,* 1935, Teil I p. 1178 and also GB1DEK, 1935, p. 99.
71. *Kirchliches Jahrbuch,* (Note III/19), p. 104.
72. Friedrich Zipfel, p. 87. See also Broszat, p. 291.
73. For a chronological list of measures taken against the Jews (non-

Aryans) see: Bruno Blau, *Das Ausnahmerecht fuer die Juden in den Europaeischen Laendern,* 1933–1945, I Teil, New York, 1952.

74. Quoted from a copy, under the title *Judenfrage,* in Wilhelm Niemoeller's Bielefelder Archive.

75. From the letter of Martin Albertz (the superintendent and adviser) in Wilhelm Niemoellers Bielefelder Archive.

76. See Eberhard Bethge, p. 354.

77. *Ibid.* p. 356.

78. H. Cornelius (Hrsg), J.A. *Seuferts Archiv fuer Entscheidungen der obersten Gerichte in den deutschen Staaten:* 91 *Band (Der dritten Folge* 36. *Band),* Muenchen/Berlin, 1937, S. 65ff. See also Bruno Blau.

79. Wilhelm Niemoeller, *Kampf und Zeugnis,* Bielefeld: Vandenhoeck, 1948, p. 289.

80. John S. Conway, p. 137.

81. Wilhelm Niemoeller, *Ist die Judenfrage Beweltigt?* p. 15.

82. *Ibid.*

83. *Ibid.*

84. Eberhard Bethge, p. 406.

85. Eberhard Bethge, pp. 406–407.

86. Niemoeller (Note 1/19), p. 282.

87. Niemoeller (Note 1/19), p. 293.

88. John S. Conway, p. 137.

89. Wilhelm Niemoeller, *Die Vierte Bekenntnissynode der Deutschen Evangelischen Kirche zu Bad Oeynhausen,* Goettingen, 1960, S. 138ff.

90. Bethge, p. 427.

91. Wilhelm Niemoeller, *Dir Bekennende Kirche sagt Hitler die Wahrheit,* 1954. See also J. Beckmann, *Kirchliches Jahrbuch,* 1948, pp. 130ff.

92. 49th Occasional Letter, exclusively for members of Confessional congregations, published by the Rhineland Evangelical Confessional Synod, 2.3.1936, p. 23.

93. Bethge, p. 442.

94. *Ibid.,* p. 443.

95. Wilhelm Niemoeller, (see 108 above) p. 24.

96. Heinz Brunotte, *Die Kirchenmitgliederschaft der nichtarischen Christen im Kirchenkampf,* Hannover: Ev. Pressedienst, p. 153.

97. Alfred Rosenberg was one of the most anti-Christian and anti-Church in the NS leadership. A close confidant of Hitler, he held the important position of the Fuehrer's Delegate for the Entire Spiritual and Philosophical Education and Supervision of the Nazi Party. He wrote *The Myth of the Twentieth Century,* in which he completely dismissed Christianity.

98. Reprinted in John S. Conway, p. 204.

99. *Ibid.*

100. *Ibid.,* p. 205.

101. On February 15, 1937, Hitler issued a decree in which he admitted that measures to unite the Church had been unsuccessful. The decree empowered the Church Minister to establish a General Synod *(RGBI Jg.,* 1937 Teil I, Nr. 20, S. 203).

102. Hofer, p. 124.

103. Martin Niemoeller, *Of Guilt and Hope,* New York: 1946, p. 73.

104. John S. Conway, p. 80.

105. A copy of the oath as well as Dr. Werner's comments and also protests from several Provincial Churches is found in, *Kirchliches Jahrbuch* (Note II/II), p. 237ff. See also *Kirche im Kampf* (Note II/15),p. 449.

106. *Ibid.*

107. W. Niemoeller, *Kampf und Zeugnis,* p. 437.

108. Bethge, p. 505.

109. See Karl Barth, *Zum Kirchenkampf, Theologische Existenz Heute,* Nr. 49, pp. 79–83.

110. Dietrich Bonhoeffer, *Gesammelte Schriften,* Bd. II, p. 314.

111. *Rundschreiben,* Nr. 8738, III/16—Es. 3310/0/57, Abgedr,: *Kirchliches Jahrbuch* (Anm. II/11), S. 262.

112. Bruno Blau, *Das Ausnahmerecht Fuer die Juden in den Europaieschen Laendern, 1933–1945,* New York: William Kober, 1952.

113. Bethge, p. 507.

114. Bruno Blau, p. 33.

115. L. Dawidowicz, p. 134.

116. *Ibid.,* p. 135.

117. *Ibid.,* p. 135.

118. *Voelkischer Beobachter (Muenchener Ausgabe)* 51 Jg., Nr. 316.

119. Bruno Blau, pp. 51–53.

120. *Kirchliches Jahrbuch,* p. 265.

121. *Kirchliches Jahrbuch,* p. 265f.

122. Wilhelm Niemoeller, *Die Evangelische Kirche im Dritten Reich,* Bielefeld: Vandenhoeck, 1956, p. 165.

123. Bruno Blau, pp. 15–51.

124. Bethge, p. 512.

125. Theodor Dipper, *ibid.*

126. See: *Kampf Gegen Anti-Semitismus, St. Katharine Bote,* Frankfurt, Nr. 4, 2/1958, p. 8.

127. Dipper, p. 266.

128. *Ibid.,* p. 267.

129. Copy in Wilhelm Niemoeller's *Bielefelder Archives,* AKTE BK/34.

130. W. Jannasch, *Deutsche Kirchendokument,* Zuerich, 1946, p. 30.

131. Heinrich Grueber, *Dona nobis pacem,* Berlin: Union, 1958, p. 104.

132. In a sermon dated November 11, 1958. Printed in *Gemeindegruss, Karserslautern,* 1.2.59. p. 2. Copy in Bielefelder Archiv.

133. See: *"Im Kampf gegen den Antisemitismus." Erlebnis im Dritten Reich* in *St. Katharinen-Bote,* Frankfurt, Main 1.5.53. Copy in Bielefelder Archiv.

134. Heinrich Grueber, *An der Stechbahn. Erlebnisse und Berichte aus dem Buro Grueber in den Jahren der Verfolgung,* Berlin, undated, at Humbolt University Library. See also Friedrich Zipfel, p. 218ff, Henry Brunotte, p. 155f.

135. Heinz Brunotte, p. 156.

136. Kurt Meier, *Kirche und Judentum,* Berlin: Union, 1934, p. 114.

137. Friedrich Zipfel, p. 218ff.

138. Heinz Brunotte, p. 154.

139. *Ibid.,* p. 162.

140. *Ibid.*

141. *RGBI* Teil I Nr. 100, September 5, 1941, S. 547.

142. *Kirchen Kanzelei, III Akte* 1502/41, Humbolt University.

143. Heinz Brunotte, p. 165.

144. Wilhelm Niemoeller, p. 18.

145. Karl Kupisch, *Die Deutschen Landeskirchen im 19 und 20, Jahrhundert*, S. R. 10 Goettingen: Vandenhoeck, 1966.

146. The first Province to apply this measure was Schleswig-Holstein, which was under the jurisdiction of Bishop Marahrens. On January 1, 1942, his office advised all the provinces to take note of the decision of December 22, 1941. See W. Niemoeller, *Ist die Judenfrage Bewaeltigt?* p. 19.

147. Bethge, p. 593.

148. Quoted in Heinrich Hermelink (ed.), *Kirch im Kampf. Dokumente des Widerstandes und des Aufbaus in der Evangelischen Kirche Deutschlands von, 1933–1945,* Tuebingen Stuttgart: Bertelsmann, 1950, p. 654.

149. From Wilhelm Niemoeller's Bielefelder Archives. Copy (Typewritten) in Hombolt University Library, V. 10518.

150. Otto Elias, p. 219.

151. Heinz Brunotte, p. 165.

152. *Ibid.,* p. 166.

153. Heinz Brunotte, p. 14.

154. Walter Hofer, p. 126.

155. Martin Broszat, p. 300.

156. Martin Niemoeller, *Of Guilt and Hope,* p. 73.

157. See J.S. Conway, p. 26.

158. Gordon C. Zahn, *German Catholics and Hitler's Wars: A Study in Social Control,* New York: Sheed and Ward, 1962, p. 193.

Chapter 4

1. Supra. p. 75.

2. Alfred Rosenberg published a book in 1930 titled *The Myth of the Twentieth Century,* which was a strong attack on Christianity. The book became compulsory reading for all National Socialist members. However, Hitler rejected the adoption of the views expressed by Rosenberg as part of the Nazi program. Rosenberg remained one of Hitler's chief advisers until the fall of the Nazis.

3. Supra, p. 80.

4. Walther Hofer, p. 122.

5. Supra, p. 10.

6. K. Kupisch, *Quellen zur Geschichte des Deutschen Protestantismus 1871–1945,* (Goettingen: Vandenhoeck, 1960), pp. 251–253.

7. Joachim Gauger (Hrsg) *Chronik der Kirchenwirren; I. Teil: Vom Aufkommen der* Deutschen Christen 1932 bis zur Bekenntnis-Reichssynode im Mai 1934. (Gotthard-Briefe, 138. bis 145.) Elberfeld 1934, S. lll.

8. Dieter Schwarz, *Die Grosse Luege des politischen Katholizismus,* (Artikelreihe im "Schwarzen Korps," Berlin 1938) S. 3,20, 31,40.

9. Wille und Macht, *Positives Christentum,* April 15, 1935. Quoted in Wilhelm Corsten, p. 63.

10. Dieter Schwarz, p. 20.

11. Walther Hofer, p. 136.

12. Point five of the Barmen Declaration, May 29–31, 1934. See Joachim Beckmann, p. 64f.

13. Otto L. Elias, p. 214.

14. Otto Elias, p. 213.

15. Wilhelm Niemoeller, *Die Evangelische Kirche im 3. Reich,* Bielefeld, 1956, p. 383.

16. Typewritten copy of manuscript in Niemoeller's *Bielefeld Archiv,* V/10518, Humbolt University Library, Berlin.

17. *Ibid.*

18. *Kirchliches Jahrbuch* II/II, p. 20.

19. *Voelkische Beobachter,* 19 July 1933, p. 4.

20. Henry Picker, *Hitler's Tischgespraeche im Fuehrerhauptquartier* 1941–1942, Hrsg. Gerhard Ritter, Bonn: Kaiser, 1951, pp. 344, 345, 348, 366.

21. Kirchliches Jahrbuch, p. 70.

22. Friedrich Zipfel, p. 93ff.

23. *Ibid.* For text of the ban, see Zipfel, pp. 361–362.

24. *RGBl* Teil I, Nr. 20, 1937, p. 203.

25. Martin Broszat, p. 292.

26. *Ibid.* See also Friedrich Zipfel p. 93.

27. See note 25 above.

28. Gutachten des Institut fuer Zeitgeschichte (Munchen; 1958) p. 364, in John S. Conway, p. 5.

29. Friedrich Zipfel. p. 98.

30. Dibelius was charged under a law passed in 1934: RGBI, I p. 1269, Clauses 1 and 2. For a report on the case, consult Zipfel. p. 99.

31. List of reports on Niemoeller's Trial is found in Zipfel, p. 101.

32. Zipfel, p. 102.

33. For an account of what prompted Niemoeller to volunteer from the concentration camp to serve in the navy and his objection to the conspiracy to kill Hitler, see Bethge, p. 569f.

34. Copy of letter in Wilhelm Niemoeller's Bielefeld Church struggle Archives. See also Th. Wurm, *Erinnerungen,* p. 181.

35. A copy of the letter is in *Landeskirchlichen Archiv* in Stuttgart, D. Wurm, D I, Bd. 225.

36. Copy of letter in Niemoeller's Bielefeld Church Archives.

37. Typewritten copy of speech by Martin Niemoeller, 9 pages, in *Bielefeld Archiv.*

38. Fritz Soehlmann, *Treysa,* 1945, p. 19.

39. Martin Niemoeller, *Reden 1945–1954,* Darmstadt, 1958, p. IIf.

40. Karl Barth, *How My Mind Has Changed,* Bonn: Wilhelm Meyer, 1948, p. 195.

41. Letter dated 28 September 1945, in Niemoeller's Bielefeld Archives.

42. Letter dated 5 October 1945, in Niemoeller's Bielefeld Archives.

43. W. A. Visser't Hooft, *Oekum. Rundschau,* 1970, Heft 4.

44. The official text of the meeting is together with other minutes dated October 25, 1945. Niemoeller's Bielefeld Archives. Hooft noted that although all the men of the *Kirchenleitung* were obviously very capable, the leadership role lay with Niemoeller and Asmussen (a former close associate of

Bonhoeffer). He also noted the obvious differences between the two groups.

45. All those present at the conference received a copy of the *Stuttgarter Schuldbekenntnis*. These copies were, however, not signed. A signed copy, which is thought to be at the World Council of Churches in Geneva, could not be traced by the author. For a copy see: Gordon Rupp, *Erinnerungen an Stuttgart,* Munich: Gruenewald, 1962, p. 64.

46. Kirchliches Amtsblatt f.d. Ev.-luth. Landeskirche Hannovers, Nr. 9, 17. II. 1945, p. 33; See also Hans Meieser, in: Amtsblatt f.d. Ev.-luth. Kirche in Bayern rechts d. Rheins, Nr. 5, 15.3.46., S. 29.

47. In a lecture on "The Intellectual and Religious Crisis of the Occident," the theologian Hans Thielicke maintained that the "guilt of a nation is always tied together with the guilt of others." Copy of the ten-page lecture is at Humbolt University Institute for Theology.

48. Martin Niemoeller, *Das Christusbekenntnis d. K. Bielfd.* '45, p. 15.

49. Niemoeller's letter to Barth, 20.ll.45. in Blfd. Archives.

50. Copy of letter dated July 8th, 1946 at Humbolt University Library, Institute for Theology. Original in Landeskirchen Archiv. Stuttgart.

51. Kirchliches Jahrbuch, 1945–1948, S. 51–55.

52. Letter dated July 25th, 1946, in Niemoeller's Bielefeld Archives.

53. Karl Barth, *Die Christliche Verkuendigung im Heutigen Europe*, Muenchen: Chr. Kaiser, 1946, S. 14.

Chapter 5

1. W. M. Eiselens, *"Christianity and the Religious Life of the Bantu,"* in *Western Civilization and the Natives of South Africa,* ed. T. Schabera (London: George Routledge & Sons, 1934), p. 65ff.

2. John de Gruchy, *The Church Struggle in South Africa,* Michigan: Wm. B. Eerdmanns, 1979, p. 69ff.

3. These churches owe their title to their British origins. They are integrated in principle and oppose *apartheid.* de Gruchy, p. 85f.

4. R. H. Sheperd and E. W. Grant, "The Christian Council of South Africa," in *International Review of Missions,* XXXIV (July, 1944) pp. 258–266.

5. William Nicole, *Why the Christian Council Failed,* a translation of a report published in the *Transvaler* (Oct. 23, 1941), and appearing in the *South African Outlook,* LXXI, Dec. 1, 1944, p. 251.

6. "An Open Letter Concerning Nationalism, National Socialism and Christianity." *Pro Veritate Supplement,* Bramfontein: Christian Institute, July, 1971, p. 12.

7. *Ibid.*

8. G. Cronje, *Regverdige Rasse-Apartheid,* Stellenbosch: Nasionale, 1942, p. 49.

9. Ibid p. 40f.

10. P. J. Meyer, *Die Afrikaner,* Cape Town: Tafelberg, 1942, p. 92.

11. G. Eloff, *Rasse en Rassensermenging: Die Boerevolk gesian van die Rasseleer,* Bloemfontein: Nationale Pes. 1942, p. 14.

12. G. Cronje, *Tuisfe vir die Nageslag,* Stellenbosch: Nasionale, 1945, p. 79.

13. *Ibid.,* p. 11.

14. *Die Suiderstam,* September 16, 1940, Quoted by W. H. Vatcher, Jr. in *White Laager: The Rise of Afrikaner Nationalism,* New York: Frederich A. Praeger, 1965, p. 63.

15. Howard Hillegas, *Oom Paul's People,* New York: D. Appleton & Co., 1900, p. 100.

16. "Programme of Principles of the Nationalist Party." See Gwendolen Carter, *The Politics of Inequality,* New York: Octagon Books, New York, 1977, p. 467.

17. Leslie Rubin, "Apartheid in Practice," *United Nations Publication;* OPI/428, 1971.

18. Quoted by W. A. Visser't Hooft, *Christianity, Race and South African People. Report on Ecumenical Visit,* New York: Barnes and Noble, 1952, p. 22. (The original document is entitled *Naturellvragstuk,* Cape Town/Pretoria: DRC Press, April, 1950.)

19. *Ibid.*

20. Visser't Hofft, p. 23.

21. Leo Marquard, *The Peoples and Policies of South Africa,* London: Oxford University Press, 1960, p. 214.

22. Edgar Brookes, p. XXX.

23. John W. de Gruchy, *The Church Struggle in South Africa,* Grand Rapids: William B. Eerdmans Publishing Co., 1979, p. 69.

24. See: *Statement on Race Relations,* Vol. I, Johannesburg: Information Bureau of the Dutch Reformed Church, 1960.

25. *Ibid.*

26. The DRC withdrew from the World Council of Churches in 1961 after that body joined English-speaking churches in South Africa in criticizing *apartheid* and pledging support for movements dedicated to the overthrow of *apartheid.*

27. Cf. Dutch Reformed Church Africa News, Vol. 3, No. 3, March 1978, p. 6.

28. *DRC Africa News,* Vol. 3, No. 3, March 1978, p. 6.

29. *DRC Africa News,* Vol. 3, No. 3, March 1978, p. 7.

30. *DRC Africa News,* Vol. 3, No. 4, April 1978, p.1.

31. Cf. Colin and Margaret Legum, *S. A. Crisis for the West,* p. 28.

32. *Journal of Theology for Southern Africa,* Vol. 19, June 1977, p. 25.

33. *Ibid.*

34. *Ibid.,* p. 17.

35. *Journal of Theology for Southern Africa, op. cit.,* p. 16.

36. Ambrose Reeves, *South Africa: Yesterday and Tomorrow,* London: Camelot Press Ltd., 1962, p. 125.

37. Ambrose Reeves, p. 147

38. Lesley Cawood, *What My Church Has Said,* Johannesburg: Church Publications, Board of, South Africa, 1964, p. 60.

39. *Ibid.*

40. L. A. Hewson, "The Historical Background," in *The Christian Citizen in a Multiracial Society,* a report of the Rosettenville Conference, 1949, Bramfontein: Christian Council of South Africa, 1949, p. 44.

41. *Ibid.*

42. The letter was later published in: *Where We Stand, Archbishop Clayton's Charges, 1948–1957,* London: Oxford University Press, 1960. (The

Archbishop died of a heart attack a few hours after signing the letter.)

43. Cf. Cawood, pp. 92–93.

44. Reeves, p. 125.

45. *Star* November 22, 1950, P.D., ⁴/₅₂₄/70, cited in Gwendolen Carter, p. 78.

46. Cf. Reeves, p. 125·

47. *Ibid.*

48. *Ibid.*

49. Lesley Cawood, *The Churches and Race Relations in South Africa,* Johannesburg, 1964, p. 5.

50. Colin and Margaret Legum, *South Africa, Crisis for the West,* London: Pall Mall Press, 1964, p. 102.

51. Ambrose Reeves, p. 145.

52. John W. de Gruchy, *The Church Struggle in South Africa,* p. XI.

53. *Ibid.*

54. Ambrose Reeves, p. 125.

55. Desmond Adendorff, et al., "An Open Letter Concerning Nationalism National Socialism and Christianity," Christian Institute: Bramfontein, *Pro Veritate Supplement,* July 1971, p. 10.

56. Cf. Lesley Cawood, p. 61.

57.Ambrose Reeves, *South Africa: Yesterday and Tomorrow,* p. 147.

58. Robert Orr, Address to the 1963 General Assembly of the Presbyterian Church of South Africa. Cf. John de Gruchy, p. 93.

59. "Memorandum of the United Congregational Church of Southern Africa for the Congregational Church of Southern Africa for the Consultation on Human Relations." Cf. *Ecunews,* Vol. 9/1979, March 23, 1973, p. 21.

60. Eberhard Bethge, *Bonhoeffer: Exile and Martyr,* New York: Barnes and Noble, 1975, p. 171.

61. Abel Hendricks, "A Call to the Methodist Church," Cf. *Ecunews,* Vol. 21/1979, p. 4.

62. John de Gruchy, p. 95 (author's italics).

63. Andre de Villiers, ed., *English-speaking South Africa Today,*(Cape Town: Juta, 1976), P. 11f.

64. John de Gruchy, p. 236.

65. *Ibid.*

66. "Realizing the need to work out in detail the implications of the Message for our national life, The South African Council of Churches and the Christian Institute of Southern Africa in 1961 jointly sponsored the Study Project on Christianity in *Apartheid* Society (SPRO—CAS) as a follow-up to the theological work undertaken by the authors of the Message." See *Apartheid and the Church,* No. 8, Johannesburg: Institute of Race Relations, 1972, p. 1.

67. Peter Randall, *A Taste of Power,* The Final, coordinated Spro-cas Report, Johannesburg, 1973, p. 83.

68. Hermann Rauschning, *Gespraeche mit Hitler,* Zuerich: Bertelsmann, 1940, p. 61.

69. C.S. MacFarland, *The New Church and the New Germany,* London: Victor Gollancz, 1934, p. 15.

70. The DRC plays a very active role in the government's anti-Communist

program. The church journal *Antikom* was started by DRC churchmen and so was the *National Council to Combat Communism*. One of the leading DRC figures behind this Church activity is moderator of the DRC, the Rev. J.D. Vorster, brother of the former Prime Minister of South Africa, who, during the 40's was an outspoken supporter of the Nazis.

71. See above, p. 166.

72. See above, p. 165.

73. John de Gruchy, p. 94.

74. Cf. Lesley Cawood, p. 77–78.

75. *Ibid.*p. 78.

76. Denis E. Hurley: *"Is the Church Doing Anything About the Discrimination Situation?" Rand Daily Mail.* October 31, 1963.

77. Denis Hurley: "The South African Situation and the Attitude of the Church," United Nations Notes and Documents. No. 7/77, March 1977, p. 4.

78. In South African Dialogue, ed. Nic Rhoodie (Johannesburg, 1972), p. 4.

79. *Ibid.*

80. See also John de Gruchy, *The Church Struggle in South Africa;* Ambrose Reeves, *South Africa: Yesterday and Tomorrow;* Edgar Brookes, *Apartheid. A Documentary Study of Modern South Africa.*

Chapter 6

1. The "Programme of Principles" remains official policy to this day. Copies of the document may be obtained from the South African Ministry of Information, Pretoria. See also Gwendolen Carter, p. 467.

2. *Ibid.,* p. 471.

3. *Ibid.*

4. Gwendolen Carter, p. 261.

5. *Christian National Education Policy,* Johannesburg: Institute for Christian-National Education, 1949, p. 4.

6. *Ibid.,* p. 5.

7. See Colin and Margaret Legum, p. 28.

8. John de Gruchy and de Villiers (eds.), *The Message in Perspective,* Johannesburg: South African Council of Churches, 1969, p. 12.

9. See John de Gruchy, p. 118.

10. Trevor Huddleston, *Naught for Your Comfort,* London: Macmillan, 1965. He had to flee South Africa in order to escape arrest for his criticism of the South African government. Ambrose Reeves, *South Africa, Yesterday and Tomorrow; and Sharpeville.* He was arrested before being deported to his home country, Britain. Michael Scott, *A Time to Speak,* London: Faber, 1958. After appearing at the United Nations to condemn South Africa's extension of *apartheid* into South West Africa, he was not allowed back into South Africa and was forced to return to Britain, his home.

11. David Bosch, "Racism and Revolution: Response of the Church in South Africa." *Occasional Bulletin,*Vol. 3, No. 1, January 1979, pp. 13–20.

12. *DRC Africa News,* Vol. 3, No. 3, March 1978, p. 8.

13. *DRC Africa News,* Vol. 3, No. 9, 9 September 1978, p. 4.

14. *Ibid.,* p. 5.

Chapter 7

1. Ambrose Reeves, *Shooting at Sharpeville, The Agony of South Africa,* Boston: Houghton Mifflin Company, 1961, p. 35ff.

2. "Statement on the Riots in South Africa," signed by nine Dutch Reformed Church clergy, in *Statement on Race Relations,* No. 1, November 1960, Johannesburg: Information Bureau of the Dutch Reformed Church, 1960, pp. 12–14.

3. Cf. John W. de Gruchy, p. 63.

4. Leslie A. Hewson, ed., *Cottesloe Consultation: The Report of the Consultation,* Johannesburg: Institute of Race Relations, 1961.

5. Leslie A. Hewson, ed., *Cottesloe Consultation,* p. 74.

6. W. A. Visser't Hooft, *Memoirs,* London, 1973, p. 288.

7. John de Gruchy, p. 69.

8. Beyers Naude, "Die Tyd vir 'n Belydende Kerk is Daar," in *Pro Veritate,* Vol. 4, No. 6 (July 1965).

9. John de Gruchy, p. 107.

10. *Cape Times,* Nov. 4, 1963, in Colin and Margaret Legum, p. 31. See also: International Commission of Jurists, eds., *The Trial of Beyers Naude,* London and Johannesburg, 1975, pp. 68ff.

11. *Ibid.*

12. Colin and Margaret Legum, p. 31.

13. *Sunday Times,* Johannesburg, October 6, 1963, in Colin and Margaret Legum, p. 32.

14. *Cape Times,* 9 May 1966 in *Apartheid,* United Nations Publication, LC No. 71—188870 Paris, 1967, p. 181. In the CI's first annual report, Naude reported that certain Afrikaans-speaking members of the CI had felt obliged to resign from the CI because of pressure brought to bear on them by the DRC. See Muriel Horrell, *A Survey of Race Relations,* 1964, pp. 12–13.

15. John de Gruchy, p. 106.

16. *Ibid.*

17. Edgar Brookes, pp. 79–80.

18. Cf. Cawood, pp. 92–93.

19. Edgar Brookes, p. 84.

20. *Ibid.*

21. Reported in the *Rand Daily Mail,* November 22, 1963. Here quoted from Cawood, *op. cit.,* p. 63.

22. Muriel Horrell, *Laws Affecting Race Relations in South Africa, 1948–1976,* South African Institute of Race Relations, Johannesburg, 1978, pp. 17–20.

23. Some deliverances (Resolutions) adopted by the General Assembly of the Presbyterian Church of South Africa, Cape Town, September 1979. Cf. *Ecunews,* Vol. 28/1979, September 1979, p. 6.

Chapter 8

1. See: "The Sullivan Principles: Decoding Corporate Camouflage" by Elizabeth Schmidt, in Notes and Documents 4/80. UN Centre Against Apartheid. New York. pp. 9–10.

2. See: "The Case for Mandatory Economic Sanctions Against South Africa" by The African National Congress of South Africa (ANC) 23/80. 80-20182. UN Centre Against Apartheid, New York.

3. Elizabeth Schmidt, p. 10.

4. Ibid. p. 45.

5. Terrorism Act, 83/1967, As Amended.

6. Arthur D. Morse, *While Six Million Died: A Chronicle of American Apathy,* New York: Ace Publishing Corp., 1968.

7. Henry L. Feingold, *The Politics of Rescue: The Roosevelt Administration and the Holocaust, 1938-1945,* New Brunswick: Rutgers University Press, 1970, p.295.

8. David S. Wyman, *Paper Walls: America and the Refugee Crisis 1938-1941,* Amherst: University of Massachusetts Press, 1968, p.213.

9. Charles H. Coker, *"The British Reaction to Refugees from Germany 1933-1939."* unpublished dissertation for the Ph.D., University of South Carolina, 1973.

Chapter 9

1. Brian Bunting, p. 64.

2. *Ibid.* p. 65.

3. See Edgar Brookes, pp. 3-4; Bunting, p. 39. J.P.Marais who once sought to have legislation passed that would have the effect of making it a criminal offence for blacks to shake hands with whites, is the chief advocate of keeping "the numbers of blacks down."

4. The order was given by Mr. C.R. Swart, in his capacity as State President, to a graduating class of white police officers.

5. See: *Police Brutality and Torture of Political Prisoners in South Africa.* A call for urgent international action. Statement by H.E. Leslie O. Harriman (Nigeria), Chairman of the Special Committee against Apartheid, before the United Nations Commission on Human Rights. 1 March 1977. 10/77. 77-06953.

Chapter 10

1. Walther Hofer, p. 318.

Chapter 11

1. "Almighty Dollar" is used as an example. It could be "Almighty Pound"; "Almighty Mark"; "Almighty Franc," etc.

Glossary

Words and Phrases

Afrikaner Nationalists. White South Africans mainly of Dutch descent but including some with French Huguenot and German background. They have ruled South Africa since 1948 and are the authors of *apartheid*.

Apartheid. A term invented by Afrikaner theologians in the early 1940s when Afrikaner support for Naziism was at its highest. A religio-political term pointing to the Afrikaner conviction that the total oppression and exploitation of blacks by whites is ordained by God. Therefore, the inhumanity which blacks experience at the hands of whites in South Africa is consistent with the will of God.

Confessing Church. A group of Christians within the German Protestant Church that opposed the idea of the church being placed under state (Nazi) control.

Deutsche Christen. A group of Christians within the German Protestant Church that supported efforts to place the church in Germany under state (Nazi) control. They were, therefore, the direct opponents of the Confessing Church.

Dutch Reformed Church. A group made up of five federated *Nederduitse Gereformeers Kerke,* the *Nederduits de Hervormde Kerk,* and the *Gereformeerde Kerk*. The federated

233

church is the largest of all. All three churches hold essentially the same views about *apartheid* with only minor nuances of difference.

English-Speaking Churches. Churches of British origin. They are the Congregational Church, the Methodist Church, the Presbyterian Church, and the Church of the Province of South Africa (Anglican). They are all members of the South African Council of Churches and the World Council of Churches.

Natives. Indigenous South Africans. In South African official documents, they are also referred to as "non-Europeans," "non-Whites," "Bantus," and "Blacks."

How the Afrikaners Define Terms

Communist: Anyone who is opposed to *apartheid*.
Terrorist: Freedom-fighter.
Exploitation and Oppression: Plural Democracy.
Police Brutality: Law and Order.
Majority Rule: Communism.
Democracy: A government of whites, for whites, by whites, and one which has a God-given mandate to oppress and terrorize blacks.

Acronyms

ANC. African National Congress.
BK. Bekennende Kirche.
CC. Confessing Church.
ChC. Christian Council.
CI. Christian Institute.
CNE. Christian National Education.
DC. Deutsche Christen.
DRC. Dutch Reformed Church.

ESC. English-Speaking Churches.
GESTAPO. Geheime Staatspolizei.
HANSARD. House of Assembly Debates.
KM. Kirchenministerium.
NATS. Nationalist (Afrikaner) Party.
NAZIS. Nationalsozialistische Deutsche Arbeiterpartei.
PAC. Pan Africanist Congress.
PNB. Pfarrernotbund.
RGBI. Reichsgesetzblatt.
SACC. South African Council of Churches.
SA. Sturmabteilung.
SS. Schutzstafel.
VKL. Vorlaeufige Kirchenleitung.
VLDEK. Vorlaeufige Leitung der Deutsche Evangelische Kirche.
WCC. World Council of Churches.

List of United States Companies in South Africa

1. AAF-INTERNATIONAL
2. ABS Worldwide Technical Services
3. Abbot Laboratories
4. Abdelman Agencies
5. Addressograph-Multigraph Corp.
6. AFAMAL-Quadrant
7. AFIA
8. Alcan Aluminium
9. Allied Chemical Corp.
10. Allied Kelite Chemical
11. Allis Chalmers
12. Amalgamated Packaging Ind. Ltd.
13. Amchem Products, Inc.
14. American Abrasives, Inc.
15. American Bank Note
16. American Bureau of Shipping N.C.
17. American Can Co.
18. American Celanese Co.
19. American Chicle
20. American Cyanamid Co.
21. American Express Co.
22. American Home Products Corp.
23. American Insurance Co.
24. American International Group, Inc.
25. American Metal Climax, Inc.
26. American Motors Corp.
27. American Pacific
28. America South Africa Investment
29. American Steel Foundries
30. Ampex Corp.
31. Amrho International
32. Amrho International Underwriters
33. Arthur Andersen and Co.
34. Anderson, Clayton and Co.
35. Aniken (Nalco Chemical Co.)
36. Applied Power Industries
37. ARCO (Atlantic Richfield Co.)
38. Argus Africa Ltd.
39. Argus Oil
40. Amco Steel Corp.
41. Armstrong Cork Co.
42. Artnell International
43. Ashland Oil and Refining Co.
44. Audco Rockwell
45. Ault and Wiborg
46. Automated Building Components, Inc.
47. Avco
48. Avis-Incorporated World Headquart.
49. Ayerst Laboratories
50. Azolphate Corp.
51. Badger Co., Inc.
52. Balkind Agencies Ltd.
53. Bankers Trust Co.
54. Barlow Oshkosh
55. Batten, Barton, Durstine and Osborn, Inc.
56. Baxter Laboratories
57. Bechtel Corp.
58. Beckman Instruments, Inc.
59. Bedaux, Charles and Associates
60. Bellows, W.S. Construction Co.
61. Berkshire International Corp.
62. Bethlehem Steel
63. Bethlehem Steel Export Corp.
64. Black Clawson Co.
65. Black and Decker Manufacturing Co.
66. Blue Bell, Inc.
67. Boeing Corp.
68. Booz, Allen and Hamilton, Inc.
69. Borden Inc.
70. Borg-Warner Corp.
71. Born Africa
72. Boyles Drilling Co.
73. Braun Transworld Co.
74. Bristol-Myers Co.
75. Buckman Laboratories
76. Buckner Industries, Inc.
77. Bucyrus-Erie
78. Budd
79. Bulova Watch Co., Inc.
80. Bundy

81. Burlington Industries
82. Burroughs Corp.
83. Butterick Fashion Marketing Co.
84. Calabrian Co., Inc. of New York
85. California Packing Corp.
86. Caltex
87. Canada Dry International, Inc.
88. Carbone Corp.
89. Carborundum Co.
90. Carlane Corp.
91. Carnation International
92. Carrier Corp.
93. Carrier International
94. Carter Products Division
95. Cascade Corporation
96. J.L. Case Co.
97. Caterpillar Tractor Co.
98. Celanese Corp.
99. C.G.S. Scientific Corp. of America
100. Champion Spark Plug Co.
101. Charter Consolidated
102. Chase Manhattan Bank
103. Chemical Bank New York Trust Co.
104. Chemical Construction Corp.
105. Chesebrough-Pond's Inc.
106. Chicago Bridge and Iron Co.
107. Chicago Pneumatic and Tool Co.
108. Christiani and Nielsen Corp.
109. Chrysler Corp.
110. Citibank N.A.
111. Cities Service Co.
112. Clark Equipment
113. Clark, Oil and Refining
114. Coca-Cola Export Corp.
115. Colgate-Palmolive International, Inc.
116. Collier Macmillan International
117. Collier-Macmillan, Ltd.
118. Collins Radio Group
119. Colloids, Inc.
120. Columbia Broadcasting System
121. Columbus McKinnon Corp.
122. Combustion Engineering
123. Computer Sciences Corporation
124. Connell Bros. Co., Ltd.
125. Consolidated Equip. and Mfg. Co.
126. Consultant Systemation
127. Continental Corp.
128. Continental Grain Co.
129. Continental Illinois National Bank
     and Trust
130. Continental Insurance Co.
131. Control Data Corp.
132. Corn Products Co.
133. Crane-Glenfield, Ltd.
134. Crown Cork and Seal Co., Inc.
135. Cummings Diesel Int., Ltd.

136. Cutler Hammer International
137. Cyanamid International
138. Dames and Moore
139. Dana
140. Dart Industries
141. Dean Export International Ltd.
142. Deere and Co.
143. De Leuw, Cather and Co. International
     Investments
144. Del Monte Corp.
145. De Witt International Corp.
146. DHJ Industries Inc.
147. Diamond H. Switsches Ltd.
148. Diner's Club International, Ltd.
149. Diversey Corp.
150. Dobbs-Life Savers International
151. Dolein Corp.
152. Donaldson Co. Inc.
153. Doughboy Industries, Inc.
154. Dow Chemical Co.
155. Dow Corning International
156. Dresser Industries Inc.
157. Dubois-Dearborn-Vestol Chemical Co.
158. Dun and Bradstreet Co.
159. Dunlop
160. Du Pont Chemical Co.
161. Duroplastic Penta Industries
162. E.C. De Witt and Co.
163. East Newark Industrial Center
164. Eastern Stainless Steel Corp.
165. Eastman Kodak Co.
166. Echlin Manufacturing Co.
167. Emico Corp.
168. Electric Storage Battery
169. Electro-Nite Co.
170. Eli Lilly and Co.
171. Eltra Co.
172. Emery Air Freight Corp.
173. Encyclopaedia Brittanica, Inc.
174. Engelhard Hanovia
175. Engelhard Minerals and Chemicals Corp.
176. Enda Drug Corp.
177. Envirotech Corp.
178. Ernst and Ernst
179. ESN Inc.
180. Essex Corp. of America
181. ESSO Africa
182. Eutectic Welding Alloys Corp.
183. Ewing, McDonald and Co.
184. Max Factor and Co.
185. Fairbanks, Morse and Co.
186. Fand M Systems Co.
187. Farrell Lines Inc.
188. Federal-Mogul Corp.
189. Ferro Corp.
190. Fiberglass, Ltd.

191. Firder Inc.
192. Firestone Tyre and Rubber Co.
193. First Consolidated Leasing Corp. Ltd.
194. First National Bank of Boston
195. First National Bank of Chicago
196. Flintkote Co.
197. Fluor Co.
198. FMC Corp.
199. FNCB Services Corp.
200. Ford Motor Co.
201. Forsyth Udwin Ltd.
202. Fram Corp.
203. Fruehauf
204. George A. Fuller Co.
205. Galion
206. Gardner-Denver Co.
207. Gates Rubber Co.
208. General Electric Co.
209. General Foods Corp.
210. General Motors
211. General Signal Corp.
212. General Tyre and Rubber Co.
213. George Angus Co.
214. Geosource Inc.
215. J. Gerber and Co., Inc.
216. A.J. Gerrard and Co.
217. Getty Oil Co.
218. Gilbert and Barker Manuf.
219. Gillette Co.
220. Gillsevey Co.
221. Glair and Kestler Co.
222. Glidden-Durkee
223. Goodyear Tyre and Rubber Co.
224. W.R. Grace and Co.
225. Grant Advertising Inc.
226. Graver Tank and Mfg. Co.
227. Grolier Inc.
228. Gulf Oil Corp.
229. Hammond Corp.
230. Harnischfeger International Corp.
231. Harsco
232. Haskins and Sells
233. Halliburton Co.
234. Heinemann Electric Co.
235. Helena Rubinstein Inc.
236. Heller (Walter E.) Inter.
237. Hertz Rent-A-Car Co.
238. Heublein International
239. Hewitt-Robins Inc.
240. Hewlett Packard International
241. Holiday Inns of America
242. Home Products International, Ltd.
243. Honeywell, Inc.
244. Honeywell Information Systems, Inc.
245. Hoover Co.
246. Howe Richardson Scale Co.
247. Hussman Refrigerators Co.
248. Huster Co.
249. Hydro-Air International
250. IBM World Trade Corp.
251. Industrial Chem. Products
252. INA Corp.
253. Infilco Division of Fuller Co.
254. Ingersoll-Rand Co.
255. Inmont Corp.
256. Insurance Company of North America
257. Interchemical Corp.
258. International Banking Corp.
259. International Bank of Reconstruction
     and Development
260. International Bus Machines
261. Int. Flavors and Fragrances Inc.
262. Int. Group of Companies
263. Int. Harvester Co.
264. International Latex Corp.
265. International Minerals and Chemicals
266. International Nickel
267. International Packers Ltd.
268. International Staple and Machine Co.
269. International Telephone and Telegraph Corp.
270. Interpublic Group of Companies Inc.
271. Irving Chute Co. Inc.
272. Jeffrey-Gallion Mfg. Co.
273. Johns-Manville International Corp.
274. Johnson and Johnson
275. S.C. Johnson and Son Inc.
276. Joy Manufacturing Co.
277. Kaiser Industries
278. Kellogg Co.
279. Kelly-Springfield Tyre and Co.
280. Kendall Co.
281. Kennedy Van Saun Mfg. and
     Engineering Corp.
282. Placid Oil
283. Keystone Asbestos Corp.
284. Kidder, Peabody and Co., Inc.
285. Kimberley-Clark Corp.
286. King Resources
287. Koret of California
288. Lakeside Laboratories, Inc.
289. E.J. Lavino and Co.
290. Lease Plan International Corp.
291. Leo Burnett Co.
292. A.R. Lilly and Son
293. Link-Belt Co.
294. Litton Industries
295. Litwin Corp.
296. Loftus Engineering Co.
297. Lovable Co.
298. Lubrizol Corp.
299. Lykes Bros. Steamship Co., Inc.
300. Lykes Youngstown Corp.

301. Mack Trucks Worldwide
302. Macmillan, Inc.
303. Mahon International Inc.
304. P.R. Mallory and Co.
305. Manhattan Shirt Co.
306. Manufacturers Hanover Trust
307. Maremount Corp.
308. Masonite Corp.
309. Master Mechanics Co.
310. McGraw-Hill, Inc.
311. McKee Arthur G. and Co.
312. Measurex Corp.
313. Mechanite Metal Corp.
314. Merck, Sharp and Dohme International
315. Mekan Enterprises
316. Merell National Laboratories
317. Metro-Goldwyn-Mayer Intl., Inc.
318. Meyer Mfg. Co. (Geo J.)
319. Middle West Service Corp.
320. Midlands Oil
321. Miles Laboratories Inc.
322. Millburg Industrial Painters
323. Mine Safety Appliances Co.
324. Minerals and Chemicals Philipp Corp.
325. Minnesota Mining and Mfg. Co.
326. Mohawk Data Sciences
327. Mobil Oil Corp.
328. Monarch Cinnabar
329. Mono Containers
330. Monsanto Co.
331. Moore-McCormack Lines, Inc.
332. Morgan Guarantee and Trust
333. Morrison Knudson
334. Motorola Inc.
335. MSD
336. Mand T Chemicals Inc.
337. Muller and Phipps International Corp.
338. Nalco Chemicals
339. Nashua Corp.
340. National Cash Register Co.
341. National Chemsearch
342. National Standard Co.
343. National Starch and Chemical Corp.
344. National Trust and Savings Assoc.
345. Navarro Exploration Co.
346. Newmont Mining Corp.
347. New Wellington
348. A.C. Nielsen International, Inc.
349. North American Rockwell
350. Norton Co.
351. Nuclear Corp. of America
352. Oak Industries, Inc.
353. Ocean Drilling and Exploration
354. Ocean Science and Engineering Inc.
355. Olin Mathieson Chemical Corp.
356. Oshkosh Truck Corp.

357. Otis Elevator Co.
358. Owens Corning
359. Owens-Illinois
360. Ozite Corp.
361. Pacific Oilseeds Inc.
362. Robert Page and Assoc.
363. J.J. Palmer and Co.
364. Pan American World Airways Inc.
365. Parke, Davis and Co.
366. Parker Hannifin Corp.
367. Parker Pen Co.
368. Pegasus International Corp.
369. Pepsi Cola International
370. Performed Line Products
371. Perking-Elmer Corp.
372. Permatex Co. Inc.
373. Perth Products
374. Pfizer International
375. Phelps Dodge Corp.
376. Philip Morris, Inc.
377. Philips Petroleum Co.
378. Pillsbury Co.
379. Pioneer Systems
380. Pipe Line Technologists, Inc.
381. Pizza Inn, Inc.
382. Placid Oil
383. Playtex International
384. Plough, Inc.
385. P.M. Products
386. Precision Valve Corp.
387. Preload Engineering Corp.
388. Premix Asphalt Co.
389. Prentice-Hall Publishers, Inc.
390. Prestolite International
391. Price Waterhouse and Co.
392. Proctor and Gamble Co.
393. Publicker International, Inc.
394. Publishers Co., Inc.
395. Radio Corp. of America
396. Ramsey Engineering Co.
397. Reader's Digest
398. Reichhold Chemicals, Inc.
399. Reliance-Toledo
400. Remington Rand
401. Revlon, Inc.
402. Rexnord, Inc.
403. Rheem International, Co.
404. Rheem Mfg.
405. Richardson Merrell, Inc.
406. Richelieu Corp., Inc.
407. Riker Laboratories
408. Ritepoint Corp.
409. Ritter Pfandler Corp.
410. River Brand Rice Mills, Inc.
411. R.M.B. Alloys
412. A.H. Robbins Co., Inc.

413. H.H. Robertson Co.
414. A.A. Robins Co., Inc.
415. Rockwell International
416. Rockwell Standard
417. Rohm and Haas Co.
418. Royal Crown Cola Co.
419. Ruth and Strong Ltd.
420. Samincorp, Inc.
421. Schering Plough Corp.
422. Schlesinger Organization
423. Schlumberger Ltd.
424. Scholl Inc.
425. W.F. Schrafft and Sons
426. Scripto Inc.
427. G.D. Searle and Co.
428. Seaway Associates Inc.
429. Security Resources
430. Servac Laboratories
431. Sheffield Corp.
432. Shell Oil Co.
433. US Shulton, Inc.
434. Simplicity Pattern Co., Inc.
435. Singer Sewing Machine Co.
436. Skelly Oil Co.
437. Skil Corp.
438. Smith Klein and French Lab.
439. A.O. Smith Corp.
440. Southwire Co. of Georgia
441. Sperry-Rand Corp.
442. Sperry Vickers
443. Square D. Co.
444. Squibb (E.R.) and Sons
445. Standard Brands Inc.
446. Standard Oil Co. of California
447. Standard Oil Co. of New Jersey
448. Standard Pressed Steel Co.
449. Stanley Works
450. C.V. Starr and Co.
451. States Marine Lines
452. Stauffer Chemical Co.
453. Steiner Co.
454. Sterling Products Inc.
455. Stowe-Woodward Co.
456. St. Regis Paper Co.
457. D.A. Stuart Oil Co.
458. Sun Oil Co.
459. Sybron Corp.
460. Symington Wayne Corp.
461. Systematics Services Pty.
462. Tampax, Inc.
463. Tanatex Chemical Corp.
464. Taylor Instrument Co.
465. Technicon Corp.
466. Tedd-Hill Products
467. Tedd McKune Investments
468. Tenneco International

469. Texas Gulf, Inc.
470. Thermo-Electric Co., Inc.
471. Thompson Remco
472. Texaco, Inc.
473. J. Walter Thompson Co.
474. Thor Power Tool Co.
475. Tidewater Marine Service
476. Tidewater Oil Co.
477. TRW Inc.
478. Three M (3M) Corp.
479. Time International
480. Timken Co.
481. Titan Industrial Corp.
482. Tokheim Corp.
483. Toledo Scale Corp. of Ohio
484. Touche, Ross, Bailey and Smart International
485. Transalloys Ltd.
486. Trane Co.
487. Trans World Airlines, Inc.
488. Triton Chemicals Ltd.
489. Tuco Ltd.
490. Twentieth Century Fox Films Corp.
491. Twin Disc Inc.
492. Underwood
493. Unimark International
494. Union Carbide Corp.
495. Uniroyal Inc.
496. United Aircraft Corp.
497. United Artists Corp.
498. United Cargo Corp.
499. United Shoe Machinery Corp.
500. United States Filter Corp.
501. United States Gypsum Co.
502. US Industries
503. United States Steel Corp.
504. Universal Leaf Tobacco
505. Universal Mineral Discoveries
506. Upjohn Co.
507. Valeron Corp.
508. Valvoline Oil Co.
509. Van Dusen Aircraft Supplies Ltd.
510. The Vendo Co.
511. Vick Chemical, Inc.
512. Vick International
513. Wallace International
514. Warner Bros., Inc.
515. Warner-Lambert Pharmaceutical Co.
516. J.R. Watkins Products, Inc.
517. Wayne Pump Co.
518. Western Airlines, Inc.
519. Western International Hotels
520. Western Knapp Engineering Co.
521. Westinghouse Air Brake Co.
522. Westinghouse Electric Intl. Corp.
523. West Point Papperoll, Inc.
524. Weyerhaeuser Co.

240

525. Whinney Murray Ernst
526. White Motor Corp.
527. Whitney Co.
528. Wilbur-Ellis Co.
529. H.B. Wilson Co.
530. Woolworth, F.W.
531. Worldtronic Inc.
532. Worthington Air Conditioning Co.
533. Wyeth International Ltd.
534. Xerox Corp.
535. XM World Trade, Inc., One World Trade Center
536. X-Ray International Ltd.
537. Arthur Young and Co.
538. ZOE

Index

Liberation Movement, 205
Lutuli, Albert, 204
Luanda, 15

Machel, Samora, 200
Madagascar, 184
Malan, D., 23
Mandela, Nelson, 195
Marahrens, 95, 115
Marriage, 26, 31
Mein Kampf, 8
Methodists, 118, 160
Movement, Freedom of, 58ff.
Mozambique, 16, 174, 199
Mueller, L., 68ff.
Mugabe, R., 200
Multinational Corporations,
    167, 169, 181, 206, 210

Namibia, 15, 174, 178 – 79,
    199, 204
National Party, 7
National States, 203
Naude, Beyers, 158
Naziism, 1, 7, 184ff.
Nazis, xi, 1, 67ff., 97ff., 101ff.,
    106ff., 184ff.
Niemoeller, Martin, 69, 85,
    109, 140
Nienoeller, Wilhelm, 80ff.
Nobel Peace Prize, 204
November Pogrom, 88
Nuclear Weapons, 175
Nuremberg, 9, 26, 90

Obote, Milton, 196
Opinion, Freedom of, 59ff.

Oppenheimer, H., 170
Ossewa-Brandwag, 20

Pan Africanist Congress, 194
Pass Laws, 56ff.
Pentecostals, 103
Pfarrernotbund, 69ff.
Players, G., 204
Police, 61ff.
Population Registration Act,
    54
Positive Christianity, 65
Presbyterian, 118, 134, 161,
    163
Pretoria, vii, 179, 204
Programme of Principles,
    123ff., 149
Propaganda, 173, 181, 187
Property, 52ff.
Protestant Church, 65ff.,
    106ff.
Pro Veritate, 158

Race, 119, 157
Racial Classification, 53ff.
Racial Purity, 8
Reeves, Ambrose, 131
Reich, 2
Reich Church Ministry, 77, 84
Resistance Movement, 190,
    196
Rhodesia, 15
Robben Island, 195, 204
Roman Catholics, 97, 118, 146
Russian Revolution, 193

Sanctions, 178

244

Scotland, 118
Seventh-Day Adventists, 103
Sharpeville, 155, 158, 170
Smith, Ian, 15
Social Democrats, 190
South African, vii, 100, 118, 178
South African Council of Churches, 146
Soweto, 172
Sport, 60ff.
Star of David, 94
Strijdom, J., 8, 17, 37
Stuttgarter Schuldbekenntnis, 110ff.
Support Systems, 165ff.
Swaziland, 174, 199

Tanzania, 16, 199
Trade Unions, 50ff., 207
Transnational Corporations. *See* Multinational Corporations
Transvaler, 17
Treysa, 110

Uganda, 196

United Nations, vii, 14, 16, 178 – 179
United States, vii, 178 – 179, 195, 198, 212

Verwoerd, Hendrik, 8, 17ff.
Violence, 14ff.
Voelkischer Beobachter, 67, 106
Vorlaeufige Kirchenleitung, 76
Vorster, John, 15, 20

Wages, 50ff.
West Germany, 178 – 179, 197, 198, 212
Western Church, 165ff.
Western Government, 177ff.
Western Media, 195
World Council of Churches, 14, 156
Worship, 42ff.
Wurm, Bp., 111ff.

Zaire, 15
Zambia, 15, 174, 199
Zimbabwe, 15, 174, 199